THE
restaurant martín
COOKBOOK

SOPHISTICATED HOME COOKING
FROM THE CELEBRATED SANTA FE RESTAURANT

Martín Rios

WITH CHERYL AND BILL JAMISON
PHOTOGRAPHY BY KATE RUSSELL

Globe
Pequot

GUILFORD, CONNECTICUT

Globe Pequot

An imprint of Rowman & Littlefield

Distributed by NATIONAL BOOK NETWORK

Copyright © 2015 by Martín and Jennifer Rios

All photography copyright © 2015 by Kate Russell

Text design: Nancy Freeborn

British Library Cataloguing in Publication Information Available

Library of Congress Cataloging-in-Publication Data Available

ISBN 978-1-4930-1004-2 (hardcover)
ISBN 978-1-4930-2233-5 (e-book)

♾™ The paper used in this publication meets the minimum requirements of American National Standard for Information Sciences—Permanence of Paper for Printed Library Materials, ANSI/NISO Z39.48-1992.

To my wife Jennifer for supporting and believing in me from the moment we met. For your unending dedication to helping me achieve my dreams, being my partner in both life and the restaurant, and for bringing me all the joy the world has to offer.

CONTENTS

ACKNOWLEDGMENTS

When I sat down to start writing my acknowledgments for this book and express my gratitude, the first thing on my mind was my wife and children. Without these three ladies—Jennifer, Emma, and Anneliese—my life would not be complete. Every day, no matter how many hours I work in my restaurant kitchen or garden, or on this cookbook, my family is my inspiration and source of happiness. Although I do not express it enough, I am eternally grateful for them and for having them as the most important people in my life.

I am also deeply appreciative of my friends and mentors, both in the culinary arena and outside of it. Chefs with whom I have worked and from whom I have learned hands-on—especially Georges Blanc of Vonnas, France, and David Burke of New York—have helped enormously in making me the chef I am today. I'm also substantially indebted to those who educated me in their books, major chefs such as Auguste Escoffier, Marco Pierre White, and Charlie Trotter to name only a few. I would also like to thank the many talented chefs under whom I have worked since I was seventeen, each of whom taught me invaluable skills and traits along the way.

In the non-culinary world I have had the great privilege to count as my confidants and friends Paul Margetson, the late Bill Zeckendorf, the late Jan Bandler, my in-laws, Ron and Joan Finn, the late Ursula Elkins, Al Holzgruber, and Corey Fidler. I am infinitely grateful for their friendship and support. My family, parents Rafael and Guadalupe Rios, brothers Daniel and Eduardo Rios, sister Aurora Rios, and their families are also a great source of strength and encouragement for me. If my mother had not taught me the love of ingredients and the cooking process from an early age, I would not be where I am today.

I would be remiss if I did not express my gratitude to the many staff members in the front and back of the house—managers, line cooks, servers, pastry chefs, and sous chefs who have passed through my kitchens, most of whom have become lifelong friends. The following gentlemen all served skillfully and amiably as my sous chefs: Josh Baum, Carlos Alvarado, Caleb Trahan, Julio Cabrera, and Alejandro Hernandez. The front of the house at Restaurant Martín is beautifully run by Jennifer, and an outstanding team of servers and support staff, among them long-term employees Graciela Gonzales, Charles Johnson, and Bethany Morse. They have worked tirelessly alongside me to offer our guests the best dining experience Santa Fe has to offer.

Due to my plate/china obsession, I knew when it came to photographing the dishes for this book I would want to feature plates that are manufactured and supplied by some of the people and companies whom I admire most. I thank Nambé, Heath Ceramics, Larry and Maggi Hill of Hill Associates, Pam Shields and The Wasserstrom Company, and the Santa Fe School of Cooking for helping me to have just the right mix of mediums when it came to plating surfaces! On this same front, John Boos & Co. contributed a series of their beautiful cutting boards you will see throughout this book—no kitchen is complete without these! Also, my partners in business, my favorite vendors stepped up to provide ingredients upon request for this project; they included Shamrock Foods Company, Jeff and Butch at Above Sea Level, and of course my favorite farmer, Rachel Le Page at Our Farmilia in Española, New Mexico.

Jennifer and I also want to thank Cheryl and Bill Jamison, for putting my thoughts and words into a comprehensive and comprehensible book. We can't imagine having anyone else tell our story or share our food with the public. It was sometimes very difficult for me to maintain the slower pace required to write a cookbook over running a restaurant kitchen, but we never expected anything less from these highly decorated, award-winning cookbook authors than to achieve a perfect balance. Cheryl showed infinite patience and support in making sure not a detail was missed. While Cheryl was the glue, Bill was the backbone putting all the pieces together to make this dream a reality on paper. Sadly, shortly after this manuscript was turned in, Bill fell ill and a few short months later, on the day I was named a finalist for the James Beard Best Chef of the Southwest Award, he passed away. Completing the edits and the process of bringing this book to print without Bill has been bittersweet and full of wonderful memories of our dear friend. Cheryl soldiered on like a champion, but we all have felt, and will always feel keenly, his absence.

To Kate Russell, photographer extraordinaire, when we started the process of putting together a cookbook, the one thing we knew was that we didn't want to do this book if we couldn't work with you. For years we have admired and marveled at how her photography has made its subject leap off the page in the best of ways. We never wanted a food stylist because we knew Kate brought all the eyes we ever needed in order to show our product in the best light. That said, when Kate brought Tuscany Wenger along as a stylist, she only improved what we were already doing. These ladies truly made this book come alive.

Words cannot express our appreciation and gratitude to the Jamisons and Kate for their attention to detail, creativity, precision, and most importantly their friendship before and throughout this process, and beyond. None of their support would have worked successfully, however, without the able guidance of Doe Coover, our agent, our editor Amy Lyons, and the staff of Globe Pequot.

We thank everyone in our lives and our community who have stood behind us, perhaps most importantly our loyal guests, who have helped us to realize the dream that is Restaurant Martín. This cookbook is the icing on the cake.

learning to cook, a lifelong adventure

If I ever stop learning about food, I'll have to stop cooking. It's a deep-seated need, this drive I have to explore and grow. It pushes me like some powerful internal engine in all aspects of life, but the pistons really rev up when I'm preparing food or just thinking about a food idea. Even after thirty years as a professional chef, confident in my cooking, I can't just rely on what I've learned or what I've done to this point. It would feel like running in place, never moving forward. Instead I need to keep experimenting with new dishes, old dishes, odd dishes, hoping to pop every one of them to a fresh level of brilliance.

Chef friends sometimes rib me about being a "throwback" in the way I work at Restaurant Martín, where I run the kitchen as the co-owner with my wife Jennifer, the general manager. They warn me that I'm bucking the trend by not seeking celebrity stardom, or trying to build a culinary empire, or easing myself out of the "burden" of cooking in some other way. But cooking is most definitely not a burden to me. I create and refine and taste every item that's on our menu and look at every dish that goes to our Santa Fe dining room under my name. By choice, not necessity, I work the line with our other cooks, and they are my closest *compadres* rather than any would-be investors, bankers, musicians, or media moguls. If hands-on is a throwback trait these days, it's also my way of staying ahead of the crowd.

The obsession with learning and growing goes back to my early childhood. I grew up in Guadalajara, Mexico, the sixth of eight children in a working-class family. Our income, such as it was, came primarily from my father's job as an auto-body repairman, work that was never in steady supply. I saw his anxiety over money, how he was forever looking for a job or trying to make more money, and I saw how it affected my mom and older brothers and sisters. We were far from living in despair, but I realized over the years that I needed an exit from that life, from that eventual fate, one that I saw few people escape.

Despite this struggle, my memories of those young years are primarily happy—mostly because they relate to food. At home we ate well, but very cheaply. Like many Mexican home cooks, my mom spent much of her time finding inexpensive ingredients that were fresh and tasty, and then putting them together for family meals. I particularly loved her *sopes*—fried masa patties made with various toppings. My favorites were the ones filled with refried beans, grated white cheese, chorizo, crema, and tomatillo salsa, and the ones flavored with poblano chiles and potatoes. No one would call *sopes* fancy cooking, but my mom's versions tasted wonderful. Simple, yes, but delicious and nurturing.

I loved the chance to play with food, whether it was rolling out tortillas at home, sneaking fresh fruit for the family from untended orchards, or making candy with Grandpa. My mother's parents ran two food businesses in their village's daily market on the outskirts of Guadalajara. At one stall my grandmother cooked and sold traditional dishes such as *flautas*, *pozole*, and *menudo*, and from a cart that he pushed around the market, my grandfather hawked his handmade candy. Usually once a week on the busiest market days, mom assisted them with the cooking and I went along to lend a hand in any way I could. It was a long hour-and-a-half bus trip each way, involving several transfers, but even that part of the experience was exciting for me as a kid.

Grandpa had a tiny workshop at home where he made his little sugar-paste candies, forming them in traditional fiesta shapes such as Day-of-the-Dead offerings. I would help him fill his handmade clay molds and take them outside to dry in the sun. Then we would load up the cart with prepared candy and push it together down to the market and around the aisles. Mom still has his candy recipe, and she even saved and gave me his rustic old molds, which I will always cherish.

When I was around ten my grandparents retired and my mother started her own cooking business at a stall in the main Guadalajara market, the Mercado San Juan de Dios, one of the largest in Mexico. My older sister Santa helped Mom fix the dishes—similar to the ones grandma sold—and they sent me to buy ingredients for them from other vendors. My eyes probably bulged conspicuously trying to absorb everything I saw, learning about foods I had never eaten, about how to select produce, about killing and plucking chickens, about cutting meat. By financial necessity, the market was all about nose-to-tail cooking and wasting nothing edible. I carry the lessons to

"THE PEOPLE WHO GIVE YOU THEIR FOOD GIVE YOU THEIR HEART." —César Chávez

my kitchen even now, doing about 90 percent of all the butchering personally at Restaurant Martín. Before you can cut meat, poultry, or fish properly, instead of just hacking it apart, I think you must know and respect the animal.

The markets were my schools in Mexico. I went to various Catholic schools on and off as we moved around the city, but no one in my immediate family really cared about formal education. Neither of my parents had gone far in school and all my older siblings dropped out as soon as they could get a job to help support us, just like almost all our neighbors. The areas where we could afford to live were poor and troubled, always flirting with violence and often erupting with it. I knew I wanted more from life, wanted to study and learn and move on, but through my teen years it was only a far-fetched yearning.

I didn't start going to school on a daily basis until my family moved from Guadalajara to Santa Fe, New Mexico, in 1979, when I was fifteen. We went because an American in the auto body trade in Santa Fe promised my father work opportunities. It was pure luck for us, knowing nothing about the United States, that we ended up in an area settled by Spanish colonists in the sixteenth century just decades after the founding of Mexico City and Guadalajara, a place where a similar culture had thrived for four centuries. At the time—and even today to a large extent—the population was heavily Hispanic, mostly descendants of families who came to the city many generations ago when it was part of New Spain. Lots of these residents spoke Spanish, though a somewhat different version than we grew up with in Mexico. Still, in this early era of cross-border migration, it would have been tough for us to get by and stay in most other areas of the country.

THE MARKETS WERE MY SCHOOLS IN MEXICO.

One day shortly after our arrival, Dad was selling dent-fixing services in a mall parking lot, with me and my younger brother Danny tagging along as pseudo-assistants. A policeman speaking the local Spanish stopped to ask why the two of us weren't in school, explaining to our surprised father that it was obligatory at our ages. The next day my parents enrolled Danny and me in middle school, and since we didn't know a word of English and were the only immigrant kids at the school, the district provided each of us with a translator and tutor for our initial year. Fortunately, many of the other students and teachers were bilingual. My first girlfriend, who just spoke English, also motivated me because I desperately wanted to get beyond the stage where we could only communicate through smiles. By the time I reached high school I was conversationally proficient in English, but still poor at reading and writing in the new language.

In the tenth grade I began working as a weekend dishwasher in the kitchen of the Sheraton Hotel, where my brother Eduardo was a line cook. Sure, it was a menial job, but I looked at it as a real opportunity to start getting ahead. I was so totally diligent about the routine responsibilities that the executive chef began assigning me more and more tasks, from washing the lettuce to cracking and separating eggs. Before long I was doing most of the prep labor for a lot of dishes, and in any spare moments I learned about the other kitchen jobs by watching and helping the cooks. At the end of the following school year, I dropped out to work full time at the restaurant, which felt like the beginning of an entirely new life.

Growth opportunities came quickly. Within little more than a year the chef promoted me through various cooking stations up to his top assistant as the sous chef. To encourage me, he gave me one of my favorite gifts of all time, an English translation of Auguste Escoffier's *Guide Culinaire*. It immediately became my most treasured possession, and I carried it with me everywhere for years. Reading it constantly and mining it for recipes and techniques taught me more about written English than I ever could have learned in a classroom. Getting over this hurdle encouraged me to buy and borrow other cookbooks, which I began reading avidly. The most influential of these at the time was Marco Pierre White's *White Heat*, an excitingly creative update of Escoffier in my mind.

After my mentor left the Sheraton, the kitchen fell into decline and I soon moved on to a fancy new hotel in town, the four-diamond Eldorado. Again, I rose through the ranks rapidly, now learning from a half-dozen talented and experienced chefs at once. I virtually lived at the restaurant, eating all my meals there and only going to my apartment to sleep. When I was off the clock, I volunteered to assist the other cooks as a way of improving my skills. Gradually during my tenure I started understanding cooking as a profession, and from that emerged the thought that this was what I wanted to do with my life. When the hotel's general manager promoted me to executive chef at the age of twenty-eight—despite my lack of a high-school diploma and any formal culinary training—I thought I had mastered the craft of cooking. I didn't consider myself an accomplished chef, however, and only fantasized vaguely about achieving that level of artistry.

> THE HOTEL'S GENERAL MANAGER PROMOTED ME TO EXECUTIVE CHEF AT THE AGE OF TWENTY-EIGHT, DESPITE MY LACK OF A HIGH SCHOOL DIPLOMA AND ANY FORMAL CULINARY TRAINING.

It was the woman who would become my wife who helped me reach the next step. Raised in New York City and New Jersey, but a frequent visitor to Santa Fe, Jennifer was then earning an MBA at Georgetown University. As a student, she completed an apprenticeship at the Eldorado in the summer of 1993 and was sent to the kitchen for a two-week introduction to the food-and-beverage side of hotel management. I had never met anyone quite like her before. Sometimes just trying to talk with her was a challenge. I had to tell her once, "Slow down. You're on the second paragraph and I'm still on the first sentence."

The communication improved quickly, and one day when I took a few hours off to play in a soccer game, I asked her if she wanted to go watch. Rain washed out the match so I suggested we get some New Mexico enchiladas smothered in green chile. Because I wouldn't let her pay for her dinner, she decided it was our first date; by the end of the summer we were a couple.

I had never confided much of anything to other people before, but I told her about my dream of one day becoming a major chef. The first step, I felt, was going to the top culinary school in the States—which I knew was the Culinary Institute of America (CIA) in Hyde Park, New York—but I didn't have a clue about how to do it. Jennifer didn't even blink, just started figuring out the

details and helping me to put together a plan to attend. We agreed that I would save the money for my hefty tuition and would take the coursework necessary to pass a GED exam to finish high school. When I had done this by the following September, I applied to the CIA, resigned from the Eldorado, and moved with Jennifer to New Jersey in anticipation of starting classes soon.

I didn't realize how staggering the changes would be for me. I had never been separated from my family, and I broke down crying when I said goodbye to Mom. I was used to working fifteen hours a day and having plenty of money to share with my parents, but now a full week of classes occupied similar time and we were scraping by on savings until Jennifer got a job. Many people spoke Spanish and understood Hispano culture in Santa Fe, but hardly anyone did in New York. Everything even looked different. From a sparsely populated, sunny, and arid mountain plateau peppered with adobe homes, we descended into a realm teeming with hustling crowds, massive buildings, harsh humidity, and icy gray winters. Most locals consider Hyde Park bucolic, but I felt like a baby iguana dropped into Times Square on New Year's Eve.

The first few months at the school were the hardest and most stressful of my life. An introductory course on the history and future of gastronomy required me to read English at a college level and absorb the material well and quickly. Even tougher, I had to write papers in English, which I had never done before in any language. Hard work alone didn't cut it like it had for many years, and I felt like I was butting my head against the ivy-covered brick walls. I despaired about messing up our lives by leaving a secure, high-paying job. Almost daily I told Jennifer I should just quit. She was sympathetic about the challenges, but ultimately kept me on track by saying, "No fucking way."

THE FIRST FEW MONTHS AT THE [CIA] WERE THE HARDEST AND MOST STRESSFUL OF MY LIFE.

Finally I passed the class. The professor, whom I had told about my difficulties, even took me aside to say that I did an amazing job of overcoming the odds, which in my mind also included getting slowly adjusted to the clouds and crowds. After the initial course the CIA got much easier as we moved to hands-on lessons, where my chef experience and age gave me an edge over other students.

My background also helped in securing apprenticeships at top restaurants. As part of the CIA training, I had the opportunity to work for six months at New York's Park Avenue Café for David Burke, a chef I admire for his French-Asian sensibilities, his intimate feel for ingredients, and his playful imagination. Someone once said that if Willy Wonka and Albert Einstein had a baby, it would be David Burke.

After graduating from school in 1996, I was accepted for an apprenticeship at Georges Blanc, one of the most famous and respected three-star restaurants in France. It was a dream come true. We eagerly moved to its small and beautiful Burgundy home village of Vonnas, which residents like to call "Blancville."

I had learned a lot in my time with Burke, but it was much more difficult to pick up culinary knowledge at Blanc's. The Michelin-starred restaurants are overrun with free help from all over the world, and they make no effort to teach the *stagiaires* (unpaid interns) anything. We prepped ingredients for hours, plated some food, and cleaned up everything, but we rarely got a chance to cook. Blanc himself remained virtually invisible, and none of us exchanged more than a few words with him over the months we worked there. To his immense credit, though, he spent much of his time sourcing superb ingredients for the restaurant from all around the region. That in itself was incredibly inspiring.

Some of the other main chefs actively obstructed our training. They would give us lists of ingredients they wanted us to collect for them for a dish, but leave out a couple of key items so that we couldn't replicate the recipe. I became particularly frustrated with the head pastry chef over a sorbet he made regularly. He stacked up boxes all around him to block our view of what he did, and I didn't discover until years later at a French pastry workshop in Colorado which ingredients he had kept secret from us.

Determined to make the most of the experience anyway, I resorted to old observational tactics from my early years in the Guadalajara market and at the Sheraton in Santa Fe. While I prepped and cleaned, I watched the cooks carefully. I saw the steps they took in preparations, and then imagined the recipes, which I wrote down later in my composition book. As I plated different courses, I studied each dish in a similar way, figuring out the products and techniques used. Also, the older couple who rented us a cottage taught me about being resourceful with food, taking me along when they bartered fresh goat cheese from neighbors for a just-made country pâté from the local charcuterie shop. Ultimately I absorbed a great deal, particularly about the importance of staying close to the ingredients, of respecting and honoring them in my cooking.

After almost six months in France, we returned briefly to New York, but Jennifer was pregnant with our first daughter, and we didn't want to have the baby in the city. I renewed professional contacts in Santa Fe and was hired to be the first executive chef of the Eldorado's signature restaurant, The Old House. I immediately redesigned the menu, making it fresher, lighter, and more contemporary. This was my first step, still somewhat tentative, toward developing a personal cooking style. I relied on French basics, but also featured southwestern accents that seemed appropriate and popular. As I look back at these dishes, I barely recognize myself in them because they are so different from my cooking today.

The Old House eventually earned Zagat's recognition as the best place to eat in New Mexico. To handle the new attention, the hotel execs hired Jennifer to manage our public relations, providing us our first opportunity to work together officially. It was a happy period in almost all respects, capped by my acquiring American citizenship and Jennifer giving birth to our second daughter.

After almost a decade at The Old House, I itched for a new challenge. A smaller Rosewood luxury resort, the Inn of the Anasazi, offered me a job as executive chef and director of food and beverage, with responsibilities largely concentrated in the latter area. It was another remarkable learning opportunity, because I had no previous experience with the business side of restaurant operations. At first I really enjoyed participating in meetings, traveling to food events, and even writing reports, but I increasingly missed real kitchen work. After two years in the job, I found myself complaining to Jennifer regularly, "I didn't even pick up a knife today."

Both of us knew that at some point we wanted a place of our own, and we had looked at possible sites for years. Now we began pursuing the idea more seriously, while in the meantime I ran the kitchen at the respected Geronimo Restaurant. We eventually found a vacant historic house that we liked near downtown, and bought it in March 2009, hoping to open by the summer. Looking ahead to the annual Santa Fe Wine and Chile Fiesta in the fall, we confidently booked a special wine dinner during the festival for September 24 and sold out all the seats far in advance. The renovation work took longer than expected, of course, and we barely opened in time for the event. The City allowed us to start prep work in the kitchen on September 21 and 22, but wouldn't let us sell food until the authorities approved our beer-and-wine license, which didn't happen until the afternoon of the 24th, just a few hours before our guests arrived.

During the construction phase, Jennifer and I refined our sense of the restaurant concept. The name troubled us some initially. We liked the idea of "Restaurant Martín," but Jennifer in particular wanted to make sure that customers noticed the accent over the "i" and pronounced it in the Spanish style. She even wondered whether I should change the spelling of my name to "Marteen" so that it didn't come out as "Martin" in the American way.

From the beginning we knew that the restaurant shouldn't be an anniversary-only place, too elegant or expensive for our friends and neighbors to visit more than once a year. It had to be comfortable and accessible, not formal or stuffy. At the same time, I knew the kitchen had to have superlative ingredients. As much as we favor affordability, our ingredients will never be cheap, even when we avoid or minimize the use of some of the most costly luxury items. I actually prefer to work with high-quality, reasonably priced goods that need care, coaxing, and creativity to shine on the plate rather than fancier foods that require minimal cooking skill. For example, I might opt for yellowfin tuna over bluefin tuna, a beef short rib over a prime rib eye steak, and lamb cheeks over lamb chops.

We opened with seating for eighty guests in three dining rooms, all small to moderate in size and casually modern in style, with prominent contemporary art on the walls. In the snowy winter months, glowing candles in a corner fireplace across from the hostess stand welcome patrons. In the warmer seasons most guests prefer to dine outside on our covered patio, rimmed by herb, vegetable, and flower gardens. From the beginning, we've been full many nights all year, leading to a recent decision to add another, larger dining room to the property—the Annex—that is enclosed in the winter and opened into the courtyard in the summer. It keeps us from needing to turn tables, and therefore rush guests, enhancing the relaxed dining experience.

My culinary goal has remained the same for almost my entire career. From my earliest days as a line cook, I've wanted to prepare and serve the most delicious and intriguing dishes appropriate to the setting and clientele. What has changed over time are the last two factors, the worldliness of restaurants where I've cooked and the sophistication of their customers. The two together have inspired a major evolution of my cooking, multiplying dimensions of tastes and textures, even though the vision remains the same.

I have a great deal of respect for all food traditions, and I look to many of them for ideas and ingredients, but I no longer feel a need to pursue one to the exclusion of others. I don't cook French food, or Mexican food, or Asian food, though many of my dishes borrow elements and flavors from these and other cuisines. Traditions can focus vision, but they also come with boundaries that delineate appropriate foods, seasonings, and cooking methodologies. I prefer to remain open to all options, to take full advantage of any product or technique that allows me to create fresh, uncommon dishes that dazzle and delight my guests. It's not about fusion,

it's not about fussiness or complexity, it's simply the quest for the most extraordinary compositions I can conceive.

At the heart of this mission is my diligently acquired knowledge of ingredients and techniques. I'm constantly nibbling foods of all kinds and imagining ways to use them differently and in unusual contexts. I'm always shopping for new items at brick-and-mortar groceries and web outlets, and reading cookbooks and online menus from around the world to find unfamiliar tidbits. Any time it's possible, we grow our own produce for the restaurant, almost annually expanding our gardens on site and at home to the maximum extent. We also contract with local farmers, such as Rachel LePage, to raise specific crops for us. Every dish I serve reflects the time and energy devoted to this exploration of ingredients. Maybe the desserts most of all reflect my commitment since I developed them originally myself instead of employing a separate pastry chef.

Classical French techniques will always remain important in our kitchen, but I also employ contemporary methods developed by me and by other chefs. We seldom use just a single technique in any preparation, often mixing old and new approaches to bring different dimensions to the dish. To limit yourself to a few tools significantly narrows your range of possibilities.

The importance I give to a thorough knowledge of ingredients and techniques drives the way I develop a new dish. I frequently start with a primary ingredient or two and a desire to bring out their essences cleanly and purely with the addition of other seasonings and accents and the application of appropriate techniques. This is the case, for example, with my many raw fish dishes. On other occasions I take another dish concept and strive to elevate it to a higher level. In this way a simple, home-style key lime pie inspired my Key Lime Vacherin with Szechuan Peppercorn Meringue and Almond-Coconut Crumbs.

In the mix of ingredients and techniques in a preparation, I always aim for multi-dimensional harmony in flavors—a satisfying integration of disparate taste sensations—and enticing contrasts in textures. I want each ingredient to speak for itself in an honest and vivid fashion, never in a loud or disproportionate voice. For me a dish should sing like an exquisite choir, not a pack of prima donnas. It must be complex to deliver serious sensual delight but also remain subtle as a smile in its mode of temptation.

My dishes often look elaborate in the way I present them in the restaurant, but they are not complicated to replicate for a motivated home cook of moderate experience. They typically have several components or sub-recipes that seldom require more than twenty minutes of active preparation time, and many of these elements can be made ahead, as I always indicate. Most of the dishes in their fully executed form are meant for special occasion dinners, but some are straightforward in their basics and suitable for everyday purposes. With my overall goal of making sophisticated food accessible to in-tune home cooks, I try in the recipes to mix sensibly the challenging and the practical.

Jennifer and I both think of the restaurant staff as family members, and they work together incredibly well as team players. The ones who stay with us for long are also eager learners, like the two of us. If you've picked up this book, Jennifer and I suspect you may have a touch of our craziness too. It's this hope that inspired us to take on a cookbook. With the restaurant settled into a steady consistency now, we figured it was time to share our passion and ideas in a new way, through words and photos. Please join us at the table for what we see as an exhilarating journey through the world of flavors.

bringing the restaurant home

Most chef's cookbooks are written for other chefs. I certainly hope some of my colleagues read this book and find a few nuggets of inspiration, but they are not my primary audience. I'm writing for home cooks who love to cook, who find joy and fulfillment in creating fine food for themselves, their families, and their friends. Cookbook publishers generally ignore this group, preferring, apparently, to classify every cook as an amateur who can only juggle three ingredients at a time, or as a restaurant professional.

This perspective seems to be supported more by prejudice than data. I'm not known for spouting numbers, but the folks behind the Harris polls do know numbers, and they confirmed that a whole lot of people really enjoy cooking. According to a recent poll, 79 percent of Americans say they enjoy cooking at home, and 30 percent say they love to do it. In another survey nearly half of the respondents believe they cook at an intermediate level and 20 percent describe their cooking skills as advanced. I think it's a shame for anyone connected to the food world to snub these serious cooks just because they choose to work at home.

By the standards of most cookbooks, my recipes are intentionally ambitious for home cooks, but ultimately simple for those with a passion for the craft. Many of the dishes, the entrees in particular, take a moderate commitment of time and energy, but accomplished home cooks have tested all the recipes in a home kitchen and helped me simplify the techniques so that everything can be made with home equipment.

The recipes typically incorporate several components or sub-recipes, but the individual elements are almost always relatively fast and easy to execute. Additionally, most of the dishes—as I consistently note—contain steps that can be done well ahead with no loss in quality. The recipes may look long, but that is largely because all the steps for the various components (except stocks) are included, allowing you to see them in one place instead of requiring you to search for sub-recipes scattered in different sections of the book.

The length of the recipes also reflects the inclusion of the essential accompaniments for each main ingredient. These are a complete meal on a plate, though they are often a little less elaborate than our restaurant versions, which are the ones shown in the photos. When this is the case, I tell you exactly what our kitchen adds in an addendum called Restaurant Embellishments. I provide a description sufficient for you to replicate any extra elements that intrigue you. I encourage you to experiment with these embellishments when you have the time or want to add a new technique to your repertoire. They make a special-occasion dish even more special.

MY COOKING

My cooking style doesn't fit any easy classification. I described it as progressive American cuisine when I opened Restaurant Martín originally, and I think that still fits as well as anything. I'm solidly grounded in French fundamentals, but I use a global array of seasonings, spices, and ingredients. I'm in awe, for instance, of classic French-style reduction sauces, but not so in awe that I can't add my own twists to the pot, such as star anise, cinnamon, a sprinkle of ancho chile, or maybe a local Nut Brown Ale. It's a decidedly personal style honed over three decades of life in professional kitchens. My dishes and recipes evolve constantly, but my style is set.

I love to combine sweet and sour, crunchy and silky, luxurious ingredients like lobster with something humble like chickpeas. I enjoy using under appreciated vegetables—such as salsify, kohlrabi, and okra—and treating ingredients in unfamiliar ways, like putting an Asian daikon radish in a Mediterranean-style crudo preparation. I always taste as I go along. It's the best way to learn how a bit more pepper can enliven a dish, how a squeeze of citrus can brighten the flavor, how one olive oil can be mellow and warm, another green and astringent. My dishes strive for fine-tuned balance, the kind you might associate with a trapeze artist. I want a spry symphony of flavors, textures, and colors, and going for that is what makes cooking so much fun for me.

I take great pride in sourcing ingredients. I grow as much produce as I can, both in gardens around my restaurant patio and on land surrounding our country home. On the restaurant patio, I have smaller plants like peppers and all kinds of herbs. There's an ancient pear tree too, with Bosc-like pears, probably planted by someone in the Ortiz family that owned this corner near downtown Santa Fe for generations. At home I have many more fruit trees and plenty of other crops such as baby lettuces that I have trouble finding elsewhere.

> I WANT A SPRY SYMPHONY OF FLAVORS, TEXTURES, AND COLORS, AND GOING FOR THAT IS WHAT MAKES COOKING SO MUCH FUN FOR ME.

Our Santa Fe Farmers' Market, a quick three blocks from the restaurant, has some amazing growers, and I often supplement my own garden and orchard items with organic produce from them. Many people who have never traveled here assume Santa Fe's climate is something like Phoenix's. Nothing could be further from the truth. At approximately seven-thousand feet in the Rocky Mountains, our summers are mild and pleasant. While the traditional growing season is short, more and more of our farmers are extending the season successfully with greenhouses and hoop houses, where they start plants early and keep them producing well beyond our early frost and snow. One of my favorite times of year is the late summer and early fall mushroom season, when foragers show up at my door with plump porcinis and other mountain mushrooms.

Just recently we've begun experimenting with having our "own" farmer and farm. We are proud to be working with Rachel LePage of Our Farmilia in the Española valley, about fifteen miles north of Santa Fe. I love the way the name of the operation mashes "farm" and the Spanish word for family. Rachel is a young, relatively new farmer, who has decided she would like to grow exclusively for us. By the time you are reading this, we should have our first mutually agreed upon cultivars and crops coming in. In working together to select what she can grow best and what we can best sell, we're helping each other.

I do bring in ingredients from elsewhere, from wherever I can find the best tasting, best raised, or best procured produce, meats, and seafood. Flavor and quality trump other considerations, as I think they should in any aspiring restaurant. My wife Jennifer, like her mother, is an animal-rights advocate, so we've been sourcing humanely raised and harvested livestock since before it became a trend. I use Beeler's Haluka pork from La Mars, Iowa, for example, raised by fifth-generation family farmers in the sunshine on a healthy vegetable diet.

We work with many different grains and make our own crackers, brioche, and burger buns. Santa Fe's excellent bread bakery, Sage, is around the corner from us and supplies other breads for our tables. Our tortillas, both corn and flour, come from Alicia's, a terrific tortilleria on Santa Fe's south side.

While preparing this book, I spent a good bit of time shopping in grocery stores and supermarkets, like home cooks do regularly, finding out what is reasonably available. I especially love to visit vibrant but funky Asian and Mexican markets in Santa Fe and Albuquerque. Seeing live seafood and hanging sides of beef seems natural to me, since I grew up with that at markets in Guadalajara. My childhood household didn't have a lot of financial resources, but our home was always rich in what we ate—real food at every meal. I learned from a young age to make use of every part of the animal and waste nothing.

I'm constantly bothered by how much food people waste. Growing up in a household where having enough for everyone was always a concern, I learned from my parents and grandparents thrifty ways of stretching key ingredients. The same lessons were repeated again in my professional training, particularly in the restaurants run by David Burke and George Blanc. We apply the principles rigorously in our own kitchen, saving everything from tough mushroom stems (for sauces) to celery leaves and carrot tops (for garnishes). Anything that is left, and there's not much, goes into compost.

OUR RESTAURANT INGREDIENTS

Salt and pepper. Our kitchen salt is Morton's coarse kosher variety. The pepper is almost always white pepper, which I prefer for its aromatic quality and the fact that it doesn't call attention to itself. When you're cooking from this book, you'll be using it a lot, so get a fresh supply from a spice store. I order it and many of my other seasonings from The Spice House, a small collection of stores based in Milwaukee, Wisconsin (thespicehouse.com). I rarely in a recipe specify the precise amount of either salt or pepper needed because it can vary considerably depending on other ingredients that are added and, to some extent, on your own taste. If you're in Santa Fe, our local downtown Savory Spice Shop has great salts, peppers, and a full array of very fresh spices.

Butter and oils. Our butter is always unsalted. When I want a neutral-flavored oil, I use canola oil. It has a clean, light texture and a reasonably high smoke point, excellent for frying and sautéing. There is concern in the food community about canola being genetically modified, but there are Certified Organic brands, such as the one from Spectrum Naturals. You can also use

grapeseed, safflower, sunflower, or other vegetable oil in place of canola. I work frequently with olive oil and always opt for a cold-pressed extra-virgin variety. When olive oil goes into a frying pan or is warmed in other ways, I use a moderately priced version, reserving a premium one for salad dressings and drizzling over the top of dishes on its own.

Herbs and greens. I can't overstate how important I think fresh herbs and greens are to my cooking. Their brightness and various aromas and tastes make them the perfect final accent. The reason I can use fresh ones so lavishly is because I grow many of my own, without pesticides, in beds that surround our patio. I recommend it highly to you too. Even in a small apartment, you can manage a few pots with parsley, sage, rosemary, thyme, and basil. Try to find room for a few others, such as chervil, lovage, and chives. I especially like lemon balm for its citrusy notes. You don't have to start them from seed, as I usually do, which can take a little babying. You can pick up lots of plants in spring and summer at nurseries or farmers' markets. I also grow amaranth, which is really a grain, as a green, picking and using the very young leaves. It comes in deep red varieties such as "Love Lies Bleeding" and "Hopi Red," and multi-colored "Rainbow," with stunning red-, green-, and cream-splotched leaves. Nasturtiums, the cheery little edible flowers, also have edible leaves with a nice peppery taste. Their fresh blossoms can be scattered on plates too, or dried to use in the winter months. Fleshy plants such as purslane and lamb's quarters grow as weeds around northern New Mexico and have been gathered by generations of local cooks, but I plant them to make sure I have them nearby. I order a lot of my seeds from Johnny's Selected Seeds (johnnyseeds.com).

Vinegars. I mostly work with Regina's aged red wine vinegar. It's mellow and inexpensive. I use rice and champagne vinegars when I want a lighter hit of acidity.

Tomato paste. We buy it in a squeezable tube so we have easy access to one tablespoon or teaspoon at a time.

Truffles. I use the occasional truffle in dishes that truly benefit from the flavor, but I've made the recipes in this book with the more commonly found truffle butter or juice. I think truffle oil has been vastly overused by chefs, in places it has no business, but I sometimes find an appropriate way to employ it.

Meat and poultry. We always look first for organic meat and poultry, but if they aren't available, we insist on them at least being well-raised by a respected source. I really like coaxing flavor out of "lesser" cuts, like cheeks, but in the book I have minimized the use of cuts that are difficult for a home cook to buy locally or even order online in small quantities.

Seafood. Our fish and seafood are mostly wild-caught. When I use luxury ingredients such as Dungeness crab or Maine lobster, I get a lot of mileage out of small quantities, and save all shells and other inedible parts for stock.

Agar agar and more. There are several products with weird names that chefs love and that you should try. Agar agar and iota carrageenan, used in some of my recipes as thickeners, are not some weird chemicals. They are both made from seaweed and are both probably sitting on the shelf in your supermarket near things like cornstarch. Soy lecithin, from the soybean, stabilizes frothy sauces. Xanthan gum, a naturally occurring substance, gives body and sheen to sauces and purees. These substances have become easy to find in the recent skyrocketing of gluten-free and vegetarian eating. They provide some of the thickening, mouth-feel, and other characteristics of white flour or gelatin. They are powders that are inexpensive given the small amounts typically used, and are shelf-stable. See Resources for sources.

Gelatin. I often avoid gelatin by using agar agar or another product to gel or thicken a liquid. True vegetarians and vegans shun gelatin because it is made from the connective tissues of animals. When I must fall back on gelatin, like most chefs I prefer gelatin sheets to the powder form. Both need to be "bloomed" in cool water. Since home cooks generally use powder, I have written the recipes to reflect that reality and the fact that the liquid in which it is bloomed will be added to the dish. In contrast, with gelatin sheets the water is wrung out of them prior to the cooking process.

TOOLS AND TECHNIQUES

At the restaurant, of course, I have an impressive *batterie de cuisine*—knives, pots, and pans, bakeware, copper saucepans from France, and much more. A good home kitchen doesn't need all that, but you should definitely invest in a few high-quality tools.

Knives. They're the key to all refined cooking. You need several superior blades of different sizes, but your workhorse should be a ten-inch chef's knife.

Blenders. My recipes include a lot of purees, mainly for sauces and vegetables. I think you can taste all the elements that go into these purees when the mixture is silky smooth, so you will be using a blender for a lot of my recipes. If you're in the market for a new one, I recommend you consider a Vitamix, a high-performance model. Immersion blenders are also handy because you can put one directly into a pot of food without transferring ingredients back and forth. While it's hard to get a fully smooth puree with them, especially if the mixture is somewhat thick, they excel at pureeing smaller amounts than you can blitz in a full-size blender. They are also great for last-minute frothing or foaming.

Strainers. I almost always pass sauces through a fine-mesh sieve. Given the number of times these are useful, having at least a couple is handy. It's a part of French tradition and you'll taste it in the types of reductions I use with most of my main dishes. A pricier but high-quality extra-fine mesh strainer for getting silky smooth mixtures is a *chinois*.

Asadors. I char or toast a lot of ingredients, such as tomatoes and onions, the way Mexican cooks have done for eons to deepen flavors. Sauces with these ingredients can be made in minutes and taste like they cooked down for hours. I plunk most ingredients whole directly over my stove burners. You might find it a little easier to work with a small, inexpensive stovetop grill called an *asador*. These are often found in Mexican markets, but you can also order them from the Santa Fe School of Cooking (santafeschoolofcooking.com).

Mandoline. When I was to be pictured recently in *New Mexico Magazine*, the photographer asked me to bring along my favorite piece of cooking equipment. I chose a mandoline. I love the beauty and texture—and even the flavor difference—that comes from thin-slicing produce and other ingredients with a mandoline. Did you know that you can taste an ingredient more fully when it is sliced thin than you can when it's in one thick piece? While commercial mandolines can be expensive, those in the thirty to fifty dollar price range do a perfectly fine job in a home kitchen. You don't need anything fancy, just one that works, like the plastic Japanese ones called *benriners*.

Kitchen scale with metrics and pounds/ounces. I know that home cooks are reluctant to give up their cups and tablespoon measurements and switch to weight measurements, but it's really worth it for accuracy, especially in baking. Cups, tablespoons, and teaspoons measure volume rather than weight or mass, so cups of sugar, salt, and flour all differ in weight. If you're going to make baked goods or pastas, you should really get a digital scale. One source for a good scale is the King Arthur Flour Company (kingarthurflour.com). In the recipes, I give measurements by volume first, but with liquids I also include a measurement by weight for any ingredient that is one ounce or more.

Spider. A kitchen spider is a mesh strainer and skimmer built to lift small items out of bubbling oil or water. Get one with a very fine mesh so you can scoop out ingredients as tiny as sesame seeds and sunflower kernels. Calphalon makes a version you can find online and in cookware stores. If you have an all-metal fine mesh sieve, you can use it in a pinch, but a spider makes it easier to get into the edges of a pot.

Microplane. It's perfect for zesting limes, lemons, and other citrus. It grates the peel finely enough that no mincing is needed. A microplane also does a great job on hard cheeses and whole nutmegs.

Kitchen torch. Julia Child once said, "Every woman should have a blowtorch." I might not go that far, but anyone (female or male) who enjoys working in a kitchen should have one.

Pasta machine. I make the pasta for all our dishes. For most of them, I use a restaurant-size electric pasta maker that rolls the dough thinner as you make successive runs through the machine. I can use the noodles for lasagna or turn them into a filled pasta such as agnolotti or tortellini. If you don't want to be bothered making your own noodles, you can find pasta sheets in places such as Whole Foods and Trader Joe's. If you really enjoy pasta, though, you should buy some kind of dedicated machine. The Atlas models that you hand crank are good, but if you own a KitchenAid mixer you may want to invest in the pasta roller attachment. It's not cheap, but it does a great job, with the machine taking on all the hard work. Cavatelli, a rounded scrolled pasta, requires a special little machine. I got mine, a small hand-crank model with wooden rollers, in New York's Little Italy years ago. I see the same inexpensive model on Amazon today.

Ice baths. Chefs use ice baths a lot, partially because making large batches of food demands quick cooling for safety as well as saving time. Ice baths can speed home preparations too. Make one with cubes and cold water in a container deep enough to come at least halfway up the container you are cooling.

High-altitude cooking. I cook at Santa Fe's lofty seven-thousand-foot altitude, well over a mile high. Since most of the world doesn't, I've taken that into account in my recipes and based the timing on sea-level altitudes. Beans and grains take a little longer to soften when cooked up here in the mountains. If deep-frying, I drop the oil temperature a few degrees. In neither case is the necessary cooking so precise that anyone should have an issue. Over the years I've worked out even my cake recipes to be compatible for kitchens at varying altitudes.

Oven temperatures. I use convection ovens in the restaurant kitchen. Typically they can run at 25°F less than traditional ovens and still cook food faster. Since most home cooks don't cook this way, the recipe instructions reflect the most common home equipment. Anyone using convection heat can choose to reduce the recommended temperatures by that 25°F and start checking for doneness a bit ahead of the prescribed cooking times.

Pan-roasting. Like in most restaurant kitchens, I sear and cook a lot of the main proteins in a sauté pan or skillet on the stovetop. In most cases, I use the French technique of adding butter and a sprig of fresh thyme to the pan at the end and then basting with the buttery pan juices. The mixture acts as a glaze of sorts for meat, seafood, and poultry. In French kitchens, a half a bay leaf is also often added to the skillet, but I think it can lend too much of its character to many dishes, so I usually skip it.

Smoking. Some of my ingredients and dishes benefit from a light smoke flavor. I use a stovetop smoker, easily available at many cookware stores and online in versions by both Cameron and Burton. They're very reasonably priced for all that you can do with them. You wouldn't barbecue a brisket in one, but they work fine for smoking nuts, salt, fish, chicken breasts, or other small ingredients.

***Sous vide* cooking.** It's become common in restaurant kitchens, including ours, but the recipes call for alternative home methods that approximate the same result. The *sous vide* (French for "under vacuum") technique of controlled, steady, low-temperature cooking in vacuum bags has two features that employ different pieces of equipment. There's a vacuum machine, which seals the food into the bags, and then a machine that warms the water bath to the appropriate low temperature and circulates that water around the bagged food. I might use the restaurant's vacuum sealing machine simply to apply pressure to mango slices to compress the texture and flavor it with a light sweet-sour pickling liquid. After resting, the mango develops an even greater silkiness in texture. I always give instructions for people who don't have this specialized equipment, but I put notes in the recipes to help those who want to make use of *sous vide*. Home versions have become reasonably priced for serious cooks in recent years. The combo of pressure with low-temperature cooking gives many foods, especially proteins, a rich silkiness and can infuse them well with flavorings sealed with them. Another advantage of *sous vide* in a restaurant kitchen is that it can be utilized to cook a protein, like a lamb rack, through so that all it needs during busy service hours is a quick sear to brown the surface. When used this way beforehand, the technique can ensure a great deal of consistency in dishes.

Presentation. I have something of a china fetish. I love the array of plates and bowls that can be used to present food. Don't feel like you need anything more than the basics, however. I love playing with my food, making compositions that use contrasting colors and textures, and nearly everything comes to the table with my herb garnishes. I like to add little touches of rusticity, maybe the green tops still attached to carrots on the plate, or an element of whimsy, like thin celery curls. You'll see photos here of many of the dishes. They may look highly composed, but we don't spend a lot of time or energy fussing with each and don't (unlike some chefs) assemble anything with tweezers. If the photographer had come another week, the dishes would look somewhat different. I tell you what we've done in each case, so that you can have a sense of creating that look, but please don't feel that you need to replicate it. Our handsome flatware, which our customers really admire, comes from a local company, Nambé, and can be ordered from them online (nambe.com).

FIVE SHORT MASTER STOCK RECIPES

I recommend you make your own stock whenever feasible. You'll be rewarded with a richness and flavor that supermarket varieties don't have, and it's a great way to use up trimmings of chicken, meat, and vegetables. On top of that, you'll save money and feel righteous about yourself. I routinely use a vegetable stock, two kinds of chicken stock, and a deeply reduced veal demi-glace, all made in our kitchen.

To make your own, it's fine to save meat trimmings and bits and pieces of vegetables in the freezer in order to make a large batch of stock at a later time, but be sure to seal them well and use them within a few weeks for the brightest flavor. Add to chicken trimmings and bones some meaty chicken parts too, maybe chicken necks, wings, and feet, and to veal bones, add at least one meaty knuckle for the best flavor and body.

The vegetable stock or light chicken stock can be replaced, in a pinch, with a low-sodium store-bought variety. The best I have found is a type that comes frozen, called Perfect Addition, sold at Whole Foods Markets and specialty food stores. Our dark chicken stock and veal demi-glace are "compound" stocks cooked down multiple times, low and slow, with lots of browned bones and onions. A store-bought demi-glace can substitute for either if needed.

Be sure to simmer the mixtures gently, rather than boil them hard. I leave them unsalted for maximum flexibility in the finished dishes. When you have reached the desired doneness, pour the liquid off from the solids right away and cool it in an ice bath. You can then refrigerate the stock for up to a week or freeze it in small containers for up to three months. I don't degrease stock until I am ready to use it in order to allow the fat to provide a seal against any air that enters a container. I don't really think anyone is going to make stock when a recipe calls for a tiny amount, but you'll love yourself for having it on hand.

VEGETABLE STOCK

We use all kinds of trimmings to make our vegetable stock. We keep the same general proportions of onions and carrots, for depth and sweetness, but the stock may also include some bits of parsnips, mushrooms, corncobs, or trimmings from mildly flavored herbs.

¼ cup (2 ounces) vegetable oil
4 ounces onions, chopped
4 ounces leeks, chopped
2 ounces carrots, chopped
2 ounces celery, chopped
2 ounces fennel, chopped

3 whole garlic cloves
8 cups (2 quarts) cold water
1 large sprig fresh thyme
2 dried bay leaves
1 teaspoon black peppercorns

Warm vegetable oil in a stockpot or Dutch oven over medium heat. Add the onions, leeks, carrots, celery, fennel, and garlic. Cover pot and sweat vegetables for 3–5 minutes. Add water and remaining ingredients. Cook at a low simmer, with just the occasional bubble bursting on the surface, for 30–40 minutes to make about 1 quart. Strain the stock through a fine-mesh sieve and use right away or chill for later use.

LIGHT CHICKEN STOCK

4 pounds meaty chicken bones or combination of bones with wings and necks, rinsed well

4 ounces onions, diced

2 ounces carrots, diced

2 ounces celery, diced

2 ounces mushroom stems or trimmings

1½ teaspoons black peppercorns

1 dried bay leaf

1 large sprig fresh thyme

1 handful parsley stems

12 cups (3 quarts) cold water

Place chicken bones in a stockpot or Dutch oven along with onions, carrots, celery, mushroom stems or trimmings, peppercorns, bay leaf, thyme, and parsley stems. Cover with cold water. Bring to a simmer over medium heat, then reduce the heat to maintain a low simmer, with just the occasional bubble bursting on the surface, for about 2 hours. You should have about 1½ quarts. Skim off any floating impurities while the stock cooks. Strain the stock through a fine-mesh sieve and use right away or chill for later use.

DARK CHICKEN STOCK

4 pounds meaty chicken bones or a combination of bones with wings and necks, rinsed well

4 ounces onions, diced

2 ounces carrots, diced

2 ounces celery, diced

2 ounces mushroom stems or trimmings

2 ounces tomato paste

1½ teaspoons black peppercorns

1 dried bay leaf

1 large sprig fresh thyme

1 handful fresh parsley stems

12 cups (3 quarts) cold water

Preheat the oven to 375°F. Mix together in a large roasting pan the bones with remaining ingredients and roast for 35–45 minutes, until deeply golden-brown. Transfer the mixture from the roasting pan to a stockpot or Dutch oven. Pour in water and bring to a simmer over medium heat, then reduce the heat to maintain a low simmer, with just the occasional bubble bursting on the surface, for 2–2½ hours. You should have about 1½ quarts. Skim off any floating impurities while the stock cooks. Strain the stock through a fine-mesh sieve and use right away or chill for later use.

VEAL DEMI-GLACE

4 pounds meaty veal bones and 1 knuckle, rinsed well

¼ cup (2 ounces) canola or vegetable oil

12 cups (3 quarts) cold water, plus additional for deglazing

4 ounces onion, cut into chunks

3 ounces mushroom stems or trimmings

2 ounces carrots, cut into chunks

2 ounces celery, cut into chunks

1 ounce whole garlic cloves

Canola or vegetable oil

3 ounces tomato paste

1. Preheat the oven to 400°F. Toss veal bones and knuckle with oil and transfer to a rimmed baking sheet. Roast for 35–45 minutes, stirring occasionally, until the bones are deeply brown.

2. Transfer to a stockpot or Dutch oven and pour in 12 cups cold water.

3. Pour about ½ cup water onto baking sheet and scrape it from the bottom to release all the browned bits, then pour that into the stockpot. Cook at a low simmer, with just the occasional bubble bursting on the surface.

4. If you have a second oven, you can simultaneously roast the vegetable mixture for the demi-glaze while cooking the veal bones. Preheat the oven to 375°F. Combine onion, mushroom stems or trimmings, carrots, celery, and garlic in a roasting pan and coat lightly with oil. Bake for 20–25 minutes, until the onion is deeply golden.

5. Stir in the tomato paste and continue baking until the paste becomes deeply rusty in color, another 10–15 minutes. Scrape the vegetable mixture into the stockpot. Ladle about ½ cup of the simmering stock from the pot into the roasting pan and scrape it up from the bottom, to release all the browned bits, and pour that, too, into the stockpot. Simmer very slowly for 3 ½–4 hours, until the liquid is reduced to about 3 amazing cups. Skim off any floating impurities while the stock cooks. Strain the stock through a fine-mesh sieve and use right away or chill for later use.

WE GET REQUESTS FROM GUESTS CONSTANTLY for two recipes in particular. Butternut squash soup is one, something easy enough for anyone to whip up for a weeknight supper (see the soup chapter). The other is for the little pearls we create of vinegar, wine, or soy sauce. Guests are fascinated by these caviar-like rounds that ping against the tongue, fashioned from some substance no one expects to looks like a tiny round egg. These are not an everyday accent, but a home cook can still accomplish them with a little time, a kitchen scale, and a trip to a well-stocked supermarket. The preparation technique is called *spherification,* and in this case it relies on agar agar (see page xxii) to gel into tiny balls. I love these added to Chilled Spring Pea Soup, where the pop of them mimics the pop of a fresh pea. Try them too on butternut squash soup, tomato salads, or even pasta. You can create this culinary sleight-of-hand up to 8 hours ahead of when you serve it. Take your time and follow the directions precisely. Magic.

BALSAMIC "CAVIAR" PEARLS

MAKES ENOUGH TO GARNISH UP TO 8 DISHES

2 cups (1 pint) extra-virgin olive oil
¼ cup plus 2 tablespoons (3 ounces)
    balsamic vinegar aged for a few years
¼ cup (2 ounces) apple juice

1 tablespoon granulated sugar
Kosher salt and ground white pepper
1.6 grams agar agar

1. Pour the olive oil into a deep container, one taller than it is wide. Place it in the freezer for 30 minutes. Meanwhile combine balsamic vinegar, apple juice, sugar, and pinches of salt and pepper in a small saucepan. Bring the mixture to a boil, stirring to dissolve the sugar. Whisk in exactly 1.6 grams agar agar.

2. Carefully pour the hot vinegar mixture into a squeeze bottle, then stand the bottle in your freezer for 2–3 minutes to cool it slightly.

3. Remove the oil from the freezer. Squeeze out a few individual droplets of the vinegar mixture slowly, from a height of about 6 inches, into the cold oil. As the droplets fall through the cold oil, they will become tiny, round, caviar-like balls. (If the balls aren't holding shape, return the squeeze bottle to the freezer for another minute or 2. Spoon out the vinegar mixture from the oil before proceeding.) Move the bottle around as you make droplets, so that they don't fall against each other and end up sticking together.

4. When all the liquid is used, strain the balls through a fine-mesh sieve (you can reuse the oil for another dish like a salad dressing), and then dunk them briefly (still in the strainer) into a bowl of cold water to rinse gently. Refrigerate for up to 8 hours if not using within 30 minutes. Spoon portions of the "caviar" over soup, salad, crudo, or other dishes just before you're ready to serve.

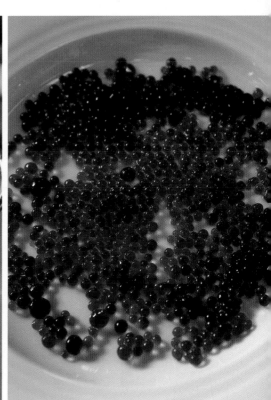

soups

CHILLED SPRING PEA SOUP WITH CRAB, SHAVED RADISH, MINT, AND BALSAMIC SYRUP

SERVES 4

You must try this soup—it's a big favorite with our guests. Part of my personal enthusiasm for it stems from the way it brings to life so much of my early summer garden—peas, pea shoots, mint, and radishes. It's an emerald-green beauty, and can be served on its own, sans accoutrements, for a simple meal. Typically though, I enhance it in various ways. Crabmeat sounds—and is—luxurious, but you only need a small spoonful per bowl to really up the wow factor. You could also substitute a couple chubby cooked shrimp for the crab. The splash of balsamic syrup almost vibrates against the green liquid.

POSSIBLE DO-AHEAD STEPS

- The vegetable stock can be made up to 1 week ahead.
- The pea soup can be made up to 8 hours ahead.
- The balsamic syrup virtually keeps forever, so it can be made any time ahead. Make more if you wish and keep it in a jar or bottle in the pantry.

FOR THE BALSAMIC SYRUP

3 ounces (¼ cup plus 2 tablespoons) balsamic vinegar, aged a few years

FOR THE PEA SOUP

½ cup packed fresh mint leaves

¼ cup packed spinach leaves

2 tablespoons (1 ounce) canola or vegetable oil

1 small leek, white and very light green portions, chopped

2 garlic cloves, chopped

1 tablespoon fresh ginger, chopped

1 pound fresh sugar snap peas or other fresh peas with edible pods

4 cups (1 quart) Vegetable Stock (see page xxvii), chilled

3 tablespoons plain, full-fat Greek yogurt

FOR THE FINISHED DISH

4 ounces cooked king crab or other lump crabmeat

4 long mild radishes, such as French Breakfast radishes, thinly sliced lengthwise

Fresh mint sprigs or pea shoots or both

Kosher salt and ground white pepper

TO PREPARE THE BALSAMIC SYRUP

Pour the vinegar into a small pan or nonreactive skillet. Bring to a boil over high heat and reduce by half. Set aside to cool.

TO PREPARE THE PEA SOUP

1. Bring a small saucepan of water to a boil over high heat. Place the mint in a strainer and dunk into the water for 5–10 seconds. Remove and run cold water over the mint to set the color. Do the same with the spinach. Drain both mint and spinach on a paper towel.

2. Warm the oil in a small saucepan over medium heat. Add the leek, garlic, and ginger and sauté until the leek is softened and translucent, about 5 minutes. Let the mixture cool briefly, then refrigerate until cold. (Having everything chilled before blending it into the soup helps keep the color at its brightest.) Scrape the mixture into a blender with the remaining ingredients and puree. Strain the soup through a fine-mesh sieve and refrigerate until needed.

PUTTING IT ALL TOGETHER

1. Arrange 4 soup plates or broad soup bowls on a work surface. Make a pretty pattern of garnishes in each bowl with the balsamic syrup, crab, radishes, and mint leaves or pea shoots. Lay a swoosh of balsamic syrup across the bottom of the bowls by dipping a spoon into the syrup and dragging it across the bowl. Form crab into 4 equal mounds and place 1 in each bowl. Dot each with a few radish slices, then scatter leaves or shoots over each. Pour the chilled soup into a pitcher. Set a bowl in front of each diner. Pour equal portions of the soup into each bowl, pooling it around the garnishes until most are submerged.

2. Alternatively, spoon the unadorned soup into the bowls. Scatter the crab, radishes, mint leaves, and/or pea shoots over each. Drizzle a squiggle of balsamic syrup over each and serve. However you assemble it, enjoy.

restaurant embellishments

They take a little fiddling, but Balsamic "Caviar" Pearls are an accent with a lot of bang for the buck. Few garnishes intrigue our customers more or stimulate more questions about how we make them. Find them on page xxx and use them in place of the balsamic syrup.

CHILLED AVOCADO-CUCUMBER SOUP WITH CARROT PANNA COTTA, WASABI TOBIKO, AND WILD RICE CRACKLINGS

SERVES 4

Another smashing soup, this evolved from a more standard cucumber and avocado gazpacho. It shines on its own as a simple soup without any adornment, but becomes a kaleidoscope of colors and excitement for your mouth with the elements we add here. The panna cotta is all creaminess and luxury, while the fried wild rice kernels are a chewy-crispy contribution to the texture. Wasabi-infused tobiko (see Kitchen Notes page 7), or flying fish roe, pops on the tongue, especially when you give it extra snap with a light touch of fresh wasabi. If you're feeling ambitious at all, consider adding the ginger granita described in Restaurant Embellishments. It sparkles, literally, in the dish and on the tongue.

POSSIBLE DO-AHEAD STEPS

- Make the Vegetable Stock up to 1 week ahead.
- The Carrot Panna Cotta can be made up to 1 day ahead.
- The Avocado-Cucumber Soup and the Wasabi-infused Tobiko can be made up to 4 hours ahead.

FOR THE PANNA COTTA

Vegetable oil or olive oil spray

1 ¼ cups (10 ounces) carrot juice

1 teaspoon granulated sugar

¼ cup plus 1 tablespoon (5 ounces) orange juice

1 tablespoon unflavored powdered gelatin

¼ teaspoon agar agar, optional

Pinch of cayenne pepper

Kosher salt

Grated zest of 2 lemons

Grated zest of 2 limes

FOR THE SOUP

2 large avocados

12-ounce English cucumber, peeled and chunked

1 large shallot, chunked

1 small rib celery, chunked

3 cups (1½ quarts) Vegetable Stock (see page xxvii), chilled

3 tablespoons plain, full-fat Greek yogurt

½ fresh jalapeño, chopped

2 tablespoons (1 ounce) rice vinegar

1 bunch (2 ounces) fresh cilantro, chopped

Juice of 1 lime

¼ cup (2 ounces) olive oil

Kosher salt and ground white pepper

FOR THE CRACKLINGS

½ cup wild rice

2 cups (1 pint) water

½ teaspoon kosher salt, or more to taste

1 cup (8 ounces) canola or vegetable oil

Ground white pepper

FOR THE TOBIKO

2 tablespoons wasabi tobiko (see Kitchen Notes page 7)

½ cup (4 ounces) olive oil

1 teaspoon wasabi paste

FOR THE FINISHED DISH

Celery leaves, chive blossoms, mustard flowers, small mint leaves, or broccolini leaves

TO PREPARE THE PANNA COTTA

1. Spray a small shallow pan, perhaps 6 or 8 inches square, with oil, and reserve.

2. Combine the carrot juice, sugar, and orange juice in a medium saucepan. Sprinkle with the gelatin and let it stand for several minutes to soften, then bring the mixture to a boil over medium heat. Whisk in agar agar (if desired), cayenne, and salt. Strain through a fine-mesh sieve, and fold in the grated lemon and lime zests.

3. Chill mixture over an ice bath until cool, then pour into the prepared pan and chill in the refrigerator for at least 1 hour, until set.

4. Before serving, cut into strips ½ x 3 inches long, or into small cubes.

TO PREPARE THE SOUP

Place all the ingredients in a blender and puree. Chill until needed.

TO PREPARE THE CRACKLINGS

1. Combine the rice, water, and salt in a medium saucepan. Bring to a boil over high heat, then reduce to a low simmer and cook until tender, about 45 minutes.

2. Drain the rice and let it dry on a clean dishtowel or paper towels. Warm the oil in a small saucepan to 375°F. With a spider, dunk the rice in the oil to fry 10 to 15 seconds, until crispy, then drain on paper towels. Season with pepper and, if you wish, a bit more salt.

TO PREPARE THE TOBIKO

Gently combine the ingredients in a small bowl. Cover and chill in the refrigerator until needed.

PUTTING IT ALL TOGETHER

1. Arrange 4 soup plates or broad soup bowls on a work surface. Make a pretty pattern of garnishes in each bowl. Arrange a strip of panna cotta off center in each bowl. Drizzle each panna cotta serving with tobiko. Sprinkle wild rice around the inside of the bowls and then scatter with leaves or blossoms. Pour the chilled soup into a pitcher.

2. Set a bowl in front of each diner. Pour equal portions of the soup into each bowl, pooling it around the garnishes until most are submerged. Eat right away.

restaurant embellishments

I love Ginger Granita melting into this soup on a hot summer day. The granita is pretty delicate, so it's best made within 4 or 5 hours of serving. But don't shy away from enjoying any leftovers on their own or over berries the next day.

GINGER GRANITA

> 8 ounces sparkling wine
> 3 ounces simple syrup
> 1½ ounces peeled sliced ginger
> 1 teaspoon gelatin
> 1 teaspoon lemon zest
> Kosher salt

Puree all ingredients together in a blender. Transfer the mixture to a small saucepan and sprinkle with gelatin. Let it sit for several minutes until the gelatin softens, then bring the mixture just to a boil over medium heat, stirring to dissolve the gelatin. Strain the mixture through a fine-mesh sieve. Stir in lemon zest and a pinch of salt. Pour into a small bowl or container and place in freezer. About every 20 minutes, go into the freezer and scrape the mixture up from the bottom with a fork to form crystals. Do this until the granita freezes, which will take a couple of hours.

Kitchen Notes

- Wasabi-infused tobiko can be found in many fish departments or, of course, on Amazon. See Resources for more information.

- Chefs prefer to use gelatin sheets instead of powdered gelatin. The sheets need to soak briefly in cold water to "bloom," or soften, so that they immediately meld with other liquids. I always use silver gelatin sheets, with a moderate level of gelling action. Instead of the powdered gelatin, I would use 3 sheets here. Home cooks can order the sheets online (see Resources) or pick them up at some restaurant supply stores.

- The agar agar makes the panna cotta creamier and, when liquid is poured over it, more stable. It can be omitted, but the mixture will take longer to firm up.

- This recipe makes more panna cotta than you need. But don't worry, it's good for lunch the next day on its own, sprinkled with some fresh basil or dill, or cubed and scattered over fresh tomato slices.

CHILLED CARROT-GINGER SOUP WITH PICKLED CARROTS AND MINT MARSHMALLOW

SERVES 4

I used to make a Thanksgiving soup with sweet potatoes and marshmallows, a fun play on the seasonally treasured sweet potato casserole. In recent years I decided to renew the idea in the form of this summery soup.

POSSIBLE DO-AHEAD STEPS

- Make the Vegetable Stock up to 1 week ahead.
- The Chilled Carrot-Ginger Soup and the Pickled Carrots can be made up to 1 day ahead.
- The Mint Marshmallow can be made up to 4 hours ahead.

FOR THE SOUP

4 tablespoons (2 ounces) olive oil

2 pounds carrots, peeled and chopped

2 medium leeks, white and pale green portions, chopped

2 garlic cloves

2 ounces fresh ginger, peeled and chopped

Pinch of dried hot red chile flakes

7 cups (1¾ quarts) Vegetable Stock (see page xxvii)

3 ounces plain full-fat Greek yogurt

2 tablespoons (1 ounce) mild-flavored honey, such as orange blossom

2 tablespoons (1 ounce) fresh lime juice

2 teaspoons grated lime zest

Kosher salt and ground white pepper

FOR THE CARROTS

1 cup (8 ounces) water

½ cup (4 ounces) champagne vinegar

½ cup granulated sugar

1 shallot, julienned

2 dried bay leaves

Small sprig of fresh thyme

Small sprig of fresh tarragon

1 tablespoon black peppercorns

2 star anise

½ teaspoon kosher salt

4 ounces slim young carrots, scrubbed and sliced thinly with a mandoline

FOR THE MARSHMALLOW

Vegetable oil spray

2 tablespoons plus 2 teaspoons unflavored powdered gelatin

¾ cup plus 2 tablespoons (7 ounces) water

1 cup (7 ounces) granulated sugar

⅔ cup (6½ ounces) light corn syrup

2 tablespoons (1 ounce) very strong mint tea (1 mint tea bag combined with ½ cup boiling water)

1 teaspoon grated lemon zest

1 teaspoon fresh lemon juice

FOR THE FINISHED DISH

Borage flowers, elderflowers, small red amaranth leaves, tarragon leaves, or tiny chervil sprigs

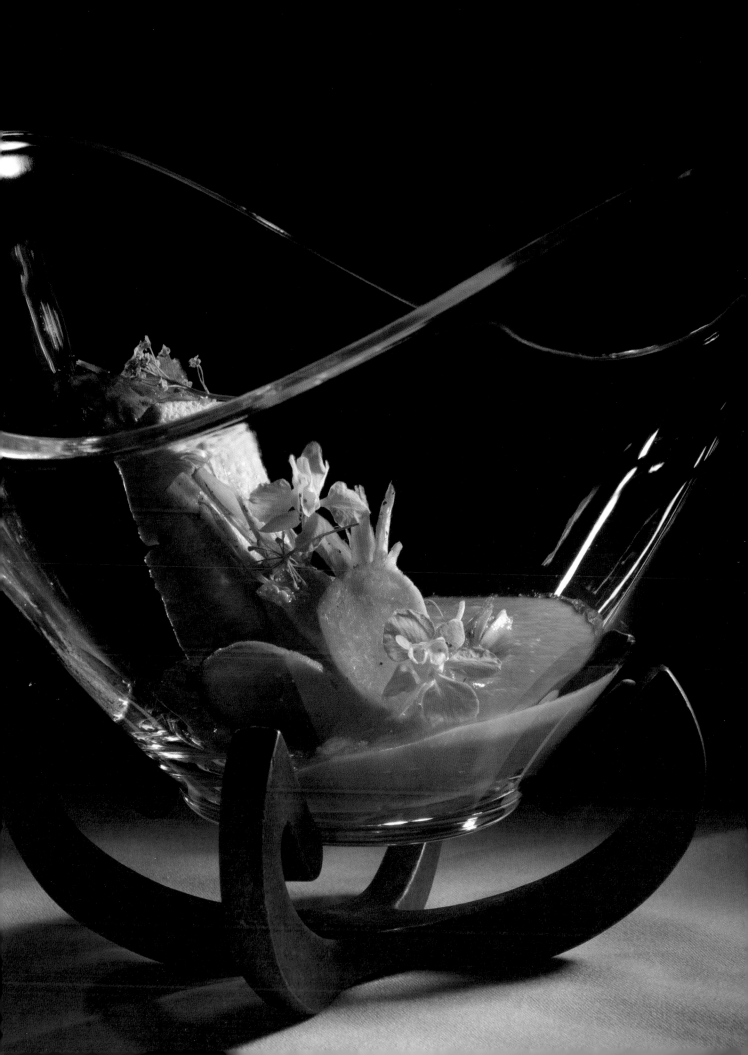

TO PREPARE THE SOUP

1. Warm the oil in a large saucepan over medium heat. Add the carrots and leeks, and sauté until the leeks begin to soften but not brown, about 5 minutes.

2. Add the garlic, ginger, and red chile flakes, and sauté 30 seconds longer.

3. Pour in the stock and bring the mixture to a boil. Reduce the heat to medium-low and simmer uncovered until the vegetables are very tender, about 20 minutes.

4. Stir in the yogurt, honey, and lime juice, and cook for 5 minutes more.

5. Transfer to a blender, in 2 batches, and puree. Pour into a large bowl, stir in the lime zest along with salt and pepper, and chill over an ice bath until cool. Refrigerate the soup until needed.

TO PREPARE THE PICKLED CARROTS

1. Combine all ingredients except the carrots in a medium saucepan over medium heat and bring to a boil.

2. Add the carrot slices and remove from the heat. Place a plate or other weight directly over the carrots, and let sit at room temperature. Once cool, refrigerate until needed.

TO PREPARE THE MARSHMALLOW

1. Line an 8-inch square pan with plastic wrap, smoothing out the wrinkles as best you can. Spray the plastic wrap with vegetable oil spray.

2. Sprinkle the gelatin into a small bowl and pour 2 tablespoons of water over it to soften; let it stand several minutes.

3. Bring the remaining ¾ cup water, sugar, and corn syrup to a boil in a small saucepan and continue boiling until a candy thermometer reaches 238°F to 240°F, the "soft ball" stage.

4. Remove the mixture from heat and immediately stir in the gelatin, watching for steam and sputters.

5. Transfer the syrupy liquid to the bowl of a stand mixer fitted with the whisk attachment. Add the tea, lemon zest, and lemon juice. Beat the mixture at medium-high speed until it is very white, shiny, and thickened but stiffly spoonable, like a soft-peaked meringue, 14–18 minutes. It will have expanded several times in volume.

6. Scrape the sticky mixture into the prepared pan, smoothing its top. Bang the pan on the counter a time or two to eliminate air bubbles. Spray again with a light coat of oil, then cover the pan with plastic wrap. Set the marshmallow aside to cool and firm, which will take at least 1 hour.

PUTTING IT ALL TOGETHER

1. Arrange 4 soup plates or broad soup bowls on a work surface. Make a pretty pattern of garnishes in each bowl. Turn the marshmallow pan upside down and unmold the marshmallow. Cut it into 1-inch cubes. Arrange 2 to the sides in each bowl. Place a mound of carrots in the center of each bowl. Pour the chilled soup into a pitcher.

2. Set a bowl in front of each diner. Pour equal portions of the soup into each bowl, pooling it around the garnishes until most are submerged. Eat right away.

restaurant embellishments

We usually serve this soup with pieces of Flaxseed Crackers. If that sounds appealing, here's the recipe.

FLAXSEED CRACKERS

½ cup flax seeds
2 tablespoons sesame seeds
2 tablespoons sunflower kernels
¼ cup unbleached all-purpose flour
1 teaspoon granulated sugar
Pinches of salt and pepper
½ cup water

1. Preheat the oven to 350°F and line a baking sheet with a non-stick mat or oiled parchment paper.

2. Place flax seeds in a food processor and process them for 30 seconds to break them down a bit.

3. Add sesame seeds and sunflower kernels and process for about 30 more seconds.

4. Add flour, sugar, salt, and pepper, and pulse a few times until they disappear into the mixture.

5. With the processor running, pour in water. For the first 30 seconds, you will have liquid and grain. Stop and then pulse several times until you have a thick batter or thin dough.

6. Use a thin metal cake spatula to spread the batter over the baking sheet to within 1–2 inches of the pan's edges.

7. Bake for 20–22 minutes or until crisp. Let the cracker mixture cool on the baking sheet on a baking rack, then reserve it at room temperature. Cover tightly if you will not be using it the same day. When you are ready to serve, break into small to moderate pieces.

Kitchen Notes

- The marshmallow recipe makes more than you will really need for the soup. The remaining marshmallows can be a snack or a take-home treat for dinner guests. They're good in hot chocolate or in a sweet potato casserole.

- If you prefer to use gelatin sheets rather than powdered gelatin, bloom 8 silver sheets.

CHERRY STONE CLAM CHOWDER WITH BACON-CHORIZO CRUMBS, FINGERLING POTATOES, AND CRISPY CLAM FRITTERS

SERVES 4

I love classic New England clam chowder, but when I make a version at the restaurant I dress it up in a somewhat whimsical fashion. Both here and in other dishes, crumbs of various breads, crackers, cakes, or cookies play a large role in my pursuit of textural contrasts. One of my friends jokingly refers to it as my "crumb program."

POSSIBLE DO-AHEAD STEPS
- Make the Light Chicken Stock up to 1 week ahead.
- Make the Bacon-Chorizo Crumbs up to 1 day ahead.

FOR THE BACON-CHORIZO CRUMBS

6 bacon slices, preferably applewood-smoked, minced

3 ounces chorizo, Spanish-style dry-cured, minced

2 tablespoons (1 ounce) water

2 ounces toasted brioche or challah bread crumbs, from about 4 small ½-inch-thick slices

1 tablespoon fresh Italian parsley

Kosher salt and ground white pepper

FOR THE POTATOES

10 ounces fingerling potatoes, sliced ¼ inch thick

2 tablespoons (1 ounce) olive oil

¼ cup (2 ounces) water

Small sprig of fresh thyme

Kosher salt and ground white pepper

FOR THE CLAM CHOWDER

2 tablespoons (1 ounce) rendered bacon fat or lard

1 small onion, finely diced

2 celery stalks, peeled and finely diced

2 garlic cloves

2 dried bay leaves

Large sprig of fresh thyme (wrapped with kitchen twine, like a bouquet garni)

12 cherry stone clams, preferably, or little neck clams

1 cup (8 ounces) dry white wine, preferably unoaked or lightly oaked

5 cups (1 quart plus 1 cup) Light Chicken Stock (see page xxviii)

1 cup (8 ounces) bottled clam juice

½ cup (4 ounces) heavy cream

Kosher salt and ground white pepper

FOR THE CLAM FRITTERS

4 ounces cherry stone or little neck clam meat, chopped

½ cup durum flour or semolina flour

2 tablespoons stone-ground yellow cornmeal

½ teaspoon baking powder

1 large egg, whisked

½ cup (4 ounces) whole milk

¼ teaspoon Cajun spice blend

¼ teaspoon chopped fresh chives

¼ teaspoon chopped fresh tarragon, optional

1 small shallot, minced

1 teaspoon grated lemon zest

⅛ teaspoon kosher salt

⅛ teaspoon ground white pepper

2 cups (1 pint) canola or vegetable oil

⅛ teaspoon xanthan gum, optional

FOR THE FINISHED DISH

Celery leaves, fennel fronds, or red amaranth leaves, or a combination

TO PREPARE THE BACON-CHORIZO CRUMBS

1. Combine the bacon, chorizo, and water in a small saucepan. Cook over low heat, stirring occasionally until the water has evaporated and the bacon and chorizo are crisp, about 10 minutes.

2. Scrape the mixture into a food processor, add the rest of the ingredients, and pulse to combine. Reserve at room temperature.

TO PREPARE THE FINGERLING POTATOES

Preheat the oven to 350°F. Place all the ingredients in a small roasting pan and cover the pan with a sheet of aluminum foil. Bake 15 minutes, then uncover and continue baking a few more minutes, until the water has evaporated and the potatoes are tender. Let rest at room temperature.

TO PREPARE THE CHOWDER

1. Warm the bacon fat in a medium saucepan over medium heat. Add the onion, celery, garlic, bay leaves, and thyme, and sauté until the vegetables begin to soften, about 5 minutes.

2. Add the clams and continue to sauté until the clams open, 3–5 minutes more. Pour in the wine and simmer until almost dry. Pour in the stock, clam juice, and cream, and reduce the liquid by about half. Season with salt and pepper.

3. Strain through a fine-mesh sieve. Pluck out the clams from the sieve, and pop the clam meat out of them with a small knife or fork. Chop the clam meat and reserve it for the clam fritters. Keep the chowder warm on low heat.

TO PREPARE THE CLAM FRITTERS

1. Combine all the clam meat with the other fritter ingredients except the oil and xanthan gum. Mix only until lightly blended. The mixture can be refrigerated an hour before you make and fry the fritters.

2. Warm the oil in a medium saucepan to 325°F to 330°F. Spoon out the batter by teaspoons, and drop gently into the oil, a half dozen or so at a time, and cook 1–2 minutes until golden brown. Stir to prevent them from sticking to each other.

3. Scoop out the fritters with a spider or slotted spoon and transfer to paper towels. Repeat with the remaining batter.

PUTTING IT ALL TOGETHER

1. Arrange 4 soup plates or broad soup bowls on a work surface. Make a pretty pattern of garnishes in each bowl. In the center of each, mound a large spoonful of bacon-chorizo crumbs, a thin line of potatoes, and 3 or so fritters per person. Scatter leaves or herbs in each bowl. Reheat the chowder briefly, if needed, then add the xanthan gum, if using, and froth the chowder with an immersion blender. Pour the soup into a pitcher.

2. Set a bowl in front of each diner. Pour equal portions of the soup into each bowl, pooling it around the garnishes until most are submerged. Eat right away.

restaurant embellishments

In the kitchen, we add a little halo of celery ribbons to the soup as a finishing garnish. We peel the outer layer of stringy celery away from a large stalk. Then it's sliced on its thinnest side on the thinnest setting of a mandoline. It looks nice but isn't essential.

Kitchen Notes

Because the bacon is such a key flavor ingredient, I prefer to use dry-aged and hickory-smoked Berkshire bacon here, from the heritage breed known for its excellent marbling. It's available from S. Wallace Edwards & Sons in Surry, Virginia (edwardsvaham.com). Another high-quality bacon can be substituted if you wish.

CURRIED BUTTERNUT SQUASH SOUP WITH PUMPKIN SEED GRANOLA AND GINGER BATONS

SERVES 4

This is the fall and winter counterpart to our spring and summer pea soup, a butternut squash soup that my daughter Emma loves as much as our guests do. We always make an ample supply of the sweet-savory granola because our diners relish it, both in the dish and passed on the side. If you don't finish it, save the leftovers for a snack or breakfast. You can turn this into a full meal by adding the roasted duck breast discussed in Restaurant Embellishments.

POSSIBLE DO-AHEAD STEPS
- Make the Vegetable Stock up to 1 week ahead.
- Make the Butternut Squash Soup up to 2 days ahead.
- Make the Pumpkin Seed Granola up to 1 day ahead.

FOR THE GRANOLA

1 cup pepitas (shelled pumpkin seeds)

½ cup old-fashioned oats

2 ounces dried cranberries

6 tablespoons (3 ounces) unsalted butter, melted

2 tablespoons (1 ounce) mild-flavored honey, such as orange blossom

2 large egg whites, whisked

1 tablespoon packed brown sugar

1 tablespoon minced rosemary

1 teaspoon ground cinnamon

½ teaspoon kosher salt, or more to taste

¼ teaspoon ground white pepper, or more to taste

Pinch of ground allspice

Pinch of ground dried mild-to-medium red chile, such as New Mexican or ancho

FOR THE SQUASH SOUP

1 tablespoon olive oil

1 pound butternut squash, peeled and chopped

½ Granny Smith apple, chopped

½ small red bell pepper, chopped

1 fresh Fresno red chile or small New Mexican red chile, seeded and chopped, or 1 teaspoon ground dried mild to medium red chile, such as New Mexican or ancho

3 tablespoons chopped onion

1½ teaspoons minced peeled fresh ginger

½ teaspoon curry powder

1 cinnamon stick

1 cup (8 ounces) apple cider

6 cups (1½ quarts) Vegetable Stock (see page xxvii)

½ cup (4 ounces) heavy cream

Kosher salt and ground white pepper

FOR THE GINGER BATONS

Canola or vegetable oil for pan-frying

Thumb-size chunk of fresh ginger, peeled and julienned

FOR THE FINISHED DISH

Thai basil leaves, small salad greens, or fennel, chive, or borage blossoms

TO PREPARE THE GRANOLA

1. Preheat the oven to 325°F. Line a baking sheet with a non-stick mat or parchment paper.

2. Combine all ingredients in a mixing bowl.

3. Spread out the granola on the prepared baking sheet and bake for about 25 minutes, until golden brown and lightly crisp. Set the baking sheet on a baking rack to cool.

TO PREPARE THE SOUP

1. You can do this while the granola bakes. Warm the oil in a medium saucepan over medium heat. Stir in the squash, apple, bell pepper, red chile, onion, ginger, and curry powder. Cook until the ingredients have some brown edges and have softened, about 7 minutes.

2. Add the cinnamon stick and cider and reduce the liquid by about half, which should take several minutes.

3. Pour in the stock and cream and continue to simmer until again reduced by about half, about 10 minutes more. Season with salt and pepper.

4. Transfer the soup, in batches, to a blender. Remember that hot soup expands quite a bit when blended. Puree. Pour the soup into a pitcher.

TO PREPARE THE GINGER BATONS

You can make this while the soup is cooking if you like. Warm a small skillet over high heat. Add enough oil to measure ¼ inch deep. When the oil shimmers, add the ginger and fry quickly, a matter of seconds, until crispy

PUTTING IT ALL TOGETHER

1. Arrange 4 soup plates or broad soup bowls on a work surface. Make a pretty pattern of garnishes in each bowl. In the center of each, mound about 3 tablespoons of the granola with a spoonful of ginger beside them. Scatter leaves or blossoms around the bowls.

2. Set a bowl in front of each diner. Pour equal portions of the soup into each bowl, pooling it around the garnishes until most are submerged. Eat right away.

Kitchen Notes

My soups use no flour, little cream (even my chowders), and a lot of vegetable essence to build depth of flavor. They are substantial without overloading you for the rest of a meal.

restaurant embellishments

Cooks should use more buttermilk. Buttermilk Curd makes a tangy complement to swirl into the soup. It's similar to a lemon curd but has more savory creaminess. Here's what you'll need.

BUTTERMILK CURD

3 ounces unsalted butter

½ cup buttermilk

1 large egg

2 large egg yolks

1 tablespoon lemon juice

1 teaspoon grated lemon zest

1 bloomed silver gelatin sheet

Kosher salt and ground white pepper

1. Whisk together in the top of a double boiler butter, the buttermilk, egg, and egg yolks. When the butter has completely melted in and disappeared, add the lemon juice and continue to whisk the mixture until it's pale in color and thick enough to coat a spoon.

2. Strain through a fine-mesh sieve. Whisk in lemon zest and bloomed gelatin sheet.

3. Season with kosher salt and a bit of ground white pepper.

4. Pour into a shallow pan, cool, and refrigerate until firm, about 1 hour. Whisk again before spooning it into the soup bowls.

I do love duck, and here's a way to use a little of it to great effect.

PAN-ROASTED DUCK BREAST

1 tablespoon canola or vegetable oil

5- to 6-ounce skin-on individual
   duck breast

Kosher salt and ground white pepper

1 tablespoon unsalted butter

1 tablespoon mild-flavored honey,
   such as orange blossom

Sprig of fresh thyme

1. Season duck with salt and pepper.

2. Warm a small sauté pan over high heat until it just starts to smoke. Turn the heat down to medium and pour in oil, swirling it around quickly.

3. Add the duck skin-side down and sauté until the skin renders some fat and becomes golden-brown and crisp, at least 4 minutes. (The browning may take twice this long, depending on the thickness of the skin and the exact heat level.) If the skin is browning before a good bit of fat is rendered, reduce the heat.

4. Turn the duck breast over and sear for about 4 minutes on the other side for rare to medium-rare doneness, an internal temperature reading of 130°F–135°F.

5. Add butter, honey, and fresh thyme. Baste the duck breast with the mixture for 30 seconds over the heat, then remove the pan from the heat and continue to spoon the honey butter over the duck for another 30 seconds.

6. Remove the duck breast from the pan and let it rest on paper towels for 2–3 minutes. Then slice down through the skin and across the grain very thinly. Add equal portions to each soup bowl before pouring in the soup.

CAULIFLOWER-APPLE SOUP WITH CHIVE PUREE AND GRUYÉRE CRISPS

SERVES 4

The cheese crisp recipe makes more than you need to top the silky stark-white soup because you, your family, and friends will definitely start nibbling them. They will disappear quickly, especially if you have a cheese-loving kid around like my daughter Anneliese.

POSSIBLE DO-AHEAD STEPS

- The Vegetable Stock can be made up to 1 week ahead.
- The Cauliflower-Apple Soup can be made up to 1 day ahead.
- The Gruyére Crisps can be made up to 8 hours ahead.

FOR THE GRUYÉRE CRISPS

1 sheet fillo dough

1 tablespoon unsalted butter, melted

2 ounces grated Gruyére cheese

Kosher salt

½ teaspoon freshly cracked black pepper

FOR THE CAULIFLOWER SOUP

¼ cup (2 ounces) olive oil

½ cup diced white onion

1 medium shallot, thinly sliced

1 garlic clove, thinly sliced

1 small stalk lemongrass, crushed lightly

Sprig of fresh thyme

1 small head cauliflower (about 1 pound after removing any leaves and tough stem)

1 Granny Smith apple, peeled and chopped

2 cups (1 pint) whole milk

1 cup (8 ounces) Vegetable Stock (see page xxvii)

½ cup (4 ounces) heavy cream

1 tablespoon fresh lemon juice

Kosher salt and ground white pepper

FOR THE CHIVE PUREE

1 cup fresh chives, blanched

¼ cup (2 ounces) ice water

¼ teaspoon xanthan gum

Kosher salt and ground white pepper

FOR THE FINISHED DISH

Small arugula or watercress leaves or radish or sunflower or red amaranth sprouts

TO PREPARE THE GRUYÉRE CRISPS

1. Preheat the oven to 350°F. Line a baking sheet with a non-stick mat or parchment paper.

2. Place the sheet of fillo horizontally on a work surface and brush lightly with about ⅓ of the butter. Be sure to cover all the edges with butter. Scatter about half of the cheese over the buttered fillo, and then sprinkle with a few grains of salt and pepper.

3. Fold the fillo in half, like a book. Top again with butter, cheese, salt, and pepper. Fold once again, so that you end up with a rectangle about 4 x 12 inches. Brush the remaining butter over the top.

4. Cut the dough lengthwise into 6 long ribbons, preferably with a fluted pastry cutter. Arrange them carefully on the baking sheet. Then cover with another non-stick mat or parchment sheet, and top with a second baking sheet. You'll have a sandwich.

5. Bake about 20 minutes until golden brown and crisp, with bits of cheese feathering out from the sides. Uncover and cool on the bottom baking sheet over a baking rack.

TO PREPARE THE SOUP

1. Warm the oil in a medium saucepan over medium heat. Stir in the onion, shallot, garlic, lemongrass, thyme, cauliflower, and apple, and cook until the onion and shallots are limp but not colored, about 5 minutes.

2. Pour in the milk, stock, cream, and lemon juice and simmer the mixture until the cauliflower is very tender and the liquid reduced by about half.

3. Discard the lemongrass and thyme sprig. Transfer the warm soup to a blender, in batches, and puree. Strain through a fine-mesh sieve back into the saucepan. Season with salt and pepper and keep warm over low heat.

TO PREPARE THE CHIVE PUREE

Combine all the ingredients together in a blender and puree. Chill in the refrigerator until needed.

PUTTING IT ALL TOGETHER

If you have 4 dark or bright colored bowls, this is a good place to use them. Pour the soup into the bowls. Set a gruyére crisp over the top of each bowl, balanced on its rim. Break off a bit at either end if the crisps look extra-long across your bowls. Spoon chive puree over the center of the crisps so that some of it spills down into the white soup. Arrange leaves over the crisps and serve right away.

restaurant embellishment

I like to make Baked Apple Slices to accompany the soup.

BAKED APPLE SLICES

> 3 cups (1 ½ pints) water
> ½ cup (4 ounces) simple syrup (see page 36)
> Juice of half a lemon
> 1 Granny Smith apple, unpeeled and sliced thin on a mandoline
> Vegetable oil spray

1. Preheat the oven to 325°F and line a baking sheet with a non-stick mat or parchment paper, spraying either with vegetable oil.

2. In a medium saucepan bring water, syrup, and juice to a boil.

3. Blanch the apple slices in the mixture until limp, less than 1 minute.

4. Place the apple slices flat on the prepared baking sheet, spray them with vegetable oil, and bake until lightly crisp, 8–10 minutes.

TISANE OF LEMON BALM AND SHIITAKE MUSHROOMS WITH CRAB-GRAPEFRUIT SALAD AND UDON NOODLE CLOUDS

SERVES 4

This makes a fine meal or starter any time of the year. A tisane is an infusion of herbs in hot water, what typically gets called an herbal tea, even though there's no tea in it. Just to make it interesting, and even tastier, I include some black tea with the herbs and mushrooms. Usually, I'm not big on brothy soups, except for Asian noodle soups like pho, which played into my thinking here. I also enjoy the combination of sweet and sour tastes in Asian dishes, which shows up here in the seafood "salad" that adorns the bowl. And speaking of adornment, the noodle nest peeking out of the top of the soup is pretty cool too.

POSSIBLE DO-AHEAD STEPS

- Make the tisane up to 8 hours ahead.
- Combine the Crab and Grapefruit Salad and fry the Udon Noodle Clouds up to 2 hours ahead.

FOR THE LEMON BALM AND MUSHROOMS

1 small onion, chopped

2 celery stalks, chopped

1 medium carrot, chopped

2 tablespoons fresh ginger, chopped

4 ounces dry shiitake mushrooms

2 tablespoons (1 ounce) tomato paste

1 tablespoon black tea leaves

1 large bunch fresh lemon balm (about 6 stems, 6–8 inches long)

1 lemongrass stalk, crushed lightly

1 cup (8 ounces) sake

2 tablespoons (1 ounce) soy sauce

2 teaspoons dry bonito flakes

8 cups (2 quarts) water

FOR THE CRAB-GRAPEFRUIT SALAD

4 ounces Dungeness crabmeat

1 Rio Star or other ruby grapefruit, peeled and cut into segments

1 Granny Smith apple, thinly sliced

½ English cucumber, thinly sliced into rounds

1 tablespoon extra-virgin olive oil

Juice of half a lime

Kosher salt and ground white pepper

FOR THE NOODLE CLOUDS

8 ounces udon noodles, cooked according to package directions and drained on paper towels

2 cups (16 ounces) canola or vegetable oil

1 teaspoon furikake or shichimi togarashi seasoning

FOR THE FINISHED DISH

Cilantro or shiso leaves, lemon balm leaves, small Bull's Blood beet tops, or feathery carrot tops

TO PREPARE THE TISANE

1. Combine all the ingredients in a medium saucepan. Warm over low heat for 30 minutes. The mixture should reduce by about half. Cook a few minutes more if needed.

2. Remove from the heat, cover, and let the mixture sit 20 more minutes to infuse.

3. Line a fine-mesh sieve with a coffee filter (to help get a very clear broth) and slowly pour the mixture through it. Don't push on the solids. Refrigerate the broth if you will not be completing the soup in the next 30 minutes.

TO PREPARE THE SALAD

Combine all the ingredients in a medium bowl, mixing them lightly. Refrigerate until needed.

TO PREPARE THE NOODLE NESTS

1. Line a baking sheet with several paper towels.

2. Warm the oil in a medium saucepan to 325°F to 330°F. Drop in a quarter of the noodles, stirring them around to fry evenly. Fry for about 30 seconds, until crisp.

3. Remove them with a spider or large slotted spoon as one nest of noodles, and transfer to the paper towels. Sprinkle with furikake seasoning. Repeat with the remaining noodles and furikake.

PUTTING IT ALL TOGETHER

1. Reheat the soup, if needed, and pour it into a pitcher.

2. Arrange 4 soup plates or broad soup bowls on a work surface. Make a pretty pattern of garnishes in each bowl. Arrange the salad in the middle of the bowl and tuck leaves around the salad. Arrange a noodle cloud over each salad.

3. Set a bowl in front of each diner. Pour equal portions of the soup into each bowl, pooling it around the garnishes. The noodle nest will be only partially submerged. Eat right away.

Kitchen Notes

Furikake and shichimi togarashi are Japanese dried spice blends. They contain seaweed and orange peel among other flavorings. Shichimi has chile too. Both are available in the Asian section of many supermarkets, in many spice shops and Asian markets, and online. Use them sprinkled over rice, sashimi, or any bowl of noodles.

salads

SPRING ASPARAGUS SALAD WITH SHEEP'S MILK CHEESE, LEMON BALM-BUTTERMILK CUSTARD, SORREL PUREE, AND POACHED QUAIL EGG

SERVES 4

I really try to push the boundaries with salads. I love greens, but there is so much else that goes well in salads to give them the same union of textures, sweet and savory flavors, and surprise elements that you find in main dishes. This salad is one of the prettiest and tastiest ways to start a spring dinner or to enjoy alone as a light lunch. When I prepare some cucumber-wrapped asparagus bundles for the dish, I often laugh about making asparagus charlotte in the Georges Blanc kitchen. It's a gelatin-gilded crown of vertical asparagus spears surrounding layers of chopped asparagus, crème fraîche, and hard-boiled eggs, and the standing spears were always falling over in my version like in a game of pick-up sticks. In comparison this salad is extraordinarily simple to compose.

POSSIBLE DO-AHEAD STEPS

• Blanch the asparagus spears and make the Lemon Balm-Buttermilk Custard up to 1 day ahead.

FOR THE CUSTARD

¼ cup chopped fresh lemon balm

1 cup (8 ounces) buttermilk

½ cup (4 ounces) heavy cream

2 large eggs

2 tablespoons cornstarch

½ teaspoon agar agar

2 tablespoons (1 ounce) unsalted butter, cut in 4 pieces

Kosher salt and ground white pepper

FOR THE SORREL PUREE

1 cup fresh sorrel leaves, or arugula, blanched with gangly stems trimmed off

¼ cup (2 ounces) olive oil

½ cup (4 ounces) ice water

½ teaspoon minced shallot

Kosher salt and ground white pepper

FOR THE ASPARAGUS AND CUCUMBER BUNDLES

16 jumbo asparagus, blanched, and trimmed of tough stems to about 6 inches in length

2 tablespoons (1 ounce) extra-virgin olive oil

½ teaspoon grated lime zest

Kosher salt and ground white pepper

1 English cucumber (unpeeled), thinly sliced lengthwise on a mandoline

FOR THE EGGS

1 tablespoon white wine vinegar or white vinegar

Kosher salt

4 quail eggs or small chicken eggs

FOR THE FINISHED DISH

Aged manchego cheese, about 4 ounces, shaved or planed into a dozen thin slices

Small radicchio leaves and arugula or watercress leaves

Kosher salt and ground white pepper

8 salted, roasted Marcona almonds

TO PREPARE THE CUSTARD

1. Warm the lemon balm, buttermilk, and cream together in a small saucepan over medium heat. Slowly bring the mixture just to a boil.

2. Meanwhile, mix together in a small bowl the eggs, cornstarch, and agar agar. Whisk about ½ cup of the hot milk mixture into the egg mixture to temper the eggs. Pour the milk-and-egg mixture back into the saucepan, whisking continually.

3. Bring the custard back to a boil, then whisk in the butter, 1 piece at a time. Season with salt and pepper.

4. When the butter is incorporated and the sauce is thick and shiny, strain it through a fine-mesh sieve. Push as much through the sieve as you can. Cool over an ice bath, stirring occasionally. Chill 20 minutes or until needed.

TO PREPARE THE SORREL PUREE

1. Combine all the ingredients in a blender and puree. Reserve at room temperature until needed.

TO PREPARE THE ASPARAGUS-CUCUMBER BUNDLES

1. In a medium bowl, toss the asparagus spears with extra-virgin olive oil to coat, then sprinkle them with lime zest and season with salt and pepper. Reserve the remaining oil mixture for a later use.

2. On a 12-inch square piece of plastic wrap, lay out 4 slices of cucumber, just overlapping, in a rectangle. You want the shorter side of this rectangle to be as wide as your asparagus is long. Bundle 4 asparagus and place them at the bottom of a shorter side of cucumber slices. Using the plastic wrap for support, roll the end of the cucumber rectangle up and over the asparagus. Pull back the plastic and keep rolling into a snug tube of cucumber-wrapped asparagus. Wrap the plastic over the completed tube. Roll the tube back and forth a time or two, if needed, to even it out. Repeat with the remaining ingredients. Refrigerate the 4 tubes until needed.

TO PREPARE THE EGGS

1. Fill a broad saucepan with about 2 inches of water, pour in the vinegar, add a big pinch of salt, and bring just to a boil.

2. Break the eggs into individual ramekins.

3. Reduce the heat to a bare simmer, then slip the eggs into the water and simmer gently for 20 seconds. Turn off the heat and cover for 1–2 minutes.

4. Remove the eggs with a slotted spoon and place each on a separate section of paper towel to drain. Trim any ragged edges off the egg whites.

PUTTING IT ALL TOGETHER

Cut each asparagus-cucumber roll with a sharp knife into 3 even pieces. For each of the 4 servings, arrange the 3 pieces more or less in a line down the center of a large shallow bowl or plate. I place the section with the asparagus tips standing, tips up, then lay one on its side, and another standing. Spoon a couple of mounds of custard to either side. Drizzle a puddle of sorrel puree to the side of the asparagus. Nudge an egg off the paper towel and onto the plate near the asparagus. Arrange manchego cheese shards over and between. Toss leaves with the remaining olive oil and lime zest from the asparagus, and arrange a few on each plate. Sprinkle a few grains of salt and pepper over the plates. With a micro-plane, grate an almond or two over each plate and serve.

Kitchen Notes

- Hollandaise sauce, as you probably know, is a frequent accompaniment for asparagus. The buttermilk custard here has some of the characteristics of that heavier French "mother" sauce, but it is lighter, brighter, can be made ahead without separating, and works chilled to taste more refreshing with a salad. The lemon balm infuses it with a subtle lemony essence and aroma without any of the citrus fruit.

- Tangy sorrel, a spring herb, has lemony undertones great with asparagus and cheese. The leaves are large, as herbs go, but can nearly dissolve in hot water, so blanch them for just a few seconds in boiling water before plunging them into ice water. One cup of packed fresh leaves should yield about ½ cup of blanched. Arugula isn't quite as lemony, but can pinch hit for sorrel if necessary. It makes a vibrant green puree but the color will fade over a few hours.

HEIRLOOM TOMATO SALAD WITH FRESH MOZZARELLA MOUSSE, BASIL GEL, AND FROZEN CITRUS VINAIGRETTE

SERVES 4

Just about everyone loves the classic summer Caprese salad, but it seems to me a restaurant chef should do something to it. Otherwise, why not stay home and tell the servers to simply slice some great garden tomatoes and combine them with a little mozzarella and basil? I don't mess with the essentials, just twist them a bit here in a way that makes the salad more exciting to serve at home too. Heirloom plum tomatoes tend to be a good bit smaller than the Roma plum tomatoes that are routinely available most of the year.

POSSIBLE DO-AHEAD STEPS

- The Fresh Mozzarella Mousse can be made up to 1 day ahead.
- The Frozen Citrus Vinaigrette can be made and frozen up to 8 hours ahead.

FOR THE MOUSSE

1 cup (8 ounces) water

2 teaspoons unflavored powdered gelatin

8 ounces fresh mozzarella, chopped

2 ounces mascarpone cheese

1 sprig medium-size fresh basil leaves

1 teaspoon fresh lemon juice

Kosher salt and ground white pepper

FOR THE VINAIGRETTE

¼ cup (2 ounces) fresh lemon juice

¼ cup (2 ounces) orange juice

2 tablespoons (1 ounce) champagne vinegar

1 teaspoon Dijon mustard

¼ cup plus 2 tablespoons (3 ounces) simple syrup

¼ cup (2 ounces) olive oil

¼ teaspoon agar agar

1 tablespoon grated lemon zest

Kosher salt and ground white pepper

FOR THE BASIL GEL

¾ cup plus 2 tablespoons (7 ounces) water

1 cup packed basil leaves, blanched (about ½ cup)

Pinch of xanthan gum

Kosher salt and ground white pepper

FOR THE TOMATO SALAD

16 heirloom plum tomatoes of varying colors, or other small to medium heirloom tomatoes

2 tablespoons (1 ounce) extra-virgin olive oil

1 tablespoon champagne vinegar

1 teaspoon minced fresh tarragon or chives or a combination

Pinch of ground coriander

Pinch of granulated sugar

Kosher salt and ground white pepper

FOR THE FINISHED DISH

Black olive crackers

Small basil leaves or sprouts, and baby spinach leaves, small amaranth leaves, or small Bull's Blood beet greens

Thinly sliced fennel, optional

Extra-virgin olive oil

Flaky sea salt, such as Maldon, or more kosher salt

TO PREPARE THE MOUSSE

1. Set aside about 2 tablespoons of the water in a ramekin, sprinkle the gelatin over it, and let it stand for several minutes.

2. Combine the remaining water, mozzarella, mascarpone, basil, and lemon juice in a small saucepan. Warm over medium-low heat, stirring occasionally, until the cheese mixture comes to a boil.

3. Reduce the heat to maintain a simmer for about 5 minutes, or as needed for the mozzarella to completely melt into the liquid.

4. Whisk in the gelatin, season with salt and pepper, and continue to simmer 2–3 more minutes, until the gelatin has dissolved into the mousse. Puree the mousse, in batches if your blender is small.

5. Strain the mousse through a fine-mesh strainer into a medium bowl. Cover and chill the mixture in the refrigerator until softly set, at least 30 minutes.

TO PREPARE THE VINAIGRETTE

1. In a small saucepan, combine the lemon and orange juices, vinegar, mustard, syrup, and olive oil. Bring the mixture to a quick boil, and whisk in the agar agar. Boil for about 2 more minutes, until the agar agar has dissolved.

2. Strain the vinaigrette through a fine-mesh sieve into a small shallow pan. Stir in the lemon zest and season with salt and pepper.

3. Transfer the vinaigrette to the freezer. After 20 minutes, and again after 40 minutes, remove the vinaigrette mixture from the freezer briefly and scrape it up from the bottom of the pan with a fork, fluffing up the ice crystals. After about 1 hour, it should be solid enough, but it can remain in the freezer for up to 7 additional hours.

TO PREPARE THE BASIL GEL

Puree the ingredients together in a blender. Chill covered in the refrigerator until needed.

TO PREPARE THE TOMATO SALAD

1. With a thin paring knife, cut a tiny x in the bottom of each tomato.

2. Bring a pot with about 3 inches of water to a boil. Dunk the tomatoes in the water, in batches if necessary, for about 20 seconds, then remove them with a spider and drain them.

3. Starting at the cuts, pull the skin away in pieces and discard it.

4. Gently combine the tomatoes in a bowl with the extra-virgin olive oil, vinegar, herbs, coriander, and sugar, and season with salt and pepper.

PUTTING IT ALL TOGETHER

Arrange 4 tomatoes down the center of each of 4 plates. I slice the bottom off of 1 or 2 per plate to stand them up, then let the others lean against them. Spoon a mound of mousse to one side, then scrape up several small spoonfuls of frozen vinaigrette to top the tomatoes. Add dots or dribbles of basil gel to each plate, tuck in a couple of crackers, then garnish with basil and other leaves. Dot with a bit of extra-virgin olive oil and a sprinkling of additional salt, and serve.

MELON SALAD WITH BRILLAT-SAVARIN CHEESE, SOYBEAN PUDDING, BLACK PEPPER–VANILLA VINAIGRETTE, AND BLACK OLIVE CRUMBS

SERVES 4

Jewel-toned summer melons balance well with the salty savor of black olives and a vinaigrette punched up with black pepper and the warm sweetness of vanilla. You can save yourself a few minutes by buying a package of Parmesan crisps at a grocery store, but they won't be as lacy and curled as your own, featured in Restaurant Embellishments.

POSSIBLE DO-AHEAD STEPS

- Make the Melon Salad up to 8 hours ahead.
- Make the Soybean Pudding up to 4 hours ahead.

FOR THE MELON SALAD

½ cup (4 ounces) simple syrup

2 tablespoons (1 ounce) Grand Marnier, Patrón Citronge, or other orange liqueur

2 tablespoons (1 ounce) olive oil

Small sprig of fresh lemon verbena

Small sprig of fresh dill

Kosher salt and ground white pepper

8 ounces of at least two kinds of seasonal melons (trimmed and cut into ½-inch blocks)

FOR THE SOYBEAN PUDDING

1 cup thawed frozen shelled soybeans (edamame)

½ cup packed Italian parsley, blanched

¾ cup (6 ounces) ice water

1 teaspoon minced shallot

¼ teaspoon minced garlic

½ teaspoon grated lemon zest

¼ teaspoon xanthan gum

¼ teaspoon kosher salt and several pinches of ground white pepper

FOR THE OLIVE CRUMBS

½ cup coarse bread crumbs or panko crumbs

2 tablespoons (1 ounce) unsalted butter, melted

1 tablespoon minced pitted Kalamata black olives

Kosher salt and ground white pepper

FOR THE VINAIGRETTE

2 tablespoons (1 ounce) rice vinegar

1 tablespoon lime juice

1 teaspoon fresh cracked black pepper

½ teaspoon grated fresh ginger

1 teaspoon Nielson-Massey vanilla bean paste, preferably, or pure vanilla extract

½ cup (4 ounces) olive oil

FOR THE FINISHED DISH

Pinches of kosher salt

4 ounces Brillat-Savarin cheese, or other triple cream cheese such as Saint André or Mt Tam, softened

Small fennel fronds, chocolate mint leaves or other small mint leaves, or small salad greens

TO PREPARE THE MELON SALAD

In a zipper-lock gallon bag, combine the simple syrup, orange liqueur, olive oil, herbs, and good pinches of salt and pepper. Stir the marinade around, then add the melon cubes. Refrigerate for at least 30 minutes, but no longer than 8 hours.

TO PREPARE THE SOYBEAN PUDDING

Puree all the ingredients in a blender. Strain the pudding through a fine-mesh sieve, scraping as needed to push it through. Chill covered in the refrigerator until needed.

TO PREPARE THE BLACK OLIVE CRUMBS

Combine all the ingredients in a small bowl. Toast them together in a sauté pan until crisp and golden. Spread the crumbs on paper towels to cool.

TO PREPARE THE VINAIGRETTE

Whisk together all the ingredients in a small bowl.

PUTTING IT ALL TOGETHER

Drain the melon cubes and sprinkle a little salt over them. Arrange a mix of all colors of melon cubes equally down the sides of 4 plates. Stack a couple of them here and there. Spoon 2 mounds of cheese next to the melons and a pool of soybean pudding to one side. Drizzle the vinaigrette around the melons. Garnish with a tablespoon of mounded olive crumbs, tuck herbs and greens in and around, and serve.

restaurant embellishments

PARMESAN CRISPS

4 ounces freshly grated Parmesan cheese
Freshly cracked black pepper

1. Preheat the oven to 400ºF.
2. Line a baking sheet with a non-stick mat or lightly oiled parchment paper.
3. Spread Parmesan cheese on the baking sheet into 8 small circles about 2 inches in diameter. Sprinkle a pinch or 2 of freshly cracked black pepper over each cheese circle.
4. Bake until the crisps start to color and set, 3–5 minutes.
5. The crisps can be used flat, but I prefer to fold them while they are still warm like a French *tuile*. Wrap each quickly around a metal cannoli tube or wooden tortilla roller to form a cylinder.
6. When your guests arrive, make a big deal about the enormous effort you expended in making the special crisps just for them.

Kitchen Notes

Simple syrup is made by boiling together equal parts of granulated sugar and water. You can buy it wherever cocktail supplies are sold, but it's so simple to make your own and it keeps forever in a bottle in the refrigerator.

BARBECUED YOUNG CARROT SALAD WITH ORANGES, BLUE CHEESE–WALNUT MILLE-FEUILLE, AND RED PEPPER CURD

SERVES 4

Carrots and oranges make a great pairing. I like to add a little more zing to their relationship, though, so I toss the carrots with a barbecue-style sauce first. Then I make a little layered mixture I whimsically call a mille-feuille, the term for a multilayered French pastry, interspersing blue cheese with candied walnuts. If you have access to Point Reyes blue cheese from northern California, use it. Otherwise, opt for another creamy but deeply flavored blue. If you are short of time, you could top the salad with crumbles of the cheese and the walnut pieces, as a substitute for the mille-feuille, or even start from store-bought candied walnuts. Look for deeply colored Cara Cara oranges in their winter season. Not only are they gorgeous, but they have very little acid and a robust sweetness. A brilliant red pepper puree blazes among all the other colors.

POSSIBLE DO-AHEAD STEPS

- Make the Red Pepper Curd, Candied Walnuts, and assemble the Layered Blue Cheese Mille-feuille up to 1 day ahead.

FOR THE RED PEPPER CURD

1 tablespoon water

1 teaspoon unflavored powdered gelatin

6 ounces red bell pepper, roasted, peeled, and pureed

1 large egg

1 large egg yolk

1 teaspoon granulated sugar

¼ teaspoon agar agar

Kosher salt and ground white pepper

FOR THE CANDIED WALNUTS

1 cup walnut pieces

2 tablespoons (1 ounce) mild-flavored honey, such as orange blossom

1 tablespoon unsalted butter

Kosher salt and ground white pepper

FOR THE BLUE CHEESE MILLE-FEUILLE

10 ounces Point Reyes blue cheese or other creamy blue cheese

2 tablespoons (1 ounce) extra-virgin olive oil

Candied walnuts

½ teaspoon fresh thyme leaves

Pinch or 2 of ground coriander

FOR THE BARBECUED CARROTS

16 young carrots, preferably of different colors, scrubbed but not peeled, gangly stems or root ends trimmed

¼ cup (2 ounces) olive oil

1 tablespoon ketchup

1 teaspoon ground dried mild to medium red chile, such as New Mexican or ancho

½ teaspoon dry mustard powder

¼ teaspoon ground dried ginger

⅛ teaspoon ground coriander

Kosher salt and ground white pepper

FOR THE VINAIGRETTE

1 small shallot, minced

2 tablespoons minced fresh chives

2 tablespoons minced fresh Italian parsley

1 teaspoon minced fresh dill

½ cup (4 ounces) olive oil

1 tablespoon fresh lemon juice

1 tablespoon roasting liquid from carrots

Kosher salt and ground white pepper

FOR THE FINISHED DISH

2 navel oranges, Cara Cara if available, peeled and cut into individual segments

Kosher salt and ground white pepper

Belgian endive leaves, dill sprigs, Italian parsley leaves, or small watercress or beet leaves

TO PREPARE THE RED PEPPER CURD

1. Pour the water into a ramekin. Sprinkle the gelatin over the water and let the mixture stand for several minutes.

2. In the top of a double boiler, combine the red pepper puree, egg, yolk, sugar, and agar agar. Place over a pan of simmering water and whisk the mixture until it thickens enough to coat the back of a spoon.

3. Stir in the gelatin and water, and continue cooking about 2 minutes more until the gelatin has dissolved into the curd.

4. Strain the curd through a fine-mesh sieve into a medium bowl, pushing on the bell pepper pulp to release as much flavor as possible.

5. Season with salt and pepper.

6. Cover the bowl and chill the mixture in the refrigerator until needed.

TO PREPARE THE CANDIED WALNUTS

1. Preheat the oven to 350°F.

2. Line a baking sheet with a non-stick mat or lightly oiled parchment paper.

3. Mix all the ingredients together in a small bowl and spoon the coated nuts onto the baking sheet.

4. Bake until lightly browned and dried out, 10–12 minutes. Leave the oven on, but remove the nuts and cool them on the baking sheet placed over a baking rack. Once they're cool, break or chop them into small pieces.

TO PREPARE THE BLUE CHEESE MILLE-FEUILLE

1. Line a baby bread loaf pan or a pair of 6- to 8-ounce ramekins with plastic wrap. Press about 2 ounces of cheese in the bottom of the pan or ramekins. Try to keep the blue veins of the cheese somewhat intact so you don't end up with gray-looking cheese. Drizzle with enough extra-virgin oil to glisten.

2. Add enough chopped walnuts to cover the cheese. Scatter with a few thyme leaves, a smidgen of coriander, and begin again with about 2 more ounces of cheese. Repeat and layer upwards, topping with cheese. Cover with plastic wrap and refrigerate until needed.

TO PREPARE THE CARROTS

1. Line a baking sheet with a non-stick mat or lightly oiled parchment paper.

2. Bring about 3 inches of lightly salted water to a boil in a broad saucepan.

3. Dunk the carrots in the water and boil for 1 minute. Cool the carrots in ice water, then dry them.

4. Transfer the carrots to a medium bowl and combine them with the oil, ketchup, chile, dry mustard, ginger, coriander, and salt and pepper.

5. Spread the carrots out on the baking sheet in a single layer, reserving the oil and ketchup mixture left in the bowl. Bake the carrots in the 350°F oven for 12–15 minutes, or until tender.

6. Reserve the carrots at room temperature. Measure 2 tablespoons of the reserved carrot oil and ketchup mixture to add to the vinaigrette.

TO PREPARE THE VINAIGRETTE

Whisk together all the ingredients in a small bowl.

PUTTING IT ALL TOGETHER

Unmold the cheese mille-feuille. Slice it into 8 equal sections. Arrange 2 pieces of cheese on 4 plates. Arrange carrots at angles over the cheese. Divide the orange segments among the plates, interspersing them with the carrots. Drizzle the vinaigrette over and around the carrots, leaving a little to coat the endive leaves and herbs. Whisk the red pepper curd vigorously, then spoon on mounds of it beside the carrots and oranges. Sprinkle lightly with salt and pepper. Dunk endive leaves and herbs in the remaining vinaigrette, scatter them around each plate, and serve.

Kitchen Notes

I blanch the carrots before roasting them because I think it helps them hold their color better and stay more evenly moist during their time in the oven.

PRAWN SALAD WITH RICE PAPER VEIL AND YUZU-GINGER COULIS

SERVES 4

I like to give a twist to expected preparations, in this case turning a traditional spring roll into a plated salad. It mixes shrimp with some of my favorite seafood pairings—mango, grapefruit, and avocado—but in a completely different fashion than any of my other dishes. It's also a darned easy recipe for the kudos it will get you.

POSSIBLE DO-AHEAD STEPS

- Make the Boiled Prawns up to 8 hours ahead.

FOR THE BOILED PRAWNS

4 ounces chopped fresh fennel

½ medium onion, chopped

½ medium lemon

Small chunk of jalapeño or serrano chile, optional

1 large sprig fresh thyme or tarragon

Kosher salt and ground white pepper

12 medium Mexican prawns or other shrimp, peeled

FOR THE COULIS

1 tablespoon yuzu juice

1 teaspoon minced fresh ginger

½ teaspoon minced fresh chives

½ teaspoon minced fresh tarragon

½ teaspoon minced jalapeño or serrano chile

2 tablespoons (1 ounce) water

¼ cup plus 2 tablespoons (3 ounces) olive oil

Kosher salt and ground white pepper

FOR THE FINISHED DISH

1 tablespoon extra-virgin olive oil

½ teaspoon grated lime zest

1 mango, thinly sliced on a mandoline

1 avocado, thinly sliced

1 grapefruit, preferably a Rio Star or other red variety, peeled and sliced into segments

4 sheets rice paper spring roll wrappers, about 8 inches in diameter, softened

Approximately 1 tablespoon white soy sauce or other Japanese soy sauce

Approximately 1 teaspoon mustard or vegetable oil

Baby pok choi, mint, or shiso leaves, fennel fronds, radish or red amaranth sprouts, or small salad greens

TO PREPARE THE BOILED PRAWNS

1. Combine the fennel, onion, lemon, chile, thyme, several good-size pinches of salt and a good pinch of pepper with about 4 inches of water in a medium saucepan.

2. Bring to a boil, then reduce the heat to a simmer and cook for 5 minutes to flavor the water.

3. Add the prawns to the pan and simmer until they turn from translucent to opaque, just a couple of minutes. Drain off the cooking liquid and chill the prawns in a covered bowl in the refrigerator.

TO PREPARE THE COULIS

Combine all the ingredients in a blender. Give a very quick on-off blitz, just to mix the ingredients up a bit, not fully puree them. Reserve at room temperature.

PUTTING IT ALL TOGETHER

1. Remove the tails from the prawns and halve each lengthwise, deveining them as you go. Arrange the prawns equally down the center of 4 plates, shingled slightly over each other, like fallen dominoes. Drizzle about ½ teaspoon of the coulis over each plate of prawns.

2. Combine the olive oil and lime zest in a small bowl. Dunk the mango slices, avocado slices, and grapefruit segments in the oil mixture. Cover the prawns with several mango slices, then lay avocado slices over the mangoes. Tuck at least 1 grapefruit segment along each long side of the prawn stacks.

3. Blot moisture from a softened rice paper and cut off the edges so you have a rectangle just larger than the prawn stacks. Lay it over the prawn stacks smoothly and tuck in around the edges. Using your fingers, rub just enough soy sauce and mustard oil over the rice paper to make it glisten.

4. Divide the remaining coulis among the plates, spooning a bit over the rice paper and more to pool around the rolls. Top each with a few leaves and serve.

Kitchen Notes

- To my taste, no other grapefruit compares to the quality of Texas Rio Grande Valley Rio Star fruit, in season generally from November to April. They are worth seeking out for their intensely refreshing taste and deep color.

- To segment a grapefruit or other citrus neatly, so that no membrane remains, first slice off enough of the peel from the top and bottom for it to set evenly on a work surface. Peel the grapefruit, working with a small thin-bladed knife. Start at the top and cut down around the side deeply enough to remove all the white pith. Repeat around the circumference of the fruit. Slice into the grapefruit along both sides of each of the membranes, cutting to the center of the fruit. Each segment should release, leaving behind the membranes. The process becomes easy with practice.

- Slightly spicy mustard oil is made from mustard seeds and used frequently in Indian cooking. A little goes a long way. Used in large quantities, it can be a real sinus clearer, like wasabi. If not available, use some canola or vegetable oil to help keep the rice paper veil glistening.

MY RAW AND COOKED GARDEN WITH FENNEL PANNA COTTA AND TOASTED ALMOND-QUINOA SALAD

SERVES 4

When two chefs got married at the restaurant recently, we put together some little "garden shots," shot glasses half-filled with carrot pudding topped with tiny carrots, greens, and blossoms, for their reception. They looked like vegetables and flowers popping up from a terra cotta pot. I expanded on the idea to make a fully plated salad that would incorporate different vegetables and textures. I feel like a child again when I get to play with multiple colors of carrots, pop open sugar snap peas, curl up cucumbers, turn beets into gel, and make little "soldiers" out of kohlrabi.

POSSIBLE DO-AHEAD STEPS

- Make the Vegetable Stock up to 1 week ahead.
- Make the Fennel Panna Cotta up to 1 day ahead.
- Assemble the Toasted Almond-Quinoa Salad up to 4 hours ahead.

FOR THE FENNEL PANNA COTTA

10 ounces fennel, chopped

1 cup (8 ounces) ice water

1 tablespoon unflavored powdered gelatin

¼ cup (2 ounces) heavy cream

1 teaspoon minced fresh ginger

1 small sprig fresh tarragon

½ teaspoon agar agar

Kosher salt and ground white pepper

2 teaspoons grated lemon zest

FOR THE ALMOND-QUINOA SALAD

¼ cup sliced almonds, toasted and finely chopped

½ cup cooked quinoa

1 teaspoon chopped chives

½ teaspoon chopped fresh mint

½ teaspoon chopped candied ginger

¼ teaspoon grated lemon zest

2 tablespoons (1 ounce) extra-virgin olive oil

1 tablespoon champagne vinegar

Kosher salt and ground white pepper

FOR THE YOUNG CARROTS

8 young carrots, scrubbed and blanched

½ cup (4 ounces) olive oil

1 tablespoon unsalted butter

Kosher salt and ground white pepper

FOR THE BRAISED KOHLRABI

8 ounces kohlrabi, peeled and cut into cubes

2 cups (1 pint) Vegetable Stock (see page xxvii)

1 tablespoon olive oil

2 tablespoons (1 ounce) champagne vinegar

1 teaspoon granulated sugar

Kosher salt and ground white pepper

FOR THE FINISHED DISH

12 sugar snap peas in pods, blanched

8 medium carrots, sliced lengthwise on a mandoline, blanched

1 English cucumber, unpeeled, sliced lengthwise on a mandoline

Extra-virgin olive oil

Kosher salt and ground white pepper

Small mint leaves or sprigs, radish sprouts, baby pok choi, or small salad greens

TO PREPARE THE FENNEL PANNA COTTA

1. Line a shallow small pan or dish (something 6 inches square is ideal) with plastic wrap.

2. Combine the fennel and ice water in a blender and puree for a good 30 seconds.

3. Strain the liquid through a fine-mesh sieve and discard the solids.

4. Pour 2 tablespoons of the fennel juice into a small ramekin. Sprinkle the gelatin over it and set it aside for several minutes.

5. In a medium saucepan over high heat warm the remaining fennel juice with the cream, ginger, and tarragon. When the mixture begins to boil, whisk in the agar agar and the gelatin liquid and cook for about 3 more minutes, until well combined.

6. Season well with salt and pepper, then strain through a fine-mesh sieve.

7. Pour the pudding into the prepared pan and sprinkle with the grated lemon zest. Cover the pan and chill the pudding in the refrigerator until firm, about 30 minutes.

TO PREPARE THE ALMOND-QUINOA SALAD

Combine all the ingredients in a medium bowl and reserve at room temperature.

TO PREPARE THE YOUNG CARROTS

1. Preheat the oven to 350°F.

2. Combine carrots and other ingredients in a small roasting pan. Bake for 15–20 minutes until tender. Remove the carrots from the pan with tongs and set them aside to cool. Reserve the oil mixture in the pan to make a salad dressing.

TO PREPARE THE KOHLRABI

Combine all the ingredients in a small saucepan. Bring to a boil over high heat, then reduce to a low simmer and cook until the kohlrabi is tender and most of the liquid is absorbed, about 10 minutes. Set aside to cool to room temperature.

PUTTING IT ALL TOGETHER

1. Split open half of the peapods and fold them open to show their peas. Combine them and the raw carrot and cucumber slices in a bowl with enough extra-virgin olive oil to coat them and sprinkle with salt and pepper. Roll up each carrot into a tight roll, then roll up 8 cucumber slices in the same fashion. Scrape the remaining oil from cooking the young carrots into the bowl with the olive oil.

2. Slice the panna cotta into 8 squares or rectangles. Place 2 in the center of each of 4 plates. Arrange the other vegetables over and around them. Sprinkle the quinoa salad in a couple of different spots on each plate using it to help some of the vegetables stand in place. Drizzle the remaining oil mixture from the vegetables over the plates. Garnish with leaves and sprouts and serve.

restaurant embellishments

I like to add Red Beet Gel to this salad.

6 ounces red beet juice	Pinch of xanthan gum
2 tablespoons balsamic vinegar	¼ teaspoon sugar
½ teaspoon low-acyl gellan gum	Pinches of kosher salt and white pepper

1. Put all ingredients into a blender and puree until smooth.

2. Transfer the liquid to a small saucepan and heat it slowly until it comes to a boil. After pressing it through a fine sieve, cover and chill the mixture in the refrigerator until it gels. It will keep for a couple of days. Smear it across the plate before adding the panna cotta and other salad ingredients to the plate.

SALT-AND-COFFEE-ROASTED BEET SALAD WITH FENNEL AND GRAPEFRUIT, FIG-BLACKBERRY PUREE, AND GOAT CHEESE

SERVES 4

This is a version of the beet salad that's on my menu almost daily in homage to my mom. She makes a brightly splendid version of ensalada de Noche Buena, the traditional Mexican holiday salad named for Christmas Eve that mixes beets with citrus, jicama, pomegranate seeds, and greens. She and my dad always have a lavish spread at midnight on Christmas Eve, with her salad, steaming bowls of posole (a hominy-like stew with loads of garnishes), savory tamales filled with shredded chicken and tomatillos, and sweet tamales stained festive red from a strawberry and raisin filling. At midnight the gathered clan offers a champagne toast to Christmas. The restaurant is open that night for the many revelers who have reserved tables before or after viewing farolitos in the nearby Canyon Road area, one of Santa Fe's biggest holiday events. I find myself watching the restaurant kitchen clock like a school kid waiting for winter break, trying my best to get to the family celebration. If I'm in danger of missing the midnight toast and feast, I make sure to stop whatever I'm doing to call my parents and wish them Feliz Navidad. They will make sure to save me some of all the dishes and bring them to the restaurant on Christmas morning.

POSSIBLE DO-AHEAD STEPS

- Salt-roast the beets, remove them from the crust, rinse them, and refrigerate them up to 1 day ahead.
- Make the Horseradish Buttermilk Gel and the Fig-Blackberry Puree up to 1 day ahead as well.

FOR THE ROASTED BEETS

4 cups kosher salt

1 cup ground coffee

½ cup granulated sugar

2 large stems each of fresh dill, tarragon, and thyme, chopped into several pieces

1½ cups egg whites (about 1 dozen large), lightly whisked

1½ pounds mixed small to medium beets, preferably red, golden, and striped Chioggia, scrubbed but tails (root ends) left on

FOR HORSERADISH BUTTERMILK GEL

1 cup (8 ounces) buttermilk

½ cup (4 ounces) heavy cream

½ small shallot, minced

1 tablespoon prepared horseradish

½ teaspoon grated lemon zest

1 teaspoon (3 grams) low-acyl gellan gum

Kosher salt and ground white pepper

FOR THE PUREE

½ cup (4 ounces) apple cider

2 teaspoons unflavored powdered gelatin

1 cup (8 ounces) dry red wine

4 fresh mission figs or rehydrated dried figs, quartered

½ cup fresh or frozen blackberries

2 tablespoons granulated sugar

2 teaspoons red wine vinegar

FOR THE FINISHED DISH

½ small fennel head, about 3 ounces, sliced thin on a mandoline

1 grapefruit, preferably a Rio Star or other red variety, peeled and sliced into segments

4 ounces creamy fresh goat cheese

Extra-virgin olive oil

Mâche sprigs, or pok choi, mizuna, watercress, or small mustard leaves, or chive blossoms

TO PREPARE THE BEETS

1. Preheat the oven to 375°F.

2. Combine the salt, coffee, sugar, and herbs in a bowl. Mix in the egg whites. The mixture will feel like wet sand.

3. Pack about 1 inch of it in the bottom of a baking pan. You will want a deep pan or pans, perhaps a pair of bread loaf pans. If any beets are appreciably larger than the others, or larger than 1 ½ inches in diameter, cut them in half.

4. Arrange the beets in the pan(s) and pack the salt mixture around them as fully as possible. Bake for 50–60 minutes, until the beets are tender. Poke around with the tip of a paring knife to check.

5. Remove the cooked beets from the salt mixture and rinse them off. Keeping the different colors separate, peel the beets, leaving a few of the better-looking beet tails in place. Place the beets in a bowl, cover them, and chill them in the refrigerator until needed.

TO PREPARE THE BUTTERMILK GEL

1. Combine the buttermilk, cream, shallot, horseradish, and lemon zest in a medium saucepan. Bring the mixture to a boil (it will bubble up).

2. Stir in the gellan gum and return the mixture to a boil.

3. Cool over an ice bath, season with salt and pepper, and chill in the refrigerator until needed.

TO PREPARE THE FIG-BLACKBERRY PUREE

1. Pour 2 tablespoons of the apple cider into a small ramekin, sprinkle the gelatin over it, and let it sit for several minutes.

2. Combine the rest of the cider, wine, both fruits, sugar, and vinegar in a small saucepan and bring to a simmer. Cook until the mixture reduces by about half, about 5 minutes.

3. Stir in the gelatin-cider mixture and bring to a boil for 1 minute, then remove from the heat. Cool over an ice bath and chill in the refrigerator until needed.

PUTTING IT ALL TOGETHER

Swoosh several spoonfuls of fig-blackberry puree across the center of each of 4 plates. Arrange the beets over the puree. You want to divide the colors out somewhat equally among the plates, and stand a beet or 2 in each serving so that its tail is wagging in the air. You can cut some of the beets in chunks if needed to portion them. Strive for a nice mixture of the different colors. Lean fennel slices around and between the beets and then add a few grapefruit segments. Spoon a couple of small mounds of buttermilk gel on each plate. Scatter cheese on each and drizzle with a bit of olive oil, enough to make everything glisten. Garnish with sprigs or leaves and serve.

Kitchen Notes

- Cooks often wonder if the salt-roasting technique is worth it, seeing how it generally requires a whole box of kosher salt and a bunch of egg whites. I do think the technique, which has been having a restaurant "moment," has merit, particularly for whole chickens, whole fish, and for root vegetables. They stay incredibly juicy and absorb a just-right salty savor. The salt-roasted food will be perfumed by anything else mixed with the salt, such as the coffee and herbs I pack in here. If you make the beets a day ahead, be sure to take them out of the salt right after cooking or you will end up with some very salty cured beets.

- If you wish though, you are welcome to simply roast your beets in foil pouches (by beet color) instead of salt-roasting, adding a portion of the herbs mentioned above to each pouch.

- The buttermilk gel is called, in chef-speak, a fluid gel. It's one that has some body and viscosity but not a lot. As with the buttermilk curd in an earlier salad recipe, it's saucy but lighter than traditional flour- or cornstarch-thickened mixtures. The thickener in it, low-acyl gellan gum, comes from the fermentation of algae, and can be used to set gels and make things like gummy candies. It is especially effective in acidic liquid, such as buttermilk. Look for it with gelatin or baking products or order it online.

restaurant embellishments

We often serve Grilled Scallions with this salad. Trim 4 medium-size scallions of any limp green tops, then slice them in half lengthwise. Coat them with oil and grill them until they're soft with browned spots. Two sections go on each plate.

This recipe is great for this dish too. We do it in place of the cheese by itself.

SEED-CRUSTED GOAT CHEESE

½ cup sunflower kernels

¼ cup pepitas (shelled pumpkin seeds)

2 tablespoons sesame seeds

2 tablespoons brown flax seeds

1 tablespoon chia seeds

4 ounces creamy fresh goat cheese

Kosher salt and ground white pepper

½ teaspoon chopped fresh thyme

1. Preheat the oven to 350°F

2. Combine sunflower kernals and seeds in a shallow baking dish and bake until all are toasted and fragrant, 7–10 minutes.

3. Let the mixture cool, then pulse it a few times in a food processor to crush the seeds lightly.

4. Roll the goat cheese into 8 small balls and sprinkle them with salt, pepper, and thyme. Refrigerate until needed.

5. Just before serving, coat a small skillet with olive oil and warm over medium heat.

6. Add the cheese balls, turning them quickly on all sides until just browned.

7. Place 2 on each salad plate.

GRILLED PEAR AND GOAT CHEESE SALAD WITH CHESTNUT HONEY, ORANGE BRIOCHE CROUTONS, AND ARUGULA OIL

SERVES 4

We have an ancient pear tree in our restaurant's courtyard, neglected for many years. With a bit of tender loving care, it now produces Bosc-type pears. We pick them in September and October for this salad and other dishes. I particularly love three-week-aged Humboldt Fog goat cheese—even its name—for this dish, but you can use another lightly aged or fresh goat cheese if you wish. Deeply flavored chestnut honey makes me think of fall in France. Orange scented croutons and arugula oil add bright notes and other textures to the plates.

POSSIBLE DO-AHEAD STEPS
- Make the Poached Pears up to 1 day ahead.
- Make the Chestnut Honey Vinaigrette up to 4 hours ahead.

FOR THE POACHED PEARS

1 cup (8 ounces) water

½ cup (4 ounces) dry white wine

¾ cup sugar

Peel of 1 lemon, in several strips

2 dried bay leaves

1 teaspoon black peppercorns

Small sprig of fresh lemon thyme or other thyme

Kosher salt and ground white pepper

2 large Bosc or Anjou pears, peeled and cut into halves vertically

FOR THE VINAIGRETTE

½ cup (4 ounces) olive oil

¼ cup (2 ounces) orange juice

¼ cup (2 ounces) apple cider

½ teaspoon fresh lemon juice

3 tablespoons (1 ½ ounces) chestnut honey, or other strong-flavored honey

1 teaspoon minced shallot

Kosher salt and ground white pepper

FOR THE BRIOCHE CROUTONS

About 8 ounces unsliced brioche, challah, or rye bread (day-old fine), cut into 1 dozen 1-inch cubes

4 tablespoons (2 ounces) unsalted butter, melted

1 ½ teaspoons grated orange zest

Kosher salt and ground white pepper

FOR THE ARUGULA OIL

½ cup blanched arugula

¼ teaspoon roasted garlic puree

¼ cup (2 ounces) ice water

½ cup (4 ounces) olive oil

¼ teaspoon grated lemon zest

Kosher salt and ground white pepper

FOR THE FINISHED DISH

1 tablespoon olive oil

Baby kale, radicchio, arugula, or watercress leaves, or a combination

TO POACH THE PEARS

1. In a medium saucepan, combine the water, wine, sugar, lemon, bay leaves, black peppercorns, thyme, and pinches of salt and pepper. Bring to a boil and then reduce the heat to a simmer and cook for about 3 minutes.

2. Add the pear halves, lower the heat so that just an occasional bubble breaks on the surface, and poach the pears for about 5 minutes, until tender.

3. Remove the pan from the stove and let the pears cool in the liquid. Refrigerate the pears in the liquid if you are not using them shortly.

TO PREPARE THE VINAIGRETTE

Whisk all the ingredients together in a small bowl. (If your honey is somewhat crystallized, it may be easier to pop the ingredients in a blender to combine them.)

TO PREPARE THE BRIOCHE CROUTONS

1. Toss the brioche cubes together in a medium bowl with the butter and orange zest. Sprinkle very lightly with salt and pepper. Let the cubes soak up the butter mixture for several minutes.

2. Meanwhile, warm a sauté pan over medium heat. Add the cubes and toast them on all sides, reducing the heat if needed to get the cubes nicely browned. Hold the brioche cubes at room temperature.

TO PREPARE THE ARUGULA OIL

Combine all the ingredients in a blender and puree.

PUTTING IT ALL TOGETHER

Preheat a grill or grill pan to medium heat. Cut the pears in quarters, removing their cores. Brush lightly with olive oil. Grill the pears quickly on all sides, to get them nicely marked by the grill. I slice a little off the bottom of four pear slices so that I can stand them up on the plates. Intersperse pear slices and brioche cubes in a line down the center of each of 4 plates. Spoon a mound of goat cheese to one side. Drizzle a puddle of arugula oil to the other side. Toss a bit of the vinaigrette with the baby kale and arugula and arrange the leaves over and around the pears and brioche croutons. Spoon some of the vinaigrette over the pears and serve.

TEXAS RUBY RED GRAPEFRUIT SALAD WITH AVOCADO, NUT BRITTLE, BLUE CHEESE, AND HONEY VINAIGRETTE

SERVES 4

Growing up in Guadalajara, we had a few fruit trees in one of our small yards. The avocado tree would ripen at about the same time as the orange, and I adored eating the two together, the smooth and buttery avocado enlivened by the hit of citrus tang. After I began to cook in restaurant kitchens, I visited Dallas, where chefs such as Stephan Pyles and Dean Fearing were starting to make headlines for their lively take on local cooking. In my dining around, I was served a grapefruit and avocado salad, which brought back the happy memory of my similar Mexican combo, but I was particularly wowed by the brightness of the Texas grapefruit. I later learned that Helen Corbitt, a Neiman-Marcus chef and renowned cookbook author and cooking instructor, had championed the combination, dressed with a sweet-sour poppy-seed–laced vinaigrette, and made it the best known starter in the state. I think I've put my own stamp on the grapefruit and avocado salad by adding the salty savor of blue cheese and a crunchy sweet nut brittle. I make my own brittle, featuring the New Mexico pine nut, called piñon in my adopted state. You can use about 4 ounces of store-bought peanut brittle bits for similar effect.

FOR THE VINAIGRETTE

½ cup (4 ounces) apple cider

2 tablespoons (1 ounce) champagne vinegar

1 tablespoon medium-flavored honey, such as wildflower

1 tablespoon minced shallots

¼ cup (2 ounces) hazelnut oil

½ cup (4 ounces) extra-virgin olive oil

Kosher salt and ground white pepper

Chopped fresh chives, at least a couple of teaspoons

FOR THE FINISHED DISH

2 large ruby red grapefruits, preferably Texas Rio Star, peeled and then cut into individual segments

2 ripe medium avocados, preferably Hass, halved and cut into ½-inch squares

Kosher salt or a flaky sea salt, such as Maldon

4 ounces Point Reyes blue cheese, or other tangy, creamy blue cheese, cut into 8 cubes

4 ounces store-bought peanut brittle, broken in bite-size pieces, or Piñon Brittle (see Restaurant Embellishments page 56)

Watercress, arugula, or nasturtium leaves

TO PREPARE THE VINAIGRETTE

In a small bowl, combine the cider, vinegar, honey, and shallots. Whisk in the oils and season with salt and pepper. Add chives to taste.

PUTTING IT ALL TOGETHER

Arrange 4 grapefruit segments in the center of each of 4 plates, interspersed with 3 avocado squares. Sprinkle lightly with salt. Place two pieces of cheese to either side of the grapefruit and avocado, then drizzle with the vinaigrette. Tuck in several pieces of nut brittle on each plate. Garnish with leaves and serve.

restaurant embellishment

Piñon Brittle is my New Mexican twist on nut brittle, using the pine nuts that come from trees that dot the Santa Fe foothills like peppercorns. We use the brittle as a garnish on this salad, but also on ice creams and over butternut squash soup. It's also great just for munching. With all these possible ways of eating it, I make about 1 pound at a time; now you can too.

PIÑON BRITTLE

½ cup granulated sugar	2 tablespoons (1 ounce) unsalted butter
¼ cup (2 ounces) light corn syrup	½ teaspoon baking soda
3 tablespoons (1 ½ ounces) water	¼ teaspoon kosher salt
1 cup pine nuts	⅛ teaspoon ground white pepper

1. Line a rimmed baking sheet with a non-stick mat or lightly oiled parchment paper.

2. In a small saucepan, combine the sugar, corn syrup, and water. Cook the mixture over high heat without stirring for about 10 minutes, until it is boiling vigorously and turns a golden amber color, 235°F–240°F on a candy thermometer.

3. Stir in the pine nuts and butter, and heat to 295°F–300°F, stirring constantly.

4. Add the baking soda, which will cause the mixture to bubble up, and salt and pepper, and pour the liquid immediately onto the prepared baking sheet, spreading it evenly about ¼ inch thick with an oiled spatula.

5. After the brittle cools for at least 15 minutes, break it into pieces and store it in a covered container if not using it all within a few hours.

crudo and ceviche appetizers

SERVES 4

So I'm a Santa Fe chef up in the mountains of northern New Mexico, and an entire chapter of my book is devoted to raw fish and seafood? Well, yes. Few dishes seem as refreshing to me as ceviche and crudo when the main ingredient is well selected and enhanced with just a few contrasting touches. My enthusiasm for this was ignited by ceviche in Mexico, where raw fish is lightly "cooked" by marinating it in acidic lime juice. I see home cooks venturing into ceviches these days, and with the accessibility of much higher quality seafood in recent years, everyone should have an opportunity to also enjoy crudo, an even more elemental preparation. In this hamachi crudo, you first taste the creamy sweetness of the fish, avocado, and lightly pickled mango, then the touch of oil associated with all of them, and then the crunch of the sprouts. At the end, the chile in the vinaigrette zings gently in your mouth.

FOR THE PICKLED MANGO

1 medium mango (about 8 ounces), sliced away from the pit in halves, then peeled and thinly sliced lengthwise into at least a dozen thin spears

¼ cup plus 2 tablespoons (3 ounces) water

¼ cup plus 2 tablespoons granulated sugar

2 tablespoons (1 ounce) champagne vinegar

FOR THE VINAIGRETTE

1 tablespoon rice vinegar

1 tablespoon champagne vinegar

1 ½ teaspoons sriracha, sambal oelek, or other Asian red chile sauce

1 tablespoon minced shallots

¼ cup plus 2 tablespoons (3 ounces) walnut oil

¼ teaspoon kosher salt

⅛ teaspoon ground white pepper

Pinch of granulated sugar

¾ pound super-fresh sashimi- or sushi-grade hamachi (yellowtail) fillet, trimmed of any bloody spots, in one more-or-less rectangular piece

FOR THE FINISHED DISH

1 ripe medium avocado, preferably Hass, peeled and cut lengthwise into eight wedges

½ cup radish sprouts, amaranth sprouts, or other tender sprouts

4 long mild radishes, such as French Breakfast radishes, thinly sliced lengthwise

Fresh mint leaves or fresh tiny shiso leaves

TO PREPARE THE PICKLED MANGO

1. Slide the mango slices side-by-side into a zipper-lock plastic bag, 1-quart-size or larger.

2. In a small bowl, stir together the water, sugar, and vinegar, and pour the pickling mixture into the bag.

3. Flatten the mango slices into a single layer as you seal the bag. Refrigerate for about 1 hour before combining with the other ingredients.

TO PREPARE THE VINAIGRETTE

1. Whisk together in a small bowl the two vinegars, sriracha, and shallots. Continue whisking as you drizzle in the oil to make an emulsion. Add salt, pepper, and sugar and whisk again. Reserve at room temperature.

2. Cut the hamachi across the grain on the diagonal very thinly (about ⅛ of an inch thick). This slicing will give the fish the most tender texture and lots of surface area. Aim for 20 slices about 2 x 3 inches.

PUTTING IT ALL TOGETHER

1. Place 5 thin slices of hamachi around the center of each of 4 plates like spokes. If you have rectangular plates, arrange the fish slices down the length. Arrange 2 slices of avocado toward the center. Then tuck in mango slices, which I like to curl around my finger before placing them on the plate, to give some height to the presentation. If you're rolling your eyes at that, like my staff does at times, simply lay them more or less equally over and around the fish.

2. Scatter with sprouts and radish slices, and tuck in herb leaves here and there. Take the time to make it look artful but don't stress over making it ultra-composed. Drizzle portions of the vinaigrette dressing around each plate and serve.

Kitchen Notes

- For the best crudo or ceviche, always keep the fish in fillet form, or cut a block of it from a fillet, until shortly before serving. Keep the wrapped fish on ice in the coolest part of your refrigerator. A flexible-bladed fillet knife or knife made for sushi is best for slicing raw fish. If the fish is skin-on, leave a very slim layer of meat on the skin because it can be a bit chewy there. Cut away and discard any bloody spots. When you're ready to use it, cut the fish into small cubes or very thin slices, across the grain and at a slight angle. Use only a smooth motion down through the fish—no sawing back and forth. If you get delayed in using the fish, cover it with plastic wrap pressed directly on its surface and refrigerate.

- California hamachi, or yellowtail (also known as amberjack), is wild-caught, a better alternative according to the Monterey Bay Aquarium Seafood Watch than farmed Japanese or Australian hamachi yellowtail. Check at a fish market for sashimi-grade hamachi or go with a substitute recommended by the fishmonger.

LIGHTLY CURED HAMACHI WITH SERRANO PESTO AND GINGERED HEIRLOOM TOMATOES

SERVES 4

Bon Appétit's recent selection of crudo as "restaurant dish of the year" seems destined to encourage even more people to try it. This version is a good place for neophytes to start because the light cure makes the fish taste slightly less raw. Also you can substitute sea bass or halibut for the hamachi if you wish, giving you a broader range of fish choices. Check out the Kitchen Note on page 62 about ceviche and crudo and their preparation if you haven't made them before.

POSSIBLE DO-AHEAD STEPS
- Make the Serrano Pesto up to 8 hours ahead.

FOR THE HAMACHI

¼ cup packed brown sugar

3½ tablespoons granulated sugar

1 tablespoon kosher salt

2 tablespoons thinly sliced fresh ginger

2 dried bay leaves

1 lemongrass stalk, crushed lightly

1 medium shallot, sliced thin

2 cups (1 pint) water

1 tablespoon rice vinegar

¾ pound super-fresh sashimi or sushi-grade hamachi (yellowtail) fillet, trimmed of any bloody spots, in one more-or-less rectangular piece

FOR THE PESTO

1 serrano chile, seeded and minced

1 teaspoon chopped fresh cilantro

½ teaspoon chopped fresh mint

1 small shallot, minced

½ teaspoon grated lemon zest

¼ teaspoon roasted garlic puree

Juice of 1 lime

2 tablespoons chopped cashews

¼ cup (2 ounces) extra virgin olive oil

Kosher salt and ground white pepper

FOR THE TOMATOES

½ pint petite heirloom tomatoes, such as grape tomatoes, in varying colors

Olive oil for pan-frying

2 tablespoons (1 ounce) extra-virgin olive oil

1 teaspoon aji panca paste, or ½ teaspoon chipotle chile puree

1 teaspoon chopped fresh chives

½ teaspoon grated fresh ginger

Kosher salt and ground white pepper

Pinch ground coriander

FOR THE YUZU BUBBLES

1 cup (8 ounces) cold water

½ cup (4 ounces) sake, chilled

¼ cup plus 2 tablespoons (3 ounces) yuzu juice

1 tablespoon rice vinegar

2 teaspoons soy lecithin powder

FOR THE FINISHED DISH

Extra-virgin olive oil

Kosher salt and ground white pepper

Black sesame seeds or black sesame crackers

Daikon radish leaves, shiso leaves, radish sprouts, fennel blossoms, or small salad greens

TO PREPARE THE CURE FOR THE HAMACHI

1. Combine all the ingredients except the fish in a saucepan. Bring the mixture to a boil over high heat, stirring a time or two, until the sugars dissolve.

2. Cool the mixture in an ice bath, then pour the cure over the hamachi in a zipper-lock plastic bag or covered shallow dish that can hold the fish flat but snugly.

3. Refrigerate and cure the hamachi for 2–3 hours.

TO PREPARE THE PESTO

While the hamachi cures, prepare the pesto. Stir together all the ingredients in a small bowl. It will be a bit chunky. Refrigerate covered until needed.

TO PREPARE THE TOMATOES

1. With a thin paring knife, cut a tiny x in the bottom end of each tomato.
2. Warm 1 inch of olive oil in a medium saucepan. When the oil shimmers, add about half the tomatoes and flash fry, for no more than 10 seconds.
3. Scoop them out with a spider or slotted spoon and set them aside on paper towels to cool. Repeat with the remaining tomatoes.
4. Pull off and discard the tomato skins.
5. Combine the peeled tomatoes in a small bowl with the extra-virgin olive oil, aji panca sauce, chives, ginger, salt and pepper, and coriander. Let the mixture sit at room temperature.

TO MAKE THE YUZU BUBBLES

Blend all the ingredients together in a blender until frothy like a bubble bath.

PUTTING IT ALL TOGETHER

1. Discard the cure liquid, rinse the fish in cold water, and pat it dry with paper towels.
2. Cut the hamachi across the grain on the diagonal very thinly (under ⅛ of an inch thick). This slicing will give the fish the most tender texture and lots of surface area. Aim for 24 slices about 2 x 3 inches.
3. Make three mounds of hamachi on each of 4 plates, twisting 2 slices together for each upward mound. Spoon tomatoes between the hamachi and drizzle the pesto over both the fish and tomatoes. Spread a few drops of extra-virgin olive oil over the fish and sprinkle it with salt and pepper. Spoon mounds of yuzu bubbles around the fish. Scatter sesame seeds lightly over the fish or tuck cracker pieces standing between the hamachi and tomatoes. Garnish with leaves and serve right away.

Kitchen Notes

- Aji panca sauce is made from a smoky, slightly sweet chile from Peru. The sauce can be found in many Latino markets and online from sources such as Tienda.com. Half the amount of Mexico's spicier chipotles en adobo can be substituted if you wish. Other uses for the aji panca sauce include stirring it into beef or pork stews, serving it with a grilled tuna steak, or rubbing it under the skin of a chicken destined for a roasting pan or rotisserie.

- The Japanese use the citrus, yuzu, the way Mexicans use limones. The flavor is like tangerine or mandarin orange with lime in the finish. Bottled versions of it are fine, and can be found in Asian food sections, Asian groceries, and online. In a pinch use a 2 to 1 mix of orange juice to lime juice as a substitute.

restaurant embellishments

- The restaurant kitchen uses *sous vide* equipment at moderate pressure to seal the hamachi in a small vacuum bag with the cure mixture. The technique ensures the hamachi will absorb the marinade's flavorings fully.

- I'm really taken by black seeds and crackers as a contrasting element to more brightly colored ingredients. For this reason I add little Black Sesame Sponge Cakes to this dish instead of sesame seeds or crackers. They are not easy to prepare at home even though they look like something from a child's Easy-Bake Oven. You'll need an iSi cream whipper with accompanying gas chargers. It's a nifty gadget to make mousses, frostings, and all kinds of froths and foams. Also, it can keep ingredients at hot or cold temperatures for long periods. If you want to experiment with an iSi cream whipper, home versions are sold at Williams-Sonoma and other high-end kitchen shops, as well as online.

BLACK SESAME SPONGE CAKES

4 ounces olive oil

3 ounces toasted sesame oil

4 ounces black sesame seeds

4 ounces egg yolks

4 ounces egg whites

⅔ cup granulated sugar

2 tablespoons unbleached all-purpose flour

Pinch of kosher salt

1. Make black sesame paste by warming olive and sesame oils in a small sauté pan over medium heat.

2. Stir in sesame seeds and toast for about 1 minute, or until fragrant.

3. Transfer to a blender and puree. Refrigerate the mixture.

4. When you're ready to make the sponge cakes, measure out 4 ounces of the black sesame paste and combine it in a blender with egg yolks and whites, sugar, flour, and salt.

5. Strain the batter through a fine-mesh sieve into an iSi cream whipper canister and charge it with two nitrous oxide chargers. Set aside for 1 hour.

6. Poke several small slashes in the bottom of 4 12-ounce paper coffee cups.

7. Pump the mixture out of the iSi whipper, filling each cup equally just over half full. Microwave each, one at a time, for 25 seconds. Let each cup cool for a couple of minutes, then dump out the small cakes from the cups.

8. Tear apart into uneven pieces ½–1 inch in size. Use immediately or cool and store in an airtight container for up to a day.

YELLOWFIN TUNA TARTARE WITH SEAWEED-OLIVE CRISPS, FRIED SHALLOTS, TOMATO-SUDACHI VINAIGRETTE, AND CURRIED APPLE PUREE

SERVES 4

Chef David Burke, my employer and mentor in New York in the 1990s, is credited with creating and popularizing the idea of tuna tartare. What a tsunami he created. Like nearly every chef since, I've had a version of it on my restaurant menu since Day 1, but I change up the presentation and the accompaniments regularly. The squid ink in the seaweed-olive crisps here enhances the color without tasting fishy, but can be left out if you don't have it. Check out the Kitchen Note on page 62 about ceviche and crudo and their preparation if you haven't made them before.

POSSIBLE DO-AHEAD STEPS

- Make the Seaweed-Olive Crisps up to 2 days ahead.
- Make the Tomato-Sudachi Vinaigrette up to 4 hours ahead.

FOR THE SEAWEED-OLIVE CRISPS

4 ounces cooked black barley (see Kitchen Notes page 71)

2 tablespoons unbleached all-purpose flour

2 tablespoons furikake seasoning or chopped toasted nori (seaweed)

¼ cup (2 ounces) water

1 ounce pitted black Kalamata olives

1 tablespoon unsalted butter, softened

½ teaspoon squid ink, optional

Pinch of granulated sugar

Pinch of kosher salt

FOR THE VINAIGRETTE

¾ pound plum tomatoes

1 medium red bell pepper, chopped and seeded

½ cup (4 ounces) water

1 tablespoon sudachi juice (or 1 of the substitutes in the Kitchen Note page 70)

1 tablespoon chopped peeled ginger

1 tablespoon packed brown sugar

1 teaspoon sriracha, sambal oelek, or other Asian red chile sauce

1 teaspoon fresh lime juice

1 teaspoon Dijon mustard

2 tablespoons (1 ounce) extra-virgin olive oil

Kosher salt and ground white pepper

FOR THE PUREE

1 Granny Smith apple, peeled and chopped

2 ounces cucumber, peeled and chopped

2 tablespoons (1 ounce) water

1 teaspoon fresh lime juice

½ teaspoon granulated sugar

Pinch or 2 of spicy curry powder

¼ teaspoon xanthan gum

Kosher salt and ground white pepper

FOR THE TUNA TARTARE

1 tablespoon minced capers

1 teaspoon minced shallot

1 teaspoon minced serrano or jalapeño chile

1 teaspoon minced fresh cilantro

1 teaspoon chopped fresh chives

1 tablespoon mustard oil, or olive oil with a dash of chile oil

1 teaspoon toasted sesame oil

¾ pound super-fresh sashimi- or sushi-grade yellowfin tuna, in very fine dice

Kosher salt and ground white pepper

Garlic chive blossoms, dill blossoms or sprigs, radish
   sprouts, or cilantro, or mint, or Bull's blood baby
   beet greens, or small watercress leaves

TO PREPARE THE CRUMBS

1. Preheat the oven to 325°F. Arrange a non-stick liner or oiled parchment paper on a baking sheet.

2. Process the barley for 30 seconds in a food processor to beat it up a little bit. Add the rest of the crumb ingredients and process until combined well.

3. Spread thinly on the baking sheet, covering most of the sheet. It will have some lacy open spots.

4. Bake the crumbs for 15–20 minutes, then let them cool on the baking sheet on a baking rack. Crumble the mixture coarsely. Reserve at room temperature.

TO PREPARE THE VINAIGRETTE

Combine all the ingredients in a blender and puree. Strain the mixture through a fine-mesh sieve, pushing on the solids to release as much flavor as possible. Reserve the vinaigrette at room temperature.

TO PREPARE THE APPLE PUREE

Rinse out the blender. Combine the puree ingredients in the blender. Spoon into a bowl, cover, and refrigerate until needed.

TO PREPARE THE TARTARE

Just before serving, mix the capers, shallot, chile, cilantro, and chives together in a medium bowl. Mix in the mustard and sesame oils. Gently mix in the chopped tuna just until combined. Season lightly with salt and pepper

I like to serve this on oblong plates, though that's by no means essential. Spoon the tartare down the center of each of 4 plates, neatly spooning it into a smooth log. Sprinkle the crumbs over the tartare. Dot the vinaigrette and apple puree down the sides of the tartare, placing some on each side. Garnish with blossoms, sprouts, or leaves and serve immediately.

restaurant embellishments

I think you'll love the additional crunch of Fried Shallots in this dish. If you can make the time for them, this is a how we make them, a customer favorite.

> 2 medium shallots, sliced thinly into rings
> ½ cup buttermilk
> ½ cup unbleached all-purpose flour
> ½ teaspoon ground coriander
> ⅛ teaspoon kosher salt
> ⅛ teaspoon ground white pepper
> Canola oil

1. Soak the shallots in the buttermilk for 30–60 minutes to make them a bit milder and softer. Drain the shallots.

2. Combine flour, coriander, salt, and pepper in a small bowl.

3. In a medium saucepan, bring 2 inches of canola oil to 330°F–335°F.

4. Dredge the shallots in the flour mixture, coating them well. Gently place them in the heated oil and fry until light golden and crisp, 3–4 minutes. Drain on a baking rack over paper towels.

5. Sprinkle with a bit more salt and serve leaning over or on top of the tartare.

Kitchen Notes

- Sudachi is a tangy green Japanese citrus used for its vibrant juice, usually available in Asian markets. The flavor reminds me of lime with notes of cumin and black pepper. It's fine to get it bottled. I sometimes use the brand Yakami Orchard, which comes in a 12-ounce bottle. You can also replace it with bottled Marukan Ponzu Premium Sudachi Citrus Marinade or just fresh juice from small Mexican limes.

- You can buy a lot of precooked grains in grocery stores today, often including black barley. Check what ones are available in your area. If you need to cook the barley, start by combining 2 tablespoons of it with 1½ cups water in a small saucepan, then cook until tender, about 45 minutes.

CITRUS-MARINATED FLUKE WITH HIJIKI, MELON, CUCUMBER-CURRY BROTH, AND BLACK SESAME BRITTLE

SERVES 4

Fluke is a flaky flatfish similar to flounder, with a nice amount of fat. How's that for alliteration? It's good with nothing more than a little lemon or lime juice, olive oil, and salt, but I like to dress it up in this manner. Good substitutes for fluke include flounder and halibut. The savory-sweet black brittle shines like obsidian, but if you don't have the time or inclination to make it, scatter some toasted black sesame seeds over this and you'll be good to go. Check out the Kitchen Note on page 62 about ceviche and crudo and their preparation if you haven't made them before.

POSSIBLE DO-AHEAD STEPS

• Make the Black Sesame Brittle and prepare the hijiki up to 8 hours ahead.

FOR THE BRITTLE

½ cup plus 2 tablespoons (5 ounces) water

1 teaspoon unflavored powdered gelatin

1 tablespoon tapioca flour

3½ tablespoons granulated sugar

1 tablespoon squid ink

2 tablespoons black sesame seeds

Kosher salt and ground black pepper

FOR THE HIJIKI

2 ounces dry hijiki seaweed

1 cup (8 ounces) water

FOR THE BROTH

4 ounces cucumber, peeled, seeded, and chopped in several pieces

1 medium celery stalk, chopped in several pieces

½ tablespoon fresh lemon juice

1 teaspoon chopped jalapeño or serrano chile

1 teaspoon fresh ginger, peeled and chopped

1 teaspoon yellow curry paste

½ cup (4 ounces) ice water

Kosher salt and ground white pepper

FOR THE MELON

8 ounces watermelon, cantaloupe, honeydew, or a combination, sliced from the rind, and cut in ½-inch cubes

½ cup simple syrup (see page 36)

2 tablespoons (1 ounce) tequila, preferably an aged or añejo version

1 tablespoon olive oil

Kosher salt and ground white pepper

FOR THE FLUKE

2 tablespoons (1 ounce) lemon-flavored olive oil or extra-virgin olive oil

1 tablespoon fresh lime juice

1 tablespoon orange juice

1 tablespoon Dijon mustard

1 teaspoon mild-flavored honey, such as orange blossom

1 tablespoon minced chopped chives

½ teaspoon grated lemon zest

Kosher salt and ground white pepper

12 ounces super-fresh sashimi- or sushi-quality fluke fillet or fillets

FOR THE FINISHED DISH

Daikon or other radish sprouts, red amaranth sprouts, or spicy small greens such as watercress

TO PREPARE THE BRITTLE

1. Preheat the oven to 300°F. Line a baking sheet with a non-stick liner or lightly oiled parchment paper.

2. Pour 1 tablespoon of water into a ramekin or other small dish and sprinkle the gelatin over it; let it stand several minutes.

3. Place the tapioca flour in a small heatproof bowl.

4. Warm the sugar in a small saucepan over medium heat until the sugar melts and becomes amber in color. Stir only if it is melting unevenly. Watching out for steam, add the remaining water and the squid ink to the sugar and bring the mixture back to a boil.

5. Pour a couple of tablespoons of the hot liquid into the tapioca flour, then quickly whisk it to remove any lumps. Pour the mixture back into the saucepan and bring it back to a boil.

6. Whisk in the gelatin and water, cook 1 minute, then add the sesame seeds, and a couple pinches of salt and pepper.

7. Pour the mixture onto the prepared baking sheet, spreading it to within 1–2 inches of the sheet's edges. Bake for approximately 15 minutes, until set and lightly crispy.

8. Cool the brittle on the baking sheet over a baking rack. It will become crisper as it sits.

TO PREPARE THE HIJIKI

Combine the seaweed with the water in a small saucepan. Bring it almost to a boil over high heat, then remove the pan from the heat and let the mixture sit until cool. Drain the liquid and refrigerate the seaweed in a covered bowl until needed.

TO PREPARE THE CUCUMBER-CURRY BROTH

Place all the ingredients in the blender and puree. Strain through a fine-mesh sieve into a bowl, cover, and refrigerate until needed.

TO PREPARE THE MELON

In a medium bowl, mix the melon with the simple syrup, tequila, olive oil, and salt and pepper to taste. Refrigerate covered bowl until needed.

TO PREPARE THE FLUKE

1. Mix together the marinade for the fluke. Stir together the oil, lime and orange juices, mustard, and honey. When combined, stir in the chives, lemon zest, and a good pinch each of salt and pepper.

2. Cut the fluke across the grain on the diagonal very thinly (between ⅛ and ¼ of an inch thick). This slicing will give the fish the most tender texture and lots of surface area. Try to get 20 slices.

3. Dunk the slices of fluke into the marinade to give them a little bath and coat evenly. Let them sit in it for a couple of minutes.

PUTTING IT ALL TOGETHER

1. This dish looks great on oval plates if you have them. Curl the fluke slices around your finger and arrange them more or less standing up in a row, spaced across the center of each of 4 plates.

2. Drain the liquid from the melon slices and arrange the cubes in the gaps between the slices of fluke.

3. Scatter pieces of hijiki over and around the fish and melon. Add small spoonfuls of the cucumber-curry broth over and around the row of fish. Spoon a bit of the fluke marinade over or around the fish.

4. Break off pieces of the black sesame brittle and stand two or three on each plate, held up by the other ingredients.

5. Garnish with sprouts or greens and serve immediately.

restaurant embellishments

I like to add a citrusy Yuzu Kosho Curd to this crudo. It's bright and silky with the fish, but a touch of butter and sour cream mellow its acid. Yuzu kosho is a Japanese paste made from yuzu and its peel with salt and a bit of chile. Here's a recipe if you'd like to make your own.

YUZU KOSHO

> 2 ounces (½ stick) unsalted butter
>
> 2 tablespoons (1 ounce) sour cream
>
> 1 large egg
>
> 1 large egg yolk
>
> 3 tablespoons juice from a jar of yuzu kosho (or just use bottled yuzu juice)
>
> 1 tablespoon granulated sugar
>
> Kosher salt and ground white pepper to taste
>
> 1 sheet bloomed silver gelatin

1. In the top of a double boiler combine butter, sour cream, egg, and egg yolk.

2. Place the mixture over the double boiler's pot of simmering water and whisk it until the butter melts in.

3. Add yuzu juice and whisk in sugar, salt, and pepper. Continue whisking until the mixture is thick and pale in color.

4. Whisk in gelatin. Pass the curd through a fine-mesh sieve, cool it, and chill it in a covered container. The curd can be made a day ahead of serving. I add several dots of it to each of the plates.

TAI SNAPPER WITH PICKLED BUTTERNUT SQUASH, PEAR AND CUCUMBER, YUZU-VERBENA OIL, AND CHILE ALMOND BRITTLE

SERVES 4

I use fresh line-caught New Zealand tai snapper for this dish, which I serve on weekends in the late summer and fall. Fishermen bring it in on Wednesday off the coast of New Zealand and I have it in my kitchen on Friday thanks to Jeff Koscomb of Santa Fe's premier fish supplier, Above Sea Level. If you don't have Jeff to deliver tai to your door, a red snapper, other snapper, or sea bream can be used with equally fine results. Check out the Kitchen Note on page 62 about ceviche and crudo and their preparation if you haven't made them before.

POSSIBLE DO-AHEAD STEPS
- Make the Pickled Butternut Squash and the Chile Almond Brittle up to 1 day ahead.

FOR THE SQUASH

1 cup (8 ounces) water

¼ cup (2 ounces) apple cider vinegar

2 tablespoons granulated sugar

1 star anise, toasted in a dry skillet until fragrant

Peel of 1 lemon

1 teaspoon black peppercorns, toasted in a dry skillet until fragrant

1 teaspoon grated peeled fresh ginger

Pinch of kosher salt

6 ounces peeled butternut squash, in small dice, blanched

FOR THE ALMOND BRITTLE

1 stick (4 ounces) unsalted butter

3 ounces packed brown sugar

¼ cup plus 2 tablespoons (3 tablespoons) light corn syrup

¼ teaspoon Chinese five-spice powder

⅛ teaspoon New Mexican or ancho dried ground red chile

Pinch of kosher salt

¼ teaspoon baking powder

1 cup roasted, salted Marcona almonds

FOR THE YUZU-VERBENA OIL

2 tablespoons (1 ounce) lemon verbena tea (see Kitchen Note page 76)

2 tablespoons (1 ounce) yuzu juice

1 tablespoon pineapple juice, or additional yuzu juice

1 teaspoon minced seeded jalapeño or serrano chile

Pinch of granulated sugar

¼ cup (2 ounces) olive oil

Kosher salt and ground white pepper

FOR THE PEAR AND CUCUMBER

1 unpeeled nashi or Asian pear, sliced very thin on a mandoline

½ unpeeled English cucumber, sliced very thin on a mandoline

2 tablespoons (1 ounce) extra-virgin olive oil

Juice of 1 lime

Kosher salt and ground white pepper

FOR THE FINISHED DISH

¾ pound tai snapper

Small shiso leaves, Italian parsley leaves, or celery leaves

TO PREPARE THE PICKLED SQUASH

1. In a small saucepan over high heat, warm the water, vinegar, sugar, star anise, lemon peel, peppercorns, ginger, and salt. Reduce the heat and simmer for 5 minutes. Set aside to cool to room temperature.

2. Strain the pickling liquid through a fine-mesh sieve into a small bowl and add the squash. Cover and refrigerate at least 1 hour.

TO PREPARE THE ALMOND BRITTLE

1. Line a baking sheet with a silicone mat or oiled parchment paper.

2. In a large saucepan, combine the butter, brown sugar, corn syrup, five-spice powder, chile, and salt. Cook over moderately high heat for 8–10 minutes, until the mixture measures 300° F (or 290°F at Santa Fe's 7,000-foot altitude) on a candy thermometer.

3. Whisk in the baking powder and almonds, and remove from the heat immediately.

4. Pour the mixture onto the prepared baking sheet and spread thinly with a spatula or the back of a spoon. Let it cool completely, about 30 minutes. Break into shards.

TO PREPARE THE YUZU-VERBENA OIL

Combine all the ingredients in a small bowl. Refrigerate covered until needed.

TO PREPARE THE PEAR AND CUCUMBER

In a medium bowl, mix together the pears and cucumber slices, oil, and lime juice. Season lightly with salt and pepper. Reserve at room temperature.

PUTTING IT ALL TOGETHER

1. Cut the snapper across the grain on the diagonal very thinly (between ⅛ and ¼ of an inch thick). This slicing will give the fish the most tender texture and lots of surface area. Try to get 20 slices.

2. Give the fish slices a little bath in about half the yuzu-verbena oil to coat them evenly. Let them marinate for a couple of minutes.

3. On 4 plates, arrange flat slices of the snapper like bike spokes, in a circle. Dunk the pear and cucumber slices in the remaining oil and stack slices over the snapper. Using a slotted spoon, arrange a mound of pickled butternut squash near the fish. Scatter the chili almond brittle around the plates. Garnish with leaves and drizzle with any remaining oil. Serve immediately.

Kitchen Notes

Make herbal lemon verbena tea for the oil by steeping the leaves from a 4- to 5-inch fresh lemon verbena stem in ¾ cup of freshly boiled water. If you don't have lemon verbena, a half-and-half combination of fresh basil and mint leaves makes an interesting substitute.

SEA SCALLOP CRUDO WITH ORANGE MARMALADE, SPICY-SWEET SUNFLOWER KERNELS, AVOCADO, AND WHITE SOY-WASABI VINAIGRETTE

SERVES 4

Plump sea scallops from cold waters off the coast of Maine are my hands-down top choice for shellfish crudo or ceviche. The savory orange marmalade, sunflower kernels, avocado, and vinaigrette bring out the flavor of the scallops and add depth to the dish. If you have some of the savory marmalade left over, it makes a great glaze for grilled salmon or roast pork. Check out the Kitchen Note on page 62 about ceviche and crudo and their preparation if you haven't made them before.

POSSIBLE DO-AHEAD STEPS

- Make the Orange Marmalade up to 3 days ahead.
- Make the Spicy-Sweet Sunflower Kernels up to 1 day ahead.

FOR THE MARMALADE

1 cup (8 ounces) orange juice

1 teaspoon unflavored powdered gelatin

1 cup orange segments (from about 2 medium oranges)

2 tablespoons (1 ounce) rice vinegar

1 teaspoon minced peeled fresh ginger

1 teaspoon minced shallots

1 star anise

1 teaspoon apple pectin powder

Kosher salt and ground white pepper

FOR THE SUNFLOWER KERNELS

½ cup sunflower kernels

1 tablespoon unsalted butter, melted

1 tablespoon mild-flavored honey, such as orange blossom

2 teaspoons sriracha, sambal oelek, or other Asian chile sauce

2 teaspoons toasted sesame oil

1 large egg white, whisked

Kosher salt and ground white pepper

FOR THE VINAIGRETTE

1 tablespoon white soy sauce, or other Japanese soy sauce

2 teaspoons minced shallots

1 teaspoon freshly grated wasabi

1 teaspoon minced, peeled fresh ginger

1 teaspoon Dijon mustard

¼ cup (2 ounces) grapeseed, canola, or vegetable oil

Kosher salt and ground white pepper

FOR THE FINISHED DISH

2 tablespoons (1 ounce) extra-virgin olive oil

½ teaspoon grated lime zest

Pinch or 2 of flaky sea salt, such as Maldon, or kosher salt

Pinch or 2 of crushed pink peppercorns

4 "dry-packed" large sea scallops, thinly sliced horizontally

1 large ripe avocado, preferably Hass, cut in ½-inch cubes

Cilantro leaves, small shiso leaves, radish sprouts, saltwort springs and chive blossoms or small spicy greens such as watercress

TO PREPARE THE MARMALADE

1. Pour 2 tablespoons of the orange juice into a ramekin or other small bowl. Sprinkle the gelatin over it and let it stand several minutes.

2. In a small saucepan combine the rest of the orange juice, orange segments, vinegar, ginger, shallots, and star anise, and simmer over high heat for 5 minutes.

3. Whisk in the pectin powder and the orange juice and gelatin mixture. Reduce the heat to medium and cook until the remaining liquid is thick. Season with salt and pepper.

4. Pour into a bowl, cool to room temperature, and refrigerate until needed.

TO PREPARE THE SUNFLOWER KERNELS

1. Preheat the oven to 325°F.

2. Line a baking sheet with a non-stick mat or lightly oiled parchment paper.

3. Combine all the ingredients in a bowl and mix well. Spread the mixture on the prepared baking sheet in a thin layer. Bake for 10–12 minutes, until dry and crisp.

4. Set aside the mixture to cool on the baking sheet on a baking rack. When it's cool, break into uneven pieces, about ½ inch in size.

TO PREPARE THE VINAIGRETTE

Whisk together the ingredients in a small bowl until emulsified.

PUTTING IT ALL TOGETHER

1. Combine the olive oil, lime zest, flaky salt, and pink peppercorns in a small bowl.

2. Place the scallops in the bowl and coat them gently.

3. Arrange an equal quantity of scallop slices curled to stand on their sides, over the center of each of 4 plates. Arrange avocado cubes over and beside the scallops. Spoon drops of marmalade next to the scallops and scatter the sunflower kernels over the scallops. Garnish with herbs or greens. Drizzle with the vinaigrette and serve immediately.

Kitchen Notes

- White soy sauce isn't really white or clear, but it is lighter in both color and flavor than regular Japanese soy sauce or shoyu. It is prized for sushi and sashimi, the reason I use it in this delicate dressing for the scallops. It's available in Asian markets, and here in Santa Fe at the shop at the Ten Thousand Waves Japanese spa. You can substitute regular Japanese soy sauce, such as Kikkoman, if you can't find it easily.

- Real wasabi isn't bright green stuff squirted from a tube accompanying grocery-store sushi. It's a root, like a mini-horseradish root, that can be grated as needed to accompany raw seafood. It has the familiar nose-clearing properties if eaten in too large a quantity, but has a softer, more balanced taste perfect with crudo. Look for it in an Asian market or order online.

- "Dry-packed" scallops have no additives or preservatives pumped into them.

restaurant embellishments

Instead of cubes of avocado, at the restaurant I prefer to offer an Avocado Curd with the dish.

AVOCADO CURD

Meat of 1 Hass avocado
¼ cup chopped cilantro
½ small serrano chile
1 small shallot
¼ teaspoon grated lemon or lime zest
juice of 1 lime
½ cup (4 ounces) ice water
½ teaspoon xanthan gum
Pinches of salt and white pepper

1. Place all ingredients into a blender and puree the mixture until it's smooth.

2. Spoon the mixture into a bowl and refrigerate it covered until serving time. It goes on the plates first, in a thick smear on which the other ingredients rest.

WILD CALIFORNIA SEA BASS CEVICHE WITH SWEET CORN PANNA COTTA AND CRISPY TEMPURA ENOKI MUSHROOMS

SERVES 4

Wild-caught California sea bass has rebounded from the time a couple of decades ago when it was considered endangered. That's happy news for fish fans, at least during its June through March season. It's not related to what is called Chilean sea bass. You might substitute another fish in its drum family, redfish for example, another fish that has come back from endangered status. I love the mild sweetness of these fish paired with summer sweet corn and the crunch of fried enoki mushrooms. Check out the Kitchen Note on page 62 about ceviche and crudo and their preparation if you haven't made them before.

POSSIBLE DO-AHEAD STEPS

- Make the Sweet Corn Panna Cotta up to 1 day ahead.

FOR THE PANNA COTTA

1½ cups (12 ounces) whole milk

1 tablespoon unflavored powdered gelatin

1 cup fresh or thawed frozen corn kernels

Juice of 1 medium lime

Kosher salt and ground white pepper

FOR THE CEVICHE

8 ounces fresh wild California sea bass, or other fresh white fish

½ large navel orange, peeled and sliced into segments

1 medium lime, peeled and sliced into segments

½ cup diced mango

2 tablespoons minced red onion

1 tablespoon chopped cilantro

1 teaspoon minced fresh chile guero (yellow hot chile), or jalapeño

Juice of 1 medium lime

2 tablespoons (1 ounce) extra-virgin olive oil

FOR THE MUSHROOMS

1 cup (8 ounces) club soda or seltzer water, chilled

1 ounce (about 1 large) egg yolk, chilled

1 teaspoon baking powder

½ cup unbleached all-purpose flour

¼ cup cornstarch

Kosher salt and ground white pepper

Grapeseed, canola, or vegetable oil for deep frying

2 ounces enoki mushrooms, separated at their root ends into 4 bundles

Small cilantro leaves or blossoms, or small shiso leaves

TO PREPARE THE PANNA COTTA

1. Pour about 2 tablespoons of the milk into a ramekin and sprinkle the gelatin over it. Let the mixture stand several minutes.

2. In a blender, puree the rest of the milk with the corn. Strain the liquid through a fine-mesh sieve, pushing on the solids to release as much of the corn's flavor and juice as you can.

3. Warm the corn liquid with the lime juice in a medium saucepan over medium heat. When heated through, stir in the gelatin mixture and bring just to a simmer, then immediately remove from the heat. Season with salt and pepper.

4. Pour the warm panna cotta into 4 clear 8-ounce glasses or bowls, filling them just about halfway full. Chill covered in the refrigerator until lightly set, about 1 hour.

TO PREPARE THE CEVICHE

Gently combine all the ingredients in a medium bowl.

TO PREPARE THE ENOKI MUSHROOMS

1. In a medium bowl, whisk together the club soda and eggs.

2. Whisk in the baking powder, flour, cornstarch, a big pinch of kosher salt, and a little white pepper.

3. Warm a small saucepan with about 2 inches of oil to 325°F–330°F. Dunk the mushrooms into the batter and fry until crisp and just lightly colored, less than 1 minute. Drain on paper towels.

PUTTING IT ALL TOGETHER

1. Using a slotted spoon, spoon equal portions of ceviche over the panna cotta.

2. Top each serving with a bundle of fried enoki sticking upward and a few leaves or blossoms. Serve right away.

Kitchen Notes

In a couple of other recipes in this chapter, a fried ingredient is considered a Restaurant Embellishment. Here, I definitely want you to enjoy the light crunch of delicate Japanese enoki mushrooms. This tempura batter is a bit lighter than the one used on avocados earlier in the chapter.

other appetizers and small plates

HAY-SMOKED OYSTERS WITH APPLE, RADISH, AND DANDELION SALAD

SERVES 4

Jennifer inherited a ranch south of Santa Fe that her mother, Jan Bandler, had established as a refuge for abandoned and abused horses. Jennifer, the girls, and I are all active with The Horse Shelter, carrying on the work that was her mother's passion. When I was thinking about smoking woods and other materials for shellfish, I saw what I needed all around me in haystacks at the ranch. This will fascinate your friends, just as it does our restaurant patrons. Smoke from grassy hay is a fine match with the minerality of cold-water oysters, such as Blue Points from Long Island's Great South Bay. All you have to do to round out the dish is serve it with the included salad. Bits of apple and radish offer cool crunch with bursts of fruit and freshness, contrasting nicely with bitter greens.

FOR THE OYSTERS

12 or 16 northeastern Blue Point or northwestern Kumamoto oysters, or other top quality oysters of moderate size

6 large handfuls of hay, preferably still a bit green, rinsed, then soaked in water for at least 30 minutes

FOR THE SALAD

1 small Granny Smith apple, julienned

2 large radishes, julienned

1 small bunch dandelion greens or other tangy, slightly bitter greens such as arugula or watercress

1 tablespoon olive oil

Zest of 1 lime and the juice of half of it

Kosher salt and ground white pepper

TO PREPARE THE SMOKED OYSTERS

1. Lay open a fish-grilling basket. Place a layer of damp hay, ½–1 inch thick, in one side of the grilling basket.

2. Arrange oysters in their shells on top in a single layer and cover with about ½–1 inch more hay. Close the basket.

3. Set a rimmed baking sheet on a work surface by the stovetop and shoo away kids, pets, and guests for a few minutes.

4. Place the grilling basket over a stove burner at medium heat. Allow the heat to ignite the hay, moving the basket around gently or turning it over as needed to smolder evenly. (Since the hay is damp it should not erupt into alarming flames and since it is a small amount, it should not smoke up your kitchen. Do stay alert.)

5. Carefully transfer the grilling basket to the baking sheet, place another rimmed baking sheet over the basket, and allow the smoke and any flames to die out, about 10 minutes. The heat will help loosen the oyster shells. A table knife should be enough to help pry open the hot oysters, but use an oyster knife if you have one.

6. Wearing heatproof gloves or using an oven mitt on one hand to hold each oyster, pop them open by sliding the knife into the opening between the shells, back near the hinge. Twist and slice under the oyster and over if needed to release it from the shell. Reserve warm oysters in their bottom shells with any liquor.

TO PREPARE THE SALAD

1. Combine the apples, radish, and greens in a medium bowl.

2. In a ramekin, stir together the oil, lime zest, and juice in a ramekin.

3. Toss the apple salad mixture with the oil-lime dressing and season with salt and pepper.

PUTTING IT ALL TOGETHER

Place 3 or 4 oysters, out of their shells, leaned together in their own little haystack, on 4 plates. Drizzle any remaining oyster liquor over them. Scatter equal amounts of apple-radish-dandelion salad around the oysters. Dot with any dressing that remains in the bowl. Serve right away.

restaurant embellishments

To turn the dish into a more filling small plate, we serve it with Cauliflower Flan. Both the salad and the shelled oysters sit on top of the flan in a large shallow bowl.

CAULIFLOWER FLAN

8 ounces chopped cauliflower florets	1 chopped garlic clove
1 cup heavy cream	½ cup Vegetable Stock (see page xxvii)
½ cup whole milk	4 ounces (about 7 large) egg yolks
1 tablespoon chopped shallots	Kosher salt and ground white pepper

1. Preheat the oven to 300°F.

2. Combine cauliflower, heavy cream, milk, shallots, garlic, and vegetable stock in a saucepan. Bring to a simmer over medium heat until the cauliflower is tender, 8–10 minutes.

3. Transfer the mixture to a blender and puree until smooth. Alternatively, puree in the pan with an immersion blender.

4. Place egg yolks in a large bowl and whisk lightly. Whisk the cauliflower puree slowly but steadily into the egg yolks. Season the custard with salt and pepper.

5. Strain the custard through a fine-mesh sieve into 4 heatproof soup bowls or 10- to 12-ounce ramekins.

6. Arrange the bowls in a roasting pan. Make a water bath, pouring warm water into the pan approximately halfway up the sides of the bowls. Cover the pan with foil and transfer carefully to the oven.

7. Bake for 25–30 minutes or until the flan becomes very lightly firm, with a tiny touch of jiggle still at the center. Remove the pan from the oven and uncover. Let the flan bowls sit in the water bath to keep warm for up to 30 minutes.

MUSSELS IN AJI PANCA–MUSTARD BROTH WITH ACORN SQUASH "FRIES" AND ARUGULA PISTOU

SERVES 4

As I recall it today, the mussels my younger brother and I used to scavenge when my family lived by the beach in Baja California, were the best I have ever eaten. It could be, though, that my memory of them is so strong partially because they were the first mussels I ever ate and were a personally plucked feast from the wild. In the restaurant, I mostly use Prince Edward Island (or PEI) mussels, cultured in cold Canadian waters. The Belgian and French favorite, moules frites, or steamed mussels with fries, was probably somewhere in the back of my head when this came together. Cubes of acorn squash are cooked confit-style in duck fat. If you want the squash crispy like the french fries they resemble, sear the batons at the end in a skillet or on a griddle.

POSSIBLE DO-AHEAD STEPS
- Make the Arugula Pistou up to 4 hours ahead.

FOR THE ARUGULA PISTOU

1 cup arugula, blanched

½ cup pine nuts (piñones)

¼ cup (2 ounces) ice water

2 anchovy fillets

1 teaspoon roasted garlic puree

½ teaspoon each grated lemon zest and lemon juice

½ cup (4 ounces) extra-virgin olive oil

Kosher salt and ground white pepper

FOR THE ACORN SQUASH "FRIES"

4 ounces duck fat

2 tablespoons (1 ounce) unsalted butter

½ pound acorn squash, peeled, sliced into 8 blocks like thick french fries about 3 inches long

2 dried bay leaves

Large sprig of fresh thyme

Kosher salt and ground white pepper

FOR THE BROTH

20 cleaned and de-bearded mussels

1 tablespoon unsalted butter

1 tablespoon olive oil

¼ cup (2 ounces) sparkling wine or dry white wine

¼ cup (2 ounces) pineapple juice

2 ounces small heirloom tomatoes, chopped

½ teaspoon aji panca paste

1 teaspoon whole-grain mustard

Kosher salt and ground white pepper

FOR THE FINISHED DISH

Radish or arugula sprouts, or small arugula leaves

TO PREPARE THE PISTOU

1. Combine the arugula, pine nuts, ice water, anchovy fillets, garlic, and lemon zest and juice in a blender.

2. With the blender running, pour in the oil in a steady stream until well combined.

3. Season with salt and pepper. Reserve at room temperature for up to 1 hour or refrigerate covered until needed.

TO PREPARE THE ACORN SQUASH "FRIES"

1. Warm the duck fat in a medium saucepan almost to the smoking point.

2. Add the butter, then the squash batons and herbs and reduce the heat to a lightly bubbling simmer. Cook the squash through, about 10 minutes. Drain on paper towels and reserve.

TO PREPARE THE MUSSELS AND BROTH

1. In a medium saucepan, heat the mussels, butter, oil, sparkling wine, and pineapple juice over medium-high heat. Cover the pan for about 3 minutes, then uncover and stir the mixture around. Mussels should open within the next couple of minutes.

2. Remove the pan from the heat and scoop out the mussels with a spider or slotted spoon. When cool enough to handle, pop the meat out of the mussel shells, discarding the shells.

3. Reduce the cooking liquid by about a third to give it a bit more body, then stir in the tomatoes, aji panca, and mustard. Heat through, then add the mussels back into the broth and season with salt and pepper.

PUTTING IT ALL TOGETHER

Spoon a pool of arugula pistou into the middle of each of 4 plates. Place a pair of squash "fries" in the middle of the pistou. Arrange mussels at angles around the squash, spoon on some of the mussels broth with tomatoes. Top with a few sprouts or greens and serve.

Kitchen Notes

Aji panca paste is made from a Peruvian red chile. It's likely available with other jarred hot stuff in your supermarket, at a Latin American market, or online. Use a splash or 2 of a Mexican hot sauce as a substitute if needed.

BRAISED GRAINS AND SEEDS WITH MUSHROOMS, MANCHEGO, AND RED BELL PEPPER CRISPS

SERVES 4

One of the companies that provides my china asked me to do a demonstration using mixed grains and cheese. This was the result, although that version was suitable for vegetarians, since it used vegetable stock and had no ham accompaniment. You could switch back to that easily if you wish.

POSSIBLE DO-AHEAD STEPS

- Make the Light Chicken Stock up to 1 week ahead.
- Cook the barley, farro, and quinoa for the Braised Grains and Seeds (see Kitchen Notes page 95) up to 2 days ahead.
- Make the Braised Grains and Seeds up to 1 day ahead.

FOR THE RED BELL PEPPER CRISPS

Approximately ½ cup pureed peeled and roasted red bell pepper (1 small red bell pepper)

½ teaspoon crushed dried Aleppo red pepper or other dried red chile flakes

2 tablespoons (1 ounce) olive oil

3 ounces almond flour or meal

FOR THE BRAISED GRAINS AND SEEDS

3 tablespoons pepitas (shelled pumpkin seeds)

4 tablespoons sunflower kernels

½ cup cooked black barley

½ cup cooked farro

½ cup cooked quinoa

3 ounces porcini, chanterelle, or brown button mushrooms, sliced thin

1 tablespoon minced shallots

Pinch of ground allspice

2 cups (1 pint) Light Chicken Stock (see page xxviii)

2 tablespoons mascarpone cheese

½ teaspoon grated lemon zest

1 teaspoon grated horseradish

Kosher salt and ground white pepper

FOR THE CHICKEN-TRUFFLE REDUCTION

1 teaspoon canola or vegetable oil

½ medium onion, chopped

1 small carrot, chopped

1 tablespoon green peppercorns

2 garlic cloves

Small sprig fresh thyme

1 dried bay leaf

1 cup (8 ounces) port

2 cups (1 pint) Dark Chicken Stock (see page xxviii)

1 tablespoon truffle juice

1 teaspoon truffle oil

Kosher salt and ground white pepper

FOR THE HAM

1 teaspoon extra-virgin olive oil

4 ounces paper-thin serrano ham slices

1 teaspoon chopped chives

FOR THE FINISHED DISH

6 ounces thinly sliced manchego cheese, softened

Fennel, cucumber, or borage blossoms or tiny sorrel or chard leaves, or dill sprigs or minced chives

TO PREPARE THE CRISPS

1. Preheat the oven to 300°F.

2. Line a baking sheet with a non-stick mat or lightly oiled parchment paper.

3. Combine all the ingredients in a food processor and mix until you have a well-blended thin dough/thick batter.

4. With a spatula, spread the mixture on the baking sheet to within 1 or 2 inches of the edges. Bake for 15–18 minutes, or until dried out and crisp. The crisps should only darken a shade. Let cool on the baking sheet over a baking rack. Break into small shards. They hold their crispness best if spread out rather than stacked.

TO PREPARE THE BRAISED GRAINS AND SEEDS

1. Combine the pepitas and sunflower kernels in a medium saucepan and toast over medium heat for about 3 minutes, until fragrant.

2. Add the rest of the ingredients and cook until the liquid is absorbed and the mixture is creamy, about 10 more minutes. Cover and keep warm on low heat unless you are making the mixture more than 1 hour ahead, in which case you should cool, cover, and refrigerate it.

TO PREPARE THE REDUCTION SAUCE

1. Warm the oil in a saucepan over medium heat.

2. Stir in the onion, carrot, peppercorns, garlic, thyme, and bay leaf and cook until lightly caramelized, 7–10 minutes.

3. Pour in the port and reduce the liquid until the mixture is almost dry, about 5 minutes.

4. Pour in the stock and reduce by about half to a light sauce consistency, another 5–10 minutes.

5. Stir in the truffle juice and truffle oil and cook for about 1 more minute. Season with salt and pepper.

6. Strain the sauce through a fine-mesh sieve and keep it warm on low heat.

7. While the sauce is reducing, prepare the ham.

TO PREPARE THE HAM

Rub the oil over each slice and sprinkle lightly with chives. Cut each slice long-ways into 1-inch wide slices. Roll up each slice, from one of the short sides, to make a little tube. Repeat with the remaining ingredients.

PUTTING IT ALL TOGETHER

If you have rectangular plates, you might want to use 4 of them here. Divide the braised grains and seeds among the plates. With a spatula or the back of a spoon, level out the mixture into a rectangle about 3 by 6 inches. Arrange the manchego slices over the grains and seeds, to cover them. Melt the cheese with your trusty little blowtorch (alternatively, by warming the plates in the oven). Arrange the ham rolls equally over the cheese toppings, standing some upright and some on their side. Spoon the reduction sauce over the plates, garnish with blossoms and leaves, and arrange a few bell pepper crisps leaning against the ham or blossoms. Serve right away.

restaurant embellishments

I like the plate to have something green so I add Chive Pudding.

CHIVE PUDDING

> 1 cup fresh chives
> ½ cup Italian parsley
> ½ cup (4 ounces) ice water
> ¼ teaspoon xanthan gum
> Kosher salt and ground white pepper

1. Blanch the chives and parsley, then combine the blanched greens in a blender with the ice water, xanthan gum, and a bit of salt and pepper.

2. Puree the mixture until smooth.

3. Pass the pudding through a fine-mesh sieve and refrigerate it covered until serving time.

Kitchen Notes

When cooking grains for a dish like this, I always make enough to have leftovers for morning cereals and other dishes. They keep well in the refrigerator for days. To cook them, simply add salted water to barley, farro, or quinoa in a saucepan and set the heat to medium. For barley, use 1 cup of the grain with 3 cups of water and cook 45–55 minutes, which will yield about 3 ½ cups cooked. One cup of farro with 2 ½ cups of water yields 3 cups at the end of 30–40 minutes on the stove. With quinoa combine 1 cup of the grain with 2 cups of water and cook for just 10–15 minutes to get 3 cups prepared.

SALSIFY IN COUNTRY HAM WITH APPLE-FENNEL PUREE AND PORCINI MUSHROOM-SHERRY VINAIGRETTE

SERVES 4

If you are not familiar with the fall-into-winter root vegetable called salsify (pronounced "sal-sa-fee"), it's a good time to find out about it. I understand that it was a popular American ingredient a century ago, but fell out of favor, maybe because it was called oyster plant or because it resembles a long, straight, shaggy twig. When you peel off the root's outer dark brown skin, you find a creamy white vegetable that tastes like a cross between an artichoke heart and a parsnip. I like it paired with hearty flavors such as ham, mushrooms, and apples. I thought of candied hazelnuts for the plate too, because I wanted something crunchy and ham is so compatible with a sugar glaze. If you're short on time, skip candying the hazelnuts and simply scatter a few chopped toasted ones over the plates.

POSSIBLE DO-AHEAD STEPS

- Make the Light Chicken Stock up to 1 week ahead.
- Simmer the salsify until tender and refrigerate it up to 2 days ahead.
- Make the Candied Hazelnuts and cool them thoroughly before storing in an airtight container up to 2 days ahead.
- Make the Apple-Fennel Puree up to 4 hours ahead.

FOR THE CANDIED HAZELNUTS

½ cup (4 ounces) water

½ cup granulated sugar

¼ cup (2 ounces) light corn syrup

1 cup (about 4½ ounces) toasted hazelnuts, loose skins rubbed off

Pinch ground allspice

Pinch dried red chile flakes

¼ teaspoon kosher salt

Ground white pepper

FOR THE VINAIGRETTE

2 ounces fresh porcini mushrooms, sliced, or fresh shiitake mushrooms

Vegetable oil spray

¼ cup (2 ounces) sherry vinegar

1 small shallot

½ teaspoon brown sugar

¼ teaspoon grated lemon zest

½ cup (4 ounces) olive oil

Kosher salt and ground white pepper

FOR THE SALSIFY

4 salsify roots, peeled and cut in 4 sections each

2 cups (1 pint) whole milk

Kosher salt and ground white pepper

16 thin slices country ham (one with some age but not super dry and salty), at least 3 inches wide

FOR THE APPLE-FENNEL PUREE

2 tablespoons (1 ounce) olive oil

2 Granny Smith apples, peeled and chopped

6-ounce fennel head, chopped

1 small shallot, chopped

1 garlic clove, halved

2 cups (1 pint) Light Chicken Stock (see page xxviii)

Juice of 1 lemon

2 tablespoons (1 ounce) unsalted butter

Kosher salt and ground white pepper

FOR THE FINISHED DISH

¼ cup (2 ounces) olive oil

2 tablespoons (1 ounce) unsalted butter

Watercress or Italian parsley leaves

TO CANDY THE HAZELNUTS

1. Line a baking sheet with a non-stick baking mat or lightly oiled parchment paper.

2. Combine the water, sugar, and corn syrup in a small saucepan and warm over high heat. Swirl the pan to help dissolve the sugar, but don't stir the syrup mixture. Boil the mixture until it turns medium amber, 4–5 minutes.

3. Stir in the hazelnuts, allspice, chile, salt, and a few shakes of pepper. Keep stirring until well coated, about 1 additional minute.

4. Pour the nuts onto the prepared baking sheet in a single layer and let cool at room temperature.

TO PREPARE THE VINAIGRETTE

1. Spray the porcini mushrooms lightly with oil, then grill or sauté them over medium heat until tender.

2. Transfer the mushrooms to a blender and add the rest of the ingredients. Puree the mixture with a few quick bursts, until combined but with a bit of texture. Reserve the vinaigrette at room temperature.

TO PREPARE THE SALSIFY AND HAM

1. Place the salsify pieces in a high-sided medium saucepan. Pour in the milk, season generously with salt and pepper, and bring to a simmer over medium-high heat. Cook the salsify for 15–20 minutes, until tender.

2. Drain the salsify and pat it dry. Wrap a slice of ham, from one of its short sides, snugly around a section of salsify. Trim off the ham extending beyond the ends of the salsify. Repeat with the remaining ham and salsify. Cover the ham-wrapped logs with plastic wrap and let sit at room temperature.

TO PREPARE THE APPLE-FENNEL PUREE

1. Warm the oil in a medium saucepan over medium heat. Add the apples, fennel, shallot, and garlic and cook about 5 minutes, until softened and lightly colored.

2. Pour in the stock and lemon juice and reduce the mixture until only about a quarter of the liquid remains, 5–10 minutes.

3. Transfer the mixture to a blender, in batches if necessary. Add the butter, and puree. Season with salt and pepper and reserve at room temperature. (If making the puree more than 1 hour ahead, refrigerate it covered and then reheat it before serving.)

1. Warm the oil in a medium to large sauté pan or skillet. Place the ham-wrapped salsify logs in the skillet, seam-sides down. Using tongs, turn the logs as needed to sear and lightly crisp on all sides, several minutes. Add the butter to the pan and baste the logs about 30 seconds with the buttery pan juices. Drain the logs on paper towels.

2. Spoon ¼ of the puree in the center of each of 4 plates. Arrange 4 ham-and-salsify logs leaning on each other, sort of Lincoln Log style, on each plate. Spoon the vinaigrette over the logs, and sprinkle the hazelnuts around the plate. Garnish each plate with watercress or parsley leaves and serve.

Kitchen Notes

The salsify I get is typically 10–12 inches long. I have seen it at Whole Foods and Sprouts markets as well as at some farmers markets. Once a root is peeled, it should be held in acidulated water or cooked right away so it doesn't oxidize. The roots are pretty dense, so it can take 20 minutes or so to become tender. If the cooking liquid runs low before the salsify is soft, add some hot water to the pan. You can also simply steam it rather than simmering it.

CARPACCIO OF SMOKED DUCK BREAST WITH WINE-POACHED FIGS, SPICED WALNUT SAUCE, CHANTERELLES, AND STILTON

SERVES 4

I conceived this dish while thinking of a fairly classic French combination of duck and figs, though I opted for the king of British cheeses to accompany it because I prefer a semi-firm cow's milk blue here to France's esteemed sheep's milk Roquefort. The walnut sauce could have had a different pedigree of its own. As a friend pointed out to me it resembles Mexican nogada, the sauce that accompanies the famous Puebla dish called chiles en nogada.

POSSIBLE DO-AHEAD STEPS

- Make the Wine-Poached Figs up to 1 day ahead.
- Brine the duck breasts for 2 hours, then smoke them up to 4 hours ahead.

FOR THE WINE-POACHED FIGS

8 black mission figs, or other fresh figs, cut in lengthwise quarters

1 cup (8 ounces) dry red wine

½ cup (4 ounces) red wine vinegar

2 tablespoons granulated sugar

1 tablespoon chopped fresh ginger

1 dried bay leaf

2 whole cloves

1 teaspoon black peppercorns

3 tablespoons (1 ½ ounces) extra-virgin olive oil

FOR THE DUCK BREAST

Two (6- to 8-ounce) skin-on individual duck breasts

2 cups (1 pint) water

½ cup (4 ounces) apple cider

¼ cup granulated sugar

2 tablespoons kosher salt

1 teaspoon black peppercorns

2 dried bay leaves

Olive oil

FOR THE WALNUT SAUCE

1 cup walnut pieces, toasted

1 cup (8 ounces) Light Chicken Stock (see page xxviii)

1 teaspoon Dijon mustard

2 quarter-size slices peeled fresh ginger

¼ teaspoon ground dried ginger

Pinch of ground dried mild or medium red chile, such as New Mexican or ancho

Pinch of ground cloves

Pinch of ground allspice

Pinch of ground cinnamon

Kosher salt and ground white pepper

FOR THE SAUTÉED CHANTERELLES

2 teaspoons olive oil

2 ounces fresh chanterelle mushrooms, or other fresh meaty mushrooms such as porcini or maitake

2 tablespoons (1 ounce) unsalted butter

Small sprig of fresh thyme

Kosher salt and ground white pepper

½ teaspoon chopped fresh chives

4 ounces Stilton cheese, cut in 4 blocks

2 tablespoons (1 ounce) extra-virgin olive oil

1 teaspoon chopped fresh chives

½ teaspoon grated lemon zest

½ teaspoon Dijon mustard

4 ounces small mustard leaves, or watercress or arugula leaves

Kosher salt and ground white pepper

TO PREPARE THE FIGS

1. Place figs in a heatproof medium bowl.

2. In a saucepan, combine the wine, vinegar, sugar, ginger, bay leaf, cloves, and peppercorns. Bring the mixture to a boil over high heat, then reduce the heat to a low simmer and cook for 5 minutes.

3. Strain the liquid through a fine-mesh sieve into the bowl of figs. Let the mixture cool to room temperature, then mix in the olive oil and refrigerate covered until needed.

TO PREPARE THE DUCK BREASTS

1. Score the skin-side of the breasts in a 1-inch diamond or crosshatch pattern. Make crisscross cuts through the skin but not into the flesh. This promotes gradual and easy rendering of fat and gives more surfaces for the seasonings to flavor.

2. Warm the water, cider, sugar, salt, peppercorns, and bay leaves in a small saucepan over medium heat. Stir until the sugar and salt dissolve to make a brine. Set aside to cool.

3. Place the duck breasts in a shallow dish, and pour the brine over them. Cover and refrigerate the duck to marinate for 2–3 hours, then rinse and pat the breasts dry with paper towels.

4. Set up a stovetop smoker, or other smoker, using apple wood.

5. Warm a medium skillet over high heat. Add a thin coat of olive oil to the pan. Sear the duck breasts in the skillet, skin-sides down. Reduce the heat to medium and sauté until the skin renders some fat, and becomes golden-brown, about 2 minutes. (The browning may take twice this long, depending on the thickness of the skin and the exact heat level.) If the skin is browning before some fat is rendered, reduce the heat.

6. Transfer the duck to the smoker. If the smoker has a thermostat, you want it in the range of 180°F–200°F. Otherwise, use the lowest heat you can manage and still have smoke. Smoke the duck breasts for 5 minutes, then let sit in the smoker for another 10 minutes. The duck should emerge rare. Cool and refrigerate covered until needed.

TO PREPARE THE WALNUT SAUCE

1. Combine all the ingredients in a small saucepan and bring the mixture to a boil over high heat. Reduce the sauce by about half, about 5 minutes.

2. Transfer the mixture to a blender and puree. It will take a good 30–60 seconds to get it truly smooth. Let the sauce sit at room temperature.

TO PREPARE THE CHANTERELLES

1. Warm a medium sauté pan coated with the olive oil over medium heat. Stir in the mushrooms and cook several minutes until limp and lightly colored.

2. Add the butter and thyme to the pan and spoon the melted butter over the mushrooms several times, then season with salt and pepper and remove them from the heat.

3. Transfer the mushrooms to a plate lined with paper towels and sprinkle with the chives.

PUTTING IT ALL TOGETHER

1. Slice the chilled duck breasts with the grain (lengthwise) as thinly as you can manage. Arrange the slices in an overlapping square down the middle of each of 4 plates.

2. Using a slotted spoon, arrange equal portions of the figs over the duck slices. Scatter chanterelles around the figs and duck. Drizzle on several small pools of walnut sauce. Arrange a block of cheese to one side on each plate. Whisk together the olive oil, chives, lemon zest, and mustard, and toss with the greens. Sprinkle the greens with salt and pepper, add them to each plate, and serve.

POACHED EGGS WITH MISO-RICE CONGEE, BLACK OLIVE OIL, GREEN ONIONS, AND PARMESAN FROTH

SERVES 4

This egg with rice dish began as a risotto, which morphed over time into my twist on the Asian rice porridge known as congee. It's both unexpected and comforting at the same time. There are umami tastes to Parmesan cheese, dashi broth, miso, olives, and anchovies, so while these elements might sound dissonant, they really come together in the bowl.

POSSIBLE DO-AHEAD STEPS

- Make the Light Chicken Stock up to 1 week ahead.
- Make the Black Olive Oil up to 2 days ahead.

FOR THE BLACK OLIVE OIL

½ cup pitted black Kalamata olives

¼ cup (2 ounces) olive oil

¼ teaspoon roasted garlic puree

½ teaspoon fresh lemon juice

1 anchovy or ½ teaspoon anchovy paste

½ small shallot

2 tablespoons (1 ounce) ice water

FOR THE MISO-RICE CONGEE

1 cup jasmine or other long-grain rice

Approximately 2 ½–3 cups (20–24 ounces) Light Chicken Stock (see page xxviii)

1 teaspoon yellow miso

1 teaspoon thinly sliced peeled fresh ginger

2 tablespoons (1 ounce) unsalted butter

2 tablespoons ricotta cheese

2 ounces thinly sliced shiitake mushrooms, sautéed in a bit of oil until tender

Kosher salt and ground white pepper

4 scallions, limp green tops removed, blanched and cut in 3-inch long pieces

1 tablespoon sesame seeds, toasted

FOR THE PARMESAN FROTH

1 cup (8 ounces) dashi broth

1 teaspoon grated peeled fresh ginger

1 garlic clove

1 teaspoon fresh lemon juice

2 tablespoons (1 ounce) unsalted butter

½ teaspoon soy lecithin

1 ounce grated Parmesan cheese

Kosher salt and ground white pepper

FOR THE POACHED EGGS

1 tablespoon white wine vinegar or white vinegar

Kosher salt

4 large eggs

Ground white pepper

FOR THE FINISHED DISH

Small mustard leaves, arugula, watercress, or other tangy tender greens

Smoked salt, optional

TO PREPARE THE BLACK OLIVE OIL

Combine all the ingredients in a blender and process with on-and-off turns to a somewhat coarse consistency. It will be something like a thin tapenade. Transfer the oil to a small bowl and let sit at room temperature if using shortly. Refrigerate it covered if not using within 1 hour.

TO PREPARE THE CONGEE

1. Combine the rice, 1 cup of stock, miso, ginger, and butter in a medium saucepan. Cook over medium-low heat, adding approximately ½ cup of stock whenever the previous stock is nearly absorbed. You may not need all of the stock. Stir constantly, until the mixture becomes creamy with very tender grains of rice, 25–30 minutes.

2. Stir in the ricotta and mushrooms and season with salt and pepper. Sprinkle with scallion batons and sesame seeds. Cover to keep warm.

TO PREPARE THE PARMESAN FROTH

1. Combine the dashi, ginger, garlic, and lemon juice in a small saucepan. Bring to a quick boil, then reduce the heat to maintain a gentle simmer and cook for 10 minutes.

2. Strain the mixture through a fine-mesh sieve into a blender. Add the butter, lecithin, and Parmesan, and puree. Season with salt and pepper.

TO POACH THE EGGS

1. Fill a broad saucepan with about 2 inches of water, pour in the vinegar, add a big pinch of salt, and bring to a boil.

2. Break the eggs into individual ramekins.

3. Reduce the heat of the salted water to a bare simmer, then slip the eggs into the water. Simmer the eggs gently for 30 seconds, then turn off the heat and cover for 1 ½–2 minutes.

4. Remove eggs with a slotted spoon and place each on a separate section of paper towel to drain. Trim any ragged edges off the egg whites and sprinkle with a bit more salt and some pepper.

PUTTING IT ALL TOGETHER

Divide the congee among 4 bowls, and drizzle each with black olive oil. Sprinkle smoked salt over if you wish. Nudge each egg off its paper towel and over a bowl of rice. Spoon the froth over the bowls, scatter a few greens over all, and serve right away.

pasta and risotto

SPRING PEA TORTELLINI WITH MINT, BRIE, AND ARUGULA COULIS

SERVES 4

I started making pasta regularly when I was chef at The Old House in Santa Fe. Since the restaurant is in the Eldorado Hotel, and hotel management always wants a menu that has one of everything on it, I made sure we had an interesting pasta daily. I find it pretty simple to make pasta dough and love the flexibility in flavorings that making my own gives to a dish, like these tortellini stuffed with peas, brie cheese, and nepitella, an Italian mint with a mild undertone of oregano. You can, of course, use any mint in the filling. I blanch the peas in the filling and the arugula that is the sauce's main ingredient so that they will be intensely verde in the dish. A version of this dish appeared in New Mexico Magazine *when the editors featured me in a story about the state's James Beard restaurant award nominees and winners. Note that in this chapter I list first the weight of the most essential ingredients in the pasta dough, and then the approximate cup and tablespoon measurement, because using the exact amount by weight is important in getting the desired dough consistency.*

POSSIBLE DO-AHEAD STEPS

- Make the tortellini pasta dough and filling up to 8 hours ahead.

FOR THE PASTA DOUGH

10 ounces (about 1 ¾ cups) durum flour

4 ounces (about ⅔ cup) semolina flour

2 ounces (a scant ½ cup) unbleached all-purpose flour

½ cup (about 6–7 large) egg yolks

¼ cup (2 ounces) water

2 tablespoons (1 ounce) extra-virgin olive oil

Kosher salt and ground white pepper

FOR THE TORTELLINI FILLING

10 ounces shelled fresh peas, blanched

5 ounces French brie

2 ounces ricotta cheese

4 tablespoons (2 ounces) unsalted butter, softened

1 large egg yolk

1 tablespoon chopped fresh nepitella or other mint

1 tablespoon panko bread crumbs

Kosher salt and ground white pepper

½ garlic clove

½ cup (4 ounces) ice water

2 tablespoons (1 ounce) extra-virgin olive oil

Kosher salt and ground white pepper

1 medium or large egg mixed with ½ teaspoon water

FOR THE ARUGULA COULIS

1 cup packed arugula, blanched

1 small shallot, chunked

½ garlic clove

½ cup (4 ounces) water

2 tablespoons (1 ounce) extra-virgin olive oil

Kosher salt and ground white pepper

FOR THE FINISHED DISH

1 tablespoon unsalted butter

Small mint or arugula leaves, fennel or dill fronds, or chive blossoms

TO PREPARE THE PASTA DOUGH

1. Combine all the ingredients together in a large mixing bowl, and mix together with your hands into a rough dough that holds together.

2. Transfer the dough to a work surface and knead it, pushing down on it with the heel of your hand, and then folding it back over itself continually, for about 5 minutes, until the dough is smooth and supple. It's hard to over-knead pasta dough.

3. Form the dough into a disk, then cover with plastic and refrigerate for 30–60 minutes.

TO PREPARE THE FILLING

Combine all the ingredients, except the egg-water mixture, in a food processor. Pulse multiple times, until you have a thick coarse puree. Reserve at room temperature.

TO PREPARE THE ARUGULA COULIS

Combine all the ingredients in a blender and puree until smooth. Reserve at room temperature.

TO MAKE THE TORTELLINI

1. Pat out pasta dough as needed to roll it through a pasta machine to its thinnest setting, following the manufacturer's directions.

2. Form the tortellini, first using a 3- or 4-inch-round cookie or biscuit cutter to cut out a dozen circles from the dough.

3. Spoon about 1 teaspoon of filling on each dough round. Brush the edge of each lightly with the egg-water mixture and fold one half over the other, pressing to get a good seal. Bend each half-moon around your index finger, until the two outer edges of the half-moon touch. Brush with a tiny bit more of the egg wash if the edges are not sticking together. Fold back the top ¼ inch of the tortellini to give it a little collar. Repeat with the remaining pasta and filling.

4. Bring a large pot of well-salted water to a rolling boil over high heat. Add the tortellini gently to the water and cook for about 3 minutes, until just tender but toothsome (al dente).

5. While the tortellini are cooking, melt the butter in a medium sauté pan.

6. Drain the pasta, then scoop it out with a spider or slotted spoon, rather than pouring the whole pot over a colander, which can smash the pasta.

7. Transfer the tortellini to the sauté pan and mix lightly until glazed with butter.

PUTTING IT ALL TOGETHER

Arrange 3 or 4 tortellini in the center of each of 4 plates. Drizzle the coulis around the pasta. Garnish with leaves and serve immediately.

Kitchen Notes

- Semolina flour is ground from durum wheat, but is coarser than what is called "durum flour." If you can't find durum flour, use bread flour (a higher gluten flour than all-purpose varieties) in its place. Weighing the quantities of flour rather than measuring in cups gives the most precise results.

- If you are short of time, you can purchase freshly made pasta in sheets or broad lasagna-style noodles at many well-stocked supermarkets.

- Blanching sets the color of vegetables or greens, which is important to the final appearance of a dish like this. Make an ice water bath in a large bowl by combining cold water with at least 6 ice cubes. Bring a saucepan of water to a rapid boil. (Here, you can use the same water for both the peas and the arugula, but always blanch different vegetables in different batches since they cook at different rates.) Lower vegetables into the boiling water. In this case, cook peas about 45 seconds, strain out with a spider or fine-mesh sieve, then plunge into the ice water until chilled. Set aside on a clean dishtowel to drain. Add more ice cubes if all have melted. Return water to a boil, if needed. Lower arugula into the boiling water, pushing it down to cover it. Cook just until wilted, about 20 seconds. Corral it with the spider again, and plunge into the ice water. When chilled, drain on towels.

TALEGGIO-AND-BUTTERNUT AGNOLOTTI WITH PARMESAN-PECAN CRUMBS, AND TRUFFLE-BROWN BUTTER

SERVES 4

While the previous pasta is one of my favorites for spring, this one seems perfect for the fall. It's another filled pasta, plump with butternut squash and the aromatic creamy Italian cheese, Taleggio. Agnolotti might be described as ravioli's smaller and more rectangular cousin.

POSSIBLE DO-AHEAD STEPS
- Make the Light Chicken Stock up to 1 week ahead.

FOR THE PASTA DOUGH

1 pound (about 2⅔ cups) durum flour

6 ounces (about 1 cup) semolina flour

2 ounces (a scant ½ cup) unbleached all-purpose
  flour

¾ cup (about 9 to 10 large) egg yolks

½ cup (4 ounces) water

2 tablespoons (1 ounce) olive oil

Kosher salt and ground white pepper

FOR THE FILLING

4 ounces Taleggio cheese

12 ounces cooked (baked or steamed) butternut
  squash

1 large egg, whisked

¼ teaspoon grated orange zest

Pinch freshly grated nutmeg

Kosher salt and ground white pepper

FOR THE PARMESAN-PECAN CRUMBS

¼ cup panko bread crumbs

¼ cup finely chopped pecans

2 tablespoons (1 ounce) unsalted butter

¼ cup freshly grated Parmesan cheese

1 tablespoon chopped fresh chives

Kosher salt and ground white pepper

FOR THE TRUFFLE-BUTTER SAUCE

2 tablespoons minced shallots

¼ cup (2 ounces) Madeira or Marsala wine

1 cup (8 ounces) Light Chicken Stock
  (see page xxviii)

Small sprig of fresh tarragon

1 dried bay leaf

4 tablespoons (2 ounces) truffle butter or 4 tablespoons unsalted butter with 1 teaspoon truffle
  juice or truffle oil

Kosher salt and ground white pepper

FOR THE FINISHED DISH

1 tablespoon unsalted butter

Basil blooms or small basil leaves or sage leaves

TO PREPARE THE PASTA DOUGH

1. Combine all the ingredients together in a large mixing bowl, and mix together with your hands into a rough dough that holds together.

2. Transfer the dough to a work surface and knead it, pushing down with the heel of your hand, and then folding it back over itself continually for about 5 minutes, until the dough is smooth and supple.

3. Form the dough into a disk, then cover with plastic and refrigerate for 30–60 minutes.

TO PREPARE THE FILLING

Combine all the ingredients in a food processor. Pulse multiple times, until you have a thick coarse puree. Reserve at room temperature.

TO PREPARE THE BREAD CRUMBS

1. Combine the bread crumbs, pecans, and butter in a small saucepan. Sauté over medium-low heat until light golden in color and crisp. Drain the crumbs on paper towels.

2. When cool, mix in the Parmesan and chives and sprinkle with salt and pepper. Reserve at room temperature.

TO PREPARE THE PASTA

1. Pat out the pasta dough as needed to roll it through a pasta machine to its thinnest setting, following the machine manufacturer's directions. You want long rectangles of pasta that you cut into broad ribbons 3 inches wide.

2. Place 2 teaspoons of filling every 3 inches along the length of the pasta. Begin to form the agnolotti by folding the bottom of the long pasta ribbon up over the filling and pinch to close along that edge to get a good seal.

3. Press the dough flat between the mounds of filling. Using a fluted pastry wheel, cut between the mounds of filling into puffy filled rectangles. Repeat with the remaining pasta and filling.

TO PREPARE THE BUTTER SAUCE

1. Combine the shallots, Madeira, stock, tarragon, and bay leaf in a small saucepan and heat over high heat until the liquid is reduced by about half.

2. Remove the tarragon sprig and bay leaf from the mixture, then whisk in the truffle butter until you have a sauce with a light silky consistency. Season with salt and pepper. Keep warm over low heat.

PUTTING IT ALL TOGETHER

1. Bring a large pot of well-salted water to a rolling boil over high heat. Add the agnolotti gently to the water and cook for about 3 minutes, until just tender but toothsome (al dente).

2. While the agnolotti are cooking, melt the butter in a medium sauté pan. Drain the pasta. Scoop it out with a spider or slotted spoon, rather than pouring the whole pot over a colander, which can smash the pasta. Transfer the agnolotti to the sauté pan and mix lightly until glazed with butter.

3. Arrange about a half-dozen agnolotti in the center of each of 4 plates. Drizzle the sauce around the pasta. Garnish with leaves and serve immediately.

restaurant embellishments

I often finish this dish with fall vegetables such as Cauliflower Puree, which I spoon under the pasta when I serve it.

CAULIFLOWER PUREE

12 ounces chopped cauliflower florets

6 ounces chopped parsnips

1 small chopped shallot

2 cups (1 pint) Light Chicken Stock (see page xxviii)

½ cup (4 ounces) heavy cream

4 tablespoons (2 ounces) unsalted butter

½ teaspoon xanthan gum

Kosher salt and ground white pepper

1. In a medium saucepan, combine the cauliflower, parsnips, shallot, stock, and heavy cream and cook over medium heat until the vegetables are soft, about 15 minutes.

2. Transfer the mixture to a blender, add butter and xanthan gum, and puree until smooth. Season with salt and white pepper.

Golden Cipollini Onions are another fine option, spooned around the plates.

GOLDEN CIPOLLINI ONIONS

8 blanched cipollini onions

2 tablespoons (1 ounce) unsalted butter

Small sprig of fresh thyme

¼ cup (2 ounces) Light Chicken Stock (see page xxviii)

Kosher salt and ground white pepper

Combine all ingredients in a small saucepan. Simmer the mixture slowly until the liquid evaporates and the onions turn a beautiful golden color.

Kitchen Notes

I think the idea of a whole butternut squash sometimes seems off-putting to home cooks. How hard will it be to cut it open and what can I do with the whole thing? It's not a particularly hard squash to slice, and you can bag sections of it for the freezer. Also, many produce departments today carry small bags of it already peeled, cubed, and ready to roast. I like that it has less moisture than pumpkin and a lot of other winter squashes.

DUNGENESS CRAB LASAGNA WITH ROASTED GARLIC SABAYON AND FRAGRANT HERBS

SERVES 4

This elegant lasagna is actually individually stacked portions of tender egg noodles with a crab, vegetable, and apple filling. It's crowned with a deliciously frothy sauce and served with an herb salad. Feel free to use other herbs than specified, or to mix up the quantities, depending upon what you have available.

POSSIBLE DO-AHEAD STEPS

- Make the lasagna dough up to 4 hours ahead.

FOR THE LASAGNA DOUGH

1 pound (about 2⅞ cups) durum flour

6 ounces (about 1 cup) semolina flour

2½ ounces (a generous ½ cup) unbleached all-purpose flour

¾ cup (about 9–10 large) egg yolks

½ cup (4 ounces) water

2 tablespoons (1 ounce) olive oil

Kosher salt and ground white pepper

FOR THE CRAB FILLING

4 ounces portobello mushroom caps, julienned

4 ounces peeled celery root, julienned

½ unpeeled Granny Smith apple, julienned

2 medium shallots, julienned

¼ teaspoon minced garlic

4 ounces lump Dungeness crab meat

2 ounces ricotta cheese

2 tablespoons freshly grated Parmesan cheese

1 tablespoon chopped fresh Italian parsley

½ teaspoon chopped fresh rosemary

Kosher salt and ground white pepper

FOR THE SABAYON

4 large egg yolks

¾ cup (6 ounces) crème fraîche

½ cup (4 ounces) Light Chicken Stock (see page xxviii)

½ cup (4 ounces) sparkling wine or dry white wine

1 tablespoon minced shallots

1 teaspoon roasted garlic puree

¼ teaspoon cornstarch

2 teaspoons champagne vinegar

Kosher salt and ground white pepper

FOR THE HERB SALAD

¼ cup fresh chervil sprigs

¼ cup fresh tarragon leaves

¼ cup fresh Italian parsley sprigs

¼ cup fresh bronze dill or other dill sprigs

Small handful basil, borage, or broccoli blossoms, optional

Peel of 1 Meyer lemon or other lemon, julienned and blanched

2 tablespoons extra-virgin olive oil

Kosher salt and ground white pepper

TO PREPARE THE PASTA DOUGH

Combine all the ingredients in a large mixing bowl, and mix together with your hands into a rough dough that holds together. Transfer the dough to a work surface and knead the dough, pushing down on it with the heel of your hand, and then folding it back over itself continually for about 5 minutes, until the dough is smooth and supple. Form the dough into a disk, then cover with plastic and refrigerate for 30–60 minutes.

TO PREPARE THE CRAB FILLING

1. Warm the oil in a medium sauté pan over medium heat. Stir in the mushrooms, celery root, apple, shallots, and garlic. Cook until the mixture has given up most of its liquid and is browned lightly.

2. Stir in the rest of the ingredients and cover to keep warm.

TO PREPARE THE SABAYON

1. Whisk together all the ingredients in the top pan of a double boiler and place it over its simmering water bath. Continue to whisk the mixture until it becomes silky and thick enough that you can see a trail through the bottom of the pan as you whisk.

2. Strain the sauce through a fine-mesh sieve and cover to keep warm.

TO MAKE THE PASTA

1. Pat out the pasta dough as needed to roll it through a pasta machine to its thinnest setting, according to the manufacturer's directions. Cut the pasta into 12 2 x 4-inch rectangles.

2. Bring a large pan of well-salted water to a rolling boil.

3. Spray a baking sheet with oil.

4. Add the pasta to the water and cook for about 3 minutes, until just tender but toothsome (al dente). Do not overcook.

5. Drain the pasta. Scoop it out with a spider or slotted spoon, rather than pouring the whole pot over a colander, which can smash the pasta. Lay out the noodles on the baking sheet.

PUTTING IT ALL TOGETHER

1. Place 1 pasta section in the center of a plate or a shallow pasta bowl. Top with ⅛ of the filling. Arrange another noodle over the filling and add more filling, followed by one more noodle. Repeat with the remaining ingredients to form 3 more portions. Pour sabayon equally over and around the lasagnas.

2. Combine the herb salad ingredients in a small bowl, and top each lasagna with similar portions of the salad. Serve right away.

Kitchen Notes

- One of the nice advantages of making your own pasta is the flavoring and coloring you can add to the dough. Just make sure the ingredient being added is pureed and well-drained to avoid adding moisture to the mixture. Some of my regular choices are black olives, arugula, tomatoes, and wild mushrooms. Of course, this is Santa Fe, so green or red chile is popular too.

- You can make this or any pasta dough in a stand electric mixer with the paddle attachment. It's so tactile and satisfying, though, to work the dough with your hands.

CAVATELLI WITH LATE SUMMER TOMATO-MUSHROOM RAGU

SERVES 4

Pasta with a rustic vegetable sauce and green salad are one of our favorite Sunday night suppers at home with the girls. Making cavatelli is a family treat. I prepare the dough, then each of us takes turns cranking out some of the little scrolled shells with our inexpensive metal and wood cavatelli maker. Kids are much more likely to eat what they have a hand in making.

POSSIBLE DO-AHEAD STEPS

- Make the Light Chicken Stock up to 1 week ahead.
- Make the cavatelli dough up to 4 hours ahead.

FOR THE CAVATELLI DOUGH

6 ounces (1 generous cup) durum flour

6 ounces (1 ½ scant cups) unbleached all-purpose flour

2 large eggs

1 large yolk

¼ cup ricotta cheese

¼ cup (2 ounces) water

2 tablespoons freshly grated Parmesan cheese

1 teaspoon freshly cracked black pepper

1 teaspoon kosher salt

FOR THE RAGU

8 ounces pancetta, chopped fine

1 small onion, chopped fine

6 ounces fresh porcini mushrooms or other wild mushrooms, sliced

1 pound assorted heirloom tomatoes, preferably of different colors, chopped

¼ cup (2 ounces) Light Chicken Stock (see page xxviii)

FOR THE FINISHED DISH

2 cups lightly packed arugula leaves or 1 cup lightly packed fresh basil leaves

Peel of 1 lemon, in very fine julienne

2 ounces freshly shaved Parmesan cheese

Extra-virgin olive oil

TO PREPARE THE PASTA DOUGH

Combine all the ingredients together in a bowl until you have a rough dough, then finish kneading the dough by hand on a work surface for about 8 minutes. Form the dough into a disk, wrap with plastic, and refrigerate for 45–60 minutes.

TO FORM THE CAVATELLI

1. Cut the dough into 4 sections and cover 3 of them with a damp cloth.
2. Roll out the remaining section of dough into a ½-inch-thick rope, and feed it through the cavatelli maker as its manufacturer directs. Repeat with the remaining dough.
3. Meanwhile, prepare an ice bath for the pasta and bring a large pot of salted water to a boil.
4. Cook the pasta in the water about a third at a time. It will sink to the bottom at first. When it starts to float, scoop it out with a spider or slotted spoon and chill it in the ice bath. Repeat with the remaining pasta. (If you wish, you can drain the cooled pasta, lay it out on a baking sheet, and spray it with oil. Then it can sit for up to an hour at room temperature before finishing the dish.)

TO PREPARE THE SAUCE

1. Cook the pancetta in a large sauté pan over medium-high heat until brown and almost crisp.
2. Remove it from the pan drippings with a slotted spoon. Reserve 1 tablespoon of pan drippings and pour off and discard any extra.
3. Reduce heat to medium-low. Add the onion and mushrooms and cook until caramelized to a light golden color, stirring occasionally, about 15 minutes.
4. Add the tomatoes and stock, then simmer for 2 more minutes to soften the tomatoes.

PUTTING IT ALL TOGETHER

Add the cavatelli and mix it around with the sauce. Just before removing from the heat stir in the arugula and lemon peel. Divide the pasta among 4 plates. Garnish with shaved Parmesan and a drizzle of extra-virgin olive oil and enjoy right away.

Kitchen Notes

Cavatelli can be shaped by hand, in which case bits of the dough are pressed up against the tines of a fork or a small wooden cavatelli (or gnocchi) paddle to get the distinctive scrolled shape.

BUTTER-POACHED OYSTERS AND CHORIZO GNOCCHI WITH SUGAR SNAP PEAS, ORANGES, AND VERMOUTH SAUCE

SERVES 4

We have no problem getting top quality oysters shipped into Santa Fe, and they nearly always sell out. Often we combine them with pork belly or bacon. One day I dreamed up this pork combination using spicy Spanish chorizo and mixing it into pillowy gnocchi. The emulsified vermouth sauce plays a mignonette-like role. We round out the dish with fresh peas in pods and the tang of oranges.

POSSIBLE DO-AHEAD STEPS

- Make the Light Chicken Stock up to 1 week ahead.
- Bake the potato for the gnocchi, peel it, and store it in the refrigerator up to 2 days ahead.
- Form the Chorizo Gnocchi up to 1 day ahead, but don't cook them.

FOR THE CHORIZO GNOCCHI

12-ounce russet potato, baked for 1 hour at 350°F, peeled

4 ounces cured Spanish chorizo, finely chopped

½ cup unbleached all-purpose flour

½ cup freshly grated Parmesan cheese

1 large egg, lightly whisked

Pinch ground nutmeg

Kosher salt and ground white pepper

Olive oil spray

FOR THE VERMOUTH SAUCE

1 medium shallot, thinly sliced

2 garlic cloves, bruised with the side of a chef's knife

Small sprig of fresh tarragon

Small sprig of fresh thyme

½ teaspoon black peppercorns

Pinch of granulated sugar

1 cup (8 ounces) sweet vermouth

Juice of 1 medium lemon

2 cups (1 pint) Light Chicken Stock (see page xxviii)

Kosher salt and ground white pepper

4 tablespoons (2 ounces) unsalted butter

FOR THE SUGAR SNAP PEAS AND ORANGES

4 ounces sugar snap peas (blanched)

2 medium to large navel oranges, peeled and segmented

1 tablespoon extra-virgin olive oil

¼ teaspoon grated lime zest

Kosher salt and ground white pepper

FOR THE OYSTERS AND GNOCCHI

4 tablespoons (2 ounces) plus 2 teaspoons unsalted butter (divided use)

Small sprig of fresh thyme

12 northeastern Blue Point or northwestern Kumamoto oysters, or other top quality oysters of moderate size, shucked

Kosher salt and ground white pepper

2 teaspoons olive oil

1 to 2 teaspoons minced fresh chives

FOR THE FINISHED DISH

Tender carrot tops, celery leaves, red shiso leaves, Bull's Blood beet greens, or small salad greens

TO PREPARE THE CHORIZO GNOCCHI

1. Using a ricer or a food mill, preferably, or a box grater if necessary, rice or finely grate the potato into a medium bowl.

2. Fry the chorizo in a small skillet over medium heat for about 5 minutes, until lightly crisp and releasing some oil. Scrape the chorizo and oil into the bowl with the potato. Add the flour, Parmesan, egg, nutmeg, about ½ teaspoon salt, and a few good shakes of pepper. Mix together with your hand. Use a light touch and stop as soon as the dough holds together and pulls away from the bowl.

3. Divide the dough in half and lightly roll each half into a long snake of dough, about ½ inch in diameter.

4. Slice each snake into small nuggets, about ½ inch in length. Roll each nugget into a tube-like gnocchi, about 1 ¼ inches long. Again apply just light pressure when forming the gnocchi. Place in a single layer on a parchment-covered baking sheet.

5. Prepare an ice bath in a medium bowl.

6. Bring a large pot of well-salted water to a rolling boil over high heat. Lower the heat slightly to a simmer and drop about half the gnocchi gently into the water. They will sink to the bottom. Cook for about 3 minutes, or until the gnocchi float to the surface.

7. Scoop out the gnocchi with a spider or slotted spoon and transfer them to the ice bath to cool. Repeat with the remaining gnocchi, first bringing the water back to a rolling boil, and then decreasing the heat to a simmer before adding them.

8. When all the gnocchi are cool, drain them and place in a single layer on a baking sheet or platter and spray lightly with oil. Let them sit at room temperature.

TO PREPARE THE VERMOUTH SAUCE

1. Combine the shallot, garlic cloves, tarragon, thyme, peppercorns, sugar, vermouth, and lemon juice in a small saucepan. Warm over medium-high heat and simmer for 5–10 minutes, or until 1–2 tablespoons of liquid remains.

2. Pour in the stock, and reduce the liquid by about half, 5–10 more minutes. Season with salt and pepper.

3. Strain the sauce through a fine-mesh sieve directly into a blender. Add the butter and puree to emulsify the sauce.

TO PREPARE THE PEAS AND ORANGES

Toss the ingredients together in a small bowl.

TO PREPARE THE OYSTERS AND GNOCCHI

1. Melt 4 tablespoons of butter over medium heat in a small saucepan. Add the thyme and then the oysters.

2. After about 1 minute, as the oysters begin to puff up and start to firm, remove the pan from the heat.

3. Baste the oysters a few times with the pan juices, season lightly with salt and generously with pepper, then let the oysters rest in the pan.

4. Warm the remaining 2 teaspoons of butter with the oil in a medium skillet or sauté pan over medium heat.

5. Add the gnocchi to the pan and stir gently. Sauté several minutes until the gnocchi are lightly browned, then stir in the chives.

PUTTING IT ALL TOGETHER

Line 3 oysters down one side of each of 4 plates. Spoon equal portions of gnocchi in between the oysters. Add peas and oranges to the middle of each plate. If the sauce has separated, give it another buzz in the blender, then spoon the sauce around the oysters. Garnish with leaves and serve.

Kitchen Notes

I like to use Cara Cara oranges when in season, which is late winter and spring. They have pinkish-red fruit, not as deeply colored as a blood orange, but quite pretty. Typically, Cara Caras are lusciously sweet with a little tart zing. Since they have very few seeds, they segment easily too.

CARNAROLI RISOTTO WITH MAINE LOBSTER, RED KURI SQUASH, LEEKS, MUSHROOM CHIPS, MASCARPONE CHEESE, AND BACON CRÈME FRAÎCHE

SERVES 4

I love how this dish presents a little surprise. A guest orders the risotto but none of it or the lobster or the stunningly orange squash is actually visible when the dish comes to the table. I enjoy the surprise factor partially because it replicates the effect made by the first risotto that ever wowed me, in taste as well as presentation. That was one that Chef David Burke created at the Park Avenue Café in the 1990s, when I was working there. He put a bed of porcini- and preserved-lemon-packed rice on a rectangular plate with three chicken drummette "lollipops" sprouting out of its top. The delight that dish always inspired has stayed with me for decades and influenced this risotto.

POSSIBLE DO-AHEAD STEPS

- Make the Light Chicken Stock up to 1 week ahead.
- Make the Risotto Base up to 1 day ahead.

FOR THE MUSHROOM CHIPS

1 cup (8 ounces) canola or vegetable oil

2 ounces shiitake mushrooms, stems discarded and caps thinly sliced

Pinch of ground allspice

Kosher salt and ground white pepper

FOR THE RISOTTO BASE

¼ cup (2 ounces) olive oil

2 medium shallots, minced

1 ½ cups carnaroli rice

½ cup (4 ounces) dry white wine

Sprig fresh thyme

4–5 cups (1 to 1 ¼ quarts) Light Chicken Stock (see page xxviii), kept warm on another burner

4 tablespoons (2 ounces) unsalted butter

FOR THE CRÈME FRAÎCHE SAUCE

2 cups (16 ounces) Light Chicken Stock (see page xxviii)

1 cup (8 ounces) heavy cream

2 tablespoons (1 ounce) bacon drippings

1 tablespoon lemon juice

FOR THE FINISHED DISH

1 cup (8 ounces) Light Chicken Stock (see page xxviii)

1 tablespoon mascarpone cheese

4 ounces red kuri or kabocha squash, cut into ½-inch cubes and blanched

8 ounces cooked lobster meat, preferably from the tail

2 tablespoons freshly grated Parmesan cheese

Kosher salt and ground white pepper

1 large leek, white part only, sliced into rings and blanched

Ginger Batons (see page 16) optional

Minced fresh chives

Ground allspice

TO PREPARE THE MUSHROOM CHIPS

1. Warm the oil in a small saucepan to 320°F–325°F.

2. Drop the mushrooms in gently and fry them until crisp. Drain them on paper towels, sprinkle with allspice, and season with salt and pepper.

TO PREPARE THE RISOTTO BASE

1. Warm the oil in a large saucepan over medium heat. Stir in the shallots and cook until tender, stirring constantly to prevent the shallots from burning, about 5 minutes.

2. Add the rice and continue stirring for about 2 more minutes.

3. Pour in the wine and simmer until almost dry.

4. Add the thyme and 1 cup of warm stock.

5. Reduce the heat to medium-low and continue stirring until the stock is mostly absorbed. Continue adding stock and stirring until the risotto has become partially tender but still has a bit of "bite" all the way to the core, 25–30 minutes. You may not need all 5 cups of stock to get to this stage.

6. Stir in the butter and let it melt into the risotto. Unless you plan to finish and serve the risotto immediately, spoon it out onto a baking sheet lined with a non-stick mat or lightly oiled parchment paper. Let it cool to room temperature, cover, and refrigerate.

TO PREPARE THE SAUCE

Combine the stock, cream, bacon drippings, and lemon juice in a medium saucepan. Bring to a boil over high heat and reduce the mixture by half, about 10 minutes. Keep the mixture warm over low heat.

PUTTING IT ALL TOGETHER

1. Finish the risotto by warming 1 cup of chicken stock in a large saucepan with the mascarpone cheese and squash. When the squash is tender, add the risotto and stir vigorously to make it creamy.

2. Slice the lobster into slim medallions, mix it into the risotto, and season with salt and pepper.

3. Divide the risotto among 4 large bowls. Add the Parmesan cheese to the crème fraîche sauce and froth it with a whisk or in a blender for at least 30 seconds.

4. Season with salt and pepper.

5. Pour equal portions of the sauce over the bowls. Garnish each bowl with leek rings, minced chives, a sprinkling of allspice, and the mushroom chips, and serve right away.

restaurant embellishments

To get the most loft and density in the bacon crème fraîche sauce, I foam it by adding a couple of extra steps, using an iSi cream whipper. Once the sauce is reduced by half, and before the mixture comes off the stove, I whisk in 2 bloomed silver gelatin sheets and ½ teaspoon of xanthan gum. I bring the mixture back to a boil and strain it through a fine-mesh sieve. I pour the mixture into the cream whipper and charge it with 2 nitrous oxide chargers. After shaking the canister for 20 seconds, I can spray foam over the risotto to cover it completely. That's how the surprise works.

Kitchen Notes

- Risotto rices share the characteristics of being short- to medium-grain and high in starch. Arborio is the most common in American supermarkets. You can use it here if you wish, but I prefer to use carnaroli, which absorbs a bit more liquid and results in a creamier risotto. It costs a little more and is pretty widely available in markets today too.

- The way restaurants get risotto on the table quickly is to do most of the work ahead of time. That's possible for a home cook too. The key is cooking it just until it reaches a fairly firm al dente stage, then spreading it out on a baking sheet to cool quickly. At that point it can be covered and chilled until needed, then finished off in about 5 minutes.

vegetable main and side dishes

PLUM TOMATO-CARAMELIZED ONION TART

SERVES 4

My wife and both of my daughters eat a mostly meatless diet. Jennifer kids me that when we met, my idea of feeding a vegetarian was to send out a pile of grilled peppers and onions and call it a dish. I don't think it was quite that minimal. She's right, though, that she and the girls have inspired me to think as intently about what I put together for non-meat eaters as I do for other diners. I'm delighted when I get praise for the combinations of vegetables and the inter-play of their textures, colors, shapes, and flavors in my vegetarian tasting plates. In all these plates, I include something that has a bit of heft, such as the small tarts here. In a restaurant tasting plate these would be one of several dishes similar to others in this chapter.

POSSIBLE DO-AHEAD STEPS

- Make the Caramelized Onions and the Tomato Confit up to 1 day ahead.

FOR THE ONIONS

2 tablespoons (1 ounce) olive oil

1 large onion, sliced thin

2 garlic cloves, roasted in a dry skillet until soft, then mashed with the side of a knife

1 tablespoon Dijon mustard

2 tablespoons minced fresh basil

1 teaspoon minced fresh thyme

Kosher salt and ground white pepper

FOR THE TOMATO CONFIT

2 pounds plum tomatoes, quartered, cored, and seeded

2 garlic cloves

2 teaspoons granulated sugar

1 teaspoon kosher salt

1 cup olive oil

3 sprigs of fresh thyme

1 sheet thawed frozen puff pastry

TO PREPARE THE ONIONS

1. Warm the olive oil in a medium sauté pan over low heat.

2. Mix the onions well with the oil, then sauté them slowly until medium brown and caramel-ized, about 45 minutes. Stir occasionally.

3. Mix in the roasted garlic and mustard and remove from the heat.

4. Stir in the herbs and season with salt and pepper. The mixture can sit at room temperature while you make the tomato confit.

TO PREPARE THE TOMATO CONFIT

1. Preheat the oven to 300°F.

2. Combine the tomatoes, garlic, sugar, salt, oil, and thyme in a small roasting pan. Cover the pan and bake for 25–30 minutes, until the tomatoes are softened but still hold their shape.

3. Remove the tomatoes from the oven and turn the oven up to 375°F.

4. Take the tomatoes from the pan with tongs, then pull off and discard the tomato skins. Save 1 tablespoon of the oil the tomatoes cooked in.

5. Arrange 4 individual round tart molds, about 3 inches in diameter, on a baking sheet lined with a non-stick mat or parchment paper.

6. Position 2 to 4 tomato pieces so that they cover the bottom of each mold. Flatten the pieces a bit as you go. This will be the top of the tart when finished so it should be neat.

7. When the onions are ready, spoon a thin layer of the mixture over the tomatoes, enough to almost fill the tart shells.

8. Roll out the sheet of puff pastry to about ⅛-inch thickness. Cut out rounds slightly larger than the molds. Place a pastry round over each mold. Tuck the edges down around the onion mixture inside the molds.

9. Bake the tarts for about 15 minutes, until the pastry is browned and puffed. Transfer the tarts to a baking rack to cool several minutes.

PUTTING IT ALL TOGETHER

While the tarts are still warm, run a thin-bladed knife around the inside of each mold. Give the tart a good but careful shake and place crust-down. Baste the top of each tart with a portion of the reserved oil, just enough to give it some gloss. Serve warm or at room temperature.

restaurant embellishments

In my vegetarian tasting plates, I combine a variety of vegetarian delicacies on the same plate. With the tart, one warm-weather addition might be a smear of Pea Puree under it for contrasting color and brightness. I love a little parsnip with peas, which gives them a complementary peppery note.

PEA PUREE

4 ounces peeled chopped parsnips

1 tablespoon minced shallots

1 garlic clove, roasted in a dry skillet until soft

2 cups (1 pint) Vegetable Stock (see page xxvii)

1 cup fresh or unthawed frozen peas

Kosher salt and ground white pepper

1. Combine parsnips, shallots, garlic, and stock in a small saucepan. Cook over medium heat until the parsnips are tender and most of the liquid has evaporated.

2. Transfer the mixture to a small bowl, cover, and chill in an ice bath. When cold, spoon it and peas into a blender. If the peas are fresh, add ¼ cup crushed ice to the blender along with the salt and pepper. (If the peas are frozen, skip the ice.) Puree.

3. Cover and refrigerate until 30 minutes before serving.

GRILLED ASPARAGUS WITH MEYER LEMON SABAYON, SHAVED RICOTTA SALATA, AND FURIKAKE

SERVES 4

Sabayons are traditionally light mousse-like dessert sauces. Turning the concept into a savory blend works well with asparagus or broccoli, vegetables that once might have been paired with a hearty Hollandaise or other heavy sauce. When I eat asparagus, I want really to taste it, so I prefer jumbo spears to wispy little young stalks. Ricotta salata is a stark white cheese that contrasts with the finishing bit of salty Japanese seasoning. You can choose either furikake or togarashi shichimi, since both have nori seaweed as one of their ingredients.

POSSIBLE DO-AHEAD STEPS

- Make the Light Chicken Stock up to 1 week ahead.
- Blanch and chill the asparagus up to 2 days ahead.

FOR THE GRILLED ASPARAGUS

16 jumbo asparagus, lower stems peeled, blanched

2 tablespoons (1 ounce) extra-virgin olive oil

1 tablespoon champagne vinegar

Kosher salt and ground white pepper

FOR THE SABAYON

½ cup (4 ounces) Light Chicken Stock (see page xxviii)

¼ cup (2 ounces) Meyer lemon juice or 3 tablespoons regular lemon juice plus 1 tablespoon orange juice

2 large egg yolks

1 large egg

2 tablespoons (1 ounce) crème fraîche

1 tablespoon minced shallots

½ teaspoon grated Meyer lemon zest or regular lemon zest

Kosher salt and ground white pepper

FOR THE FINISHED DISH

4-ounce wedge ricotta salata cheese, shaved into 8 triangles

Furikake or togarashi shichimi seasoning

4 Marcona almonds, optional

Baby pok choi or other small salad greens or fresh dill sprigs or amaranth sprouts

Peel of half a Meyer lemon, or other lemon, in very thin julienne, blanched

TO PREPARE THE GRILLED ASPARAGUS

Toss the asparagus with oil and vinegar, and sprinkle generously with the salt and pepper. Marinate for 15–30 minutes. Fire up a grill to medium heat or get a grill pan ready.

TO PREPARE THE SABAYON

1. Whisk all the ingredients together in the top pan of a double boiler. Place the pan over the lower pan of simmering water.

2. Continue whisking the mixture until it becomes thick enough to see a trail across the bottom of the pan as you whisk it. Turn off the heat.

3. Strain the sabayon through a fine-mesh sieve and keep it warm by returning it to the double boiler over the pan of warm water.

PUTTING IT ALL TOGETHER

1. Drain the asparagus. Grill it over medium heat for 5–7 minutes, rolling it frequently, or until tender and lightly browned in spots.

2. Pour a circle of sabayon in the center of each of 4 plates. Arrange 4 asparagus spears over the sabayon. Lean a pair of ricotta salata slices over the asparagus. Sprinkle furikake seasoning over it. Shave an almond over each plate if you wish. Tuck a few greens around the edges of the asparagus, scatter a few slivers of lemon peel over, and serve.

ROASTED PEPPERS IN POPPY-SEED CREPES

SERVES 4

I could be one of the few guys anywhere who associates crepes with boxing matches. Here's why. Boxing is a much more popular sport in Mexico than in the United States. Much of Saturday's television schedule is devoted to boxing matches. When I was growing up in Guadalajara, my dad loved to watch boxing almost as much as futbol, or soccer. Dad was not normally the cook in our house, but every Saturday afternoon he took over the kitchen, whipping up a gigante stack of crepes, a dish he had learned to make from his mother. You may not know that a variety of French dishes have been considered Mexican since the brief period that France controlled Mexico in the mid-nineteenth century. Anyway, in addition to the huge stack of crepes, Dad would set out three hefty bowls, one with strawberry jam, another with orange marmalade, and the third with cajeta, the beloved Mexican caramel often made with goat's milk. He knew the assemble-yourself dish would keep his kids and his friends there to cheer on his favorite fighters. With his inspiration I, too, learned how to make crepes.

POSSIBLE DO-AHEAD STEPS

- Roast, peel, and slice the peppers for the pepper filling up to 2 days ahead.
- Make the crepes and let them sit at room temperature up to 1 hour ahead.

FOR THE CREPES

1 cup unbleached all-purpose flour

1 ½ cups (12 ounces) whole milk

1 large egg

1 large egg yolk

1 tablespoon unsalted butter, melted

1 teaspoon kosher salt

¼ teaspoon ground white pepper

2 tablespoons chopped fresh chives

1 tablespoon poppy seeds

1 tablespoon grated lemon zest

About 2 tablespoons (1 ounce) olive oil

FOR THE PEPPER FILLING

1 pound whole red and yellow bell peppers

2 tablespoons (1 ounce) olive oil

2 tablespoons slivered shallots

1 garlic clove, slivered

6 tablespoons chopped fresh herbs, perhaps 2 tablespoons each basil, tarragon, and chives

Kosher salt and ground white pepper

2 tablespoons grated Gruyére cheese

FOR THE HERB SALAD

2 handfuls arugula or spinach or pok choi leaves

¼ cup fresh tarragon, fennel, or dill sprigs

Extra-virgin olive oil

Kosher salt and ground white pepper

Shaved fennel slices

TO PREPARE THE CREPE BATTER

1. Puree the flour, milk, egg, yolk, butter, salt, and pepper in a blender.

2. Pour mixture into a large spouted bowl or other bowl, and mix in the chives, poppy seeds, and lemon zest.

3. Refrigerate the mixture covered for at least 30 minutes. The batter should be very pourable, with a consistency between heavy cream and buttermilk. Add a bit of water if needed to get the proper consistency.

TO COOK THE CREPES

1. Warm a 7- or 8-inch crepe pan or similar sauté pan over medium-high heat, and brush lightly with oil.

2. Pour in 3–4 tablespoons of batter, just enough to thinly coat the pan. Quickly swirl the batter around to cover the pan evenly. Cook the crepe until the surface is no longer shiny and the edges begin to dry, 45–60 seconds.

3. Loosen the crepe with a table knife or small spatula and flip it over. Cook another 30–45 seconds and slide the crepe from the pan. Repeat with remaining batter and oil, stacking the crepes on top of each other.

TO PREPARE THE FILLING

1. First, roast the whole peppers over an asador or other stovetop grill, or directly over a stovetop burner. Blacken the skin of the peppers, turning on all sides to roast evenly.

2. Transfer the peppers to a plastic bag and let them steam until cool enough to handle.

3. Using your fingers and a few paper towels or a clean dish towel, pull or rub off and discard the blackened skin.

4. Slice the peppers into thin ribbons, saving any of the juices.

5. Warm the oil in a medium sauté pan over medium heat. Stir in the shallots and garlic and cook for about 3 minutes, until they have begun to soften.

6. Mix in the bell peppers and juice and simmer the mixture until most of the liquid has evaporated. The peppers, however, should still be moist.

7. Stir in the herbs and heat through, then season with salt and pepper and mix in the cheese.

PUTTING IT ALL TOGETHER

1. Place a crepe on a work surface and spoon ¼ of the filling down the center of it. Roll the crepe up, trim off the ragged ends, and slice it in half. Arrange the 2 sections on a plate, 1 laying down and the other standing, leaning on it. Repeat with the remaining crepes on 3 other plates.

2. Toss the arugula and herbs together with just enough oil to make it glisten, then sprinkle it with salt and pepper. Arrange the herb salad over the 2 sections of crepe. Lean a couple of fennel slices alongside the crepe too.

3. Dribble a bit of extra-virgin olive oil over the crepes and fennel slices. Alternatively, all the crepes can be arranged with the salad topping and fennel slices on a large plate or platter. Serve.

Kitchen Notes

The batter makes more than you need for 4 crepes, but it doesn't make sense to make it in any smaller quantity. If this is being served as a vegetable main dish, you might use 2 per serving, putting a bit less filling in each one. The batter will keep for several days in the refrigerator (reblend it before using), so you can have another crepe meal, or you can make up all the batter and freeze the remaining crepes, tightly wrapped, to use at another time. Even with the little flecks of chives in them, you can still serve them up like my Dad did, with jam, marmalade, or cajeta.

GOLDEN CORN FLAN TAMALES WITH ASADERO CHEESE FONDUE

SERVES 4

Here's my twist on a summer tamale, inspired a bit by the "green corn" tamales of the South-west, which mix fresh corn, cheese, and rajas (strips of green chile). A quivering corn flan stands in for the usual corn masa mixture. The fondue or sauce is a riff on the beloved Mexican melted cheese dish, queso fundido. *I use asadero cheese, one of the slightly tangy white cheeses common to the dish. You could also use a Mexican-style Chihuahua cheese or Monterey jack instead.*

FOR THE FLANS

6 ounces sweet yellow corn kernels, fresh or
    thawed frozen

1½ cups (12 ounces) water

5 large egg yolks

½ cup (4 ounces) heavy cream

½ teaspoon roasted garlic puree

Kosher salt and ground white pepper

FOR THE VEGETABLE MIX

2 tablespoons (1 ounce) olive oil

5- or 6-ounce summer squash, such as yellow
    crooked neck or zucchini, julienned

2 fresh medium poblano chiles, roasted, peeled and
    seeded, and julienned, with any juices

Kosher salt and ground white pepper

FOR THE FONDUE

4 ounces asadero cheese, grated

1 teaspoon cornstarch

1 tablespoon olive oil

1 small shallot, minced (really minced)

¼ cup (2 ounces) sour cream

¼ cup (2 ounces) flavorful beer, such as
    Santa Fe Pale Ale

3 tablespoons (1½ ounces) Vegetable Stock
    (see page xxvii)

Kosher salt and ground white pepper

FOR THE FINISHED DISH

8 dried corn husks

TO PREPARE THE FLANS

1. Preheat the oven to 350°F.

2. Lightly grease four 8-ounce ramekins and place them in a baking pan just a little larger than the ramekins.

3. In a blender, combine the corn and water, then strain the mixture through a fine-mesh sieve, discarding the corn solids.

4. Rinse out the blender. Return the corn juice to the blender along with the egg yolks, cream, garlic, and pinches of salt and pepper, and puree.

5. Pour the mixture into the ramekins. Add warm water to the baking dish, enough to come up about halfway on the ramekins.

6. Cover the pan with foil and bake for 30–35 minutes, just enough to set the flans, with the barest bit of jiggle at their centers. Do not overbake. Let the flans cool for about 15 minutes.

TO PREPARE THE VEGETABLE MIX

1. When the flans are ready, prepare the vegetable mixture.

2. Warm the oil in a small sauté pan over medium heat.

3. Stir in the summer squash and sauté until tender, 5–8 minutes. Stir in the poblano and accumulated juices and heat through. Season with salt and pepper.

TO PREPARE THE CHEESE FONDUE

1. Toss together the cheese with the cornstarch and reserve.

2. Warm the oil in a small saucepan over medium heat. Stir in the shallot and cook until tender, but not colored, 3–5 minutes. Whisk in sour cream followed by the beer, stock, and salt and pepper. When well mixed, add the cornstarch-covered cheese, cooking about 1 minute to let any cornstarch flavor disappear. Remove from the heat when creamy and cover to keep warm.

PUTTING IT ALL TOGETHER

Arrange a pretty dried cornhusk on each of 4 plates. Unmold the flans by running a knife between the custard and the cup. Invert over a cornhusk. Repeat with the remaining flans. Spoon the poblano mixture equally over the flans. Spoon cheese fondue over and around each flan. Serve right away.

restaurant embellishments

I might take the corn husks, dunk them in hot oil to make them pliable, and then shape them somewhat into a U by letting them cool supported by a couple of jars or cans. I also might cut an inch-or-so-wide strip of corn tortilla per serving, then wrap each around a cannoli mold, and spray them lightly with olive oil. Then I bake them at 300ºF or 325ºF for 5–8 minutes, until lightly toasted and holding the curlicue shape. They go over the dish just before serving.

ROASTED CAULIFLOWER STEAKS WITH OYSTER MUSHROOM STEW AND WALNUTS

SERVES 4

Roasted cauliflower on its own makes a great side dish, but if you add a few flourishes, as we do here, it becomes an appealing and hearty main dish for a meatless meal.

POSSIBLE DO-AHEAD STEPS

- Make the vegetable stock up to 1 week ahead.
- Make the Oyster Mushroom Stew up to 8 hours ahead.

FOR THE CAULIFLOWER STEAKS

1 head cauliflower, about 1 ¼ pounds

¼ cup plus 2 tablespoons (3 ounces) olive oil (divided use)

2 tablespoons (1 ounce) balsamic vinegar

1 tablespoon chopped fresh sage

1 tablespoon chopped fresh rosemary

Kosher salt and ground white pepper

2 tablespoons (1 ounce) unsalted butter

FOR THE MUSHROOM STEW

4 tablespoons (2 ounces) unsalted butter

2 medium shallots, thinly sliced

2 garlic cloves, sliced

3 ounces (about 2 cups) sliced oyster mushrooms, any tough stems removed

¼ cup (2 ounces) dry white wine

1 ½ cups (12 ounces) Vegetable Stock (see page xxvii)

1 teaspoon cornstarch, blended with 2 tablespoons (1 ounce) cold water

Kosher salt and ground white pepper

FOR THE FINISHED DISH

1 to 2 tablespoons toasted walnut pieces

2 handfuls small pok choi, kale, or arugula leaves, or Bull's Blood beet greens, or a combination

Extra-virgin olive oil

1–2 tablespoons chopped fresh chives

TO PREPARE THE CAULIFLOWER STEAKS

1. Preheat the oven to 400°F.

2. Set the cauliflower, stem-end down, on a work surface. Cut down through the cauliflower, making 1½-inch-thick slabs. Lay the slabs flat and cut each of them into 2–3 pieces, creating smaller 1½-inch-thick slabs.

3. Warm ¼ cup of the oil in a large cast-iron skillet over medium heat.

4. Arrange the cauliflower steaks in the skillet and cook 2–3 minutes on each side, until they develop a bit of color.

5. Drizzle the remaining olive oil and the vinegar over the steaks and sprinkle with the sage, rosemary, and salt and pepper.

6. Transfer the skillet to the oven and roast for 15–18 minutes, or until the cauliflower is nicely browned and tender. Poke one of the steaks with a paring knife to make sure it is soft. Remove from the oven, add the butter to the skillet, and baste the steaks with the pan juices. Keep warm on a stovetop burner over low heat.

TO PREPARE THE MUSHROOM STEW

1. Warm the butter in a medium saucepan over medium heat and sauté the shallots until soft but not colored, about 3 minutes. Stir in the garlic.

2. Increase the heat to medium-high, add the oyster mushrooms, and sauté for 3–5 more minutes, so the mushrooms become limp and brown in a few spots.

3. Stir in the wine, scraping up any bits on the bottom of the pan. Pour in the stock and bring to a simmer, then reduce the heat to medium again.

4. Stir in the cornstarch mixture, cook for at least another couple of minutes until the stew thickens and becomes glossy. Season with salt and pepper. Cover and keep warm over low heat.

PUTTING IT ALL TOGETHER

Arrange several cauliflower steaks in the center of each of 4 plates, leaning against each other. Spoon the mushroom stew equally over the cauliflower. Scatter walnuts over each serving. Toss the leaves with a few drops of extra-virgin olive oil and scatter around each plate. Dot with chives. Serve right away.

LEMON SAFFRON ARANCINI WITH PICKLED BEETS AND GOLDEN RAISIN HERB SALAD

SERVES 4

I love arancini, fried balls of risotto, often made with a melty little nugget of mozzarella at the center. Little ones make scrumptious nibbles and oversize ones like this delight as a meatless main dish with tangy bright salad on the side. Since arancini developed as a way to use up leftover risotto, you can certainly make the risotto itself a day or 2 ahead or even use leftovers from another risotto preparation.

POSSIBLE DO-AHEAD STEPS

- Make the Light Chicken Stock up to 1 week ahead.
- Make the Lemon Saffron Risotto and the Pickled Red Beets up to 2 days ahead.

FOR THE BEETS

1 cup (8 ounces) dry red wine

¼ cup (2 ounces) red wine vinegar

¼ cup plus 1 tablespoon granulated sugar

1 tablespoon chopped peeled fresh ginger

1 tablespoon toasted black peppercorns

Large sprig of fresh thyme

1 dried bay leaf

8 ounces cooked and peeled red beets, cut into ½-inch pieces

3 tablespoons (1 ½ ounces) extra-virgin olive oil

FOR THE RISOTTO

2 tablespoons (1 ounce) olive oil

1 large shallot, minced

1 cup carnaroli rice

¼ cup (2 ounces) dry white wine

Sprig of fresh thyme

1 dried bay leaf

Pinch of saffron threads

About 5 cups (1 quart and 8 ounces) Light Chicken Stock (see page xxviii), warmed

¼ cup freshly grated Parmesan cheese

2 tablespoons (1 ounce) unsalted butter

1 tablespoon mascarpone cheese or heavy cream

1 teaspoon grated lemon zest

Kosher salt and ground white pepper

FOR THE ARANCINI

8 small balls (bocconcini) fresh mozzarella cheese at room temperature, or eight ¾-inch cubes fresh mozzarella

Canola or vegetable oil for deep-frying

About ½ cup unbleached all-purpose flour

1 large egg, whisked with 1 teaspoon water

About 1 ½ cups dried fine bread crumbs

FOR THE FINISHED DISH

2 handfuls of fresh parsley leaves, celery leaves, radish sprouts, Bull's Blood beet greens, or a combination

Chive batons or blossoms or both, optional

⅓ cup plump golden raisins

Extra-virgin olive oil

TO PREPARE THE PICKLED BEETS

1. Combine the wine, vinegar, sugar, ginger, peppercorns, thyme, and bay leaf in a medium saucepan. Bring to a boil over high heat, then reduce the pickling liquid by half, about 5 minutes.

2. Strain the liquid and return it to the pan. Stir the beets into the liquid and continue cooking several minutes more until just about 1 tablespoon of liquid remains.

3. Add the olive oil to the beets and set aside to cool to room temperature.

TO PREPARE THE RISOTTO

1. Warm the oil in a large saucepan over medium heat. Stir in the shallot and cook until tender, stirring constantly to prevent the shallot from burning, about 5 minutes.

2. Add the rice and continue stirring for about 2 more minutes.

3. Pour in the wine and simmer until almost dry.

4. Add the thyme, bay leaf, saffron, and 1 cup of warm stock. Reduce the heat to medium-low and continue stirring until the stock is mostly absorbed. Continue adding stock and stirring until the risotto is tender and creamy.

5. Add the Parmesan, butter, mascarpone, and lemon zest, then season with salt and pepper.

6. Spread the risotto onto a small sheet pan. When cooled to room temperature, cover the risotto and refrigerate it for at least 1 hour.

TO MAKE THE ARANCINI

1. Lay a 12-inch square piece of plastic wrap on a work surface.

2. Scoop out about ½ cup of chilled risotto, enough to make about a 3½-inch wide disk about ½ inch in thickness.

3. Place a ball of mozzarella in the middle of the risotto. Using the plastic wrap to help shape, fold up the disk on all sides to enclose the mozzarella and make a snug round ball. Form 7 more balls, using more plastic wrap, risotto, and mozzarella.

4. Heat at least 5 inches of oil in a Dutch oven or large heavy saucepan to 325°F–330°F.

5. While the oil is heating, dunk each ball first in flour, then in egg, and then in bread crumbs, making sure to cover completely in crumbs.

6. Fry the arancini, in batches if needed, until deeply golden-brown, 4–6 minutes. Drain on paper towels.

PUTTING IT ALL TOGETHER

Place 2 arancini on each of 4 plates. Combine the herbs and raisins with enough extra-virgin olive oil to glisten. Arrange a portion of the salad to the side of the arancini. Spoon to the other side a mound of pickled beets. Serve.

restaurant embellishments

This puree looks pretty under the fried arancini and alongside the burgundy beets.

PARSNIP PUREE

  1 cup (8 ounces) buttermilk
  1 garlic clove
  1 small shallot, chopped
  4 ounces chopped parsnip
  ½ cup (4 ounces) Vegetable Stock (see page xxvii)
  2 tablespoons (1 ounce) unsalted butter

1. Combine buttermilk, garlic, shallot, parsnip, vegetable stock, and butter in a small saucepan. Simmer until the parsnip becomes soft.

2. Transfer the mixture to a blender, and puree until smooth. Season with salt and pepper.

I also like having an element of crunch on the plates, in this case Portobello Mushroom Chips. I slice 4 ounces of portobello mushrooms thinly with a mandoline, fry them in canola or vegetable oil heated to 325°F–330°F, stir them around until crisp, strain them on paper towels, and season with salt and pepper.

CRUSTY PARMESAN SAGE POLENTA

SERVES 4 OR MORE

You could serve this polenta, soft and creamy, just out of the pan, but I like to crust it with a quick dunk in hot oil. The deep-frying seals the moisture inside while the outside is getting crisp, the best possible combination of textures.

POSSIBLE DO-AHEAD STEPS

- Make the Vegetable Stock up to 1 week ahead.

2 ½ cups (1 pint plus 4 ounces) Vegetable Stock (see page xxvii)

1 cup (8 ounces) whole milk

4 tablespoons (2 ounces) unsalted butter

1 teaspoon roasted garlic puree

½ teaspoon ground white pepper

¼ teaspoon kosher salt

1 cup medium-grind yellow polenta cornmeal

2 tablespoons freshly grated Parmesan cheese

2 teaspoons minced fresh sage

Canola or vegetable oil for deep-frying

Additional kosher salt

Chopped fresh chives or chive batons

1. Grease an 8-inch-square baking dish, or other small baking dish.

2. Combine the stock, milk, butter, garlic, white pepper, and salt in a large saucepan.

3. Bring the mixture to a boil, then sprinkle in the cornmeal, a handful at a time, whisking constantly to avoid lumps. When all the cornmeal is mixed in, lower the heat to medium-low and continue to cook, stirring occasionally, until the cornmeal is very creamy. The time will vary a little, depending on the corn and the heat, but expect it to take 15–20 minutes. Stir in the Parmesan and sage and remove from the heat.

4. Scrape the polenta into the prepared dish and let the mixture cool to room temperature. Cover and refrigerate the polenta if you will not be finishing it within the next hour.

PUTTING IT ALL TOGETHER

1. Pour about 3 inches of oil into a saucepan and heat it to 325°F–330°F.

2. Cut the polenta into 2-inch squares and deep-fry several of the squares at a time until lightly browned and crunchy, about 1 minute. Drain on paper towels and immediately sprinkle with a bit of salt. Repeat with the remaining polenta.

3. Serve on a platter or pile 2 or 3 squares at angles on individual small plates. Scatter chives over and serve.

Kitchen Notes

If you are in Santa Fe and visiting our local farmers' market, Monte Vista Organic Farm sells a gorgeous burgundy-flecked polenta cornmeal, ground from Floriani Red Flint corn. The Fresquez family grows the corn on their La Mesilla property outside of Española. The medium-grind corn requires 50 percent more milk and water to start, and at least 30 minutes of cooking time to get to its scrumptious, creamy best.

ORZO MACARONI AND CHEESE

SERVES 4 OR MORE

I'm finishing the chapter with two starchy sides that have been on our menu since we opened in 2009, at the height of America's love affair with comfort food. This and the previous polenta remain two accompaniments that we will never be able to remove from the menu. I guess you might see this macaroni and cheese preparation as an extension of the pasta chapter, but the dishes there are really entrees, and this is meant to be eaten on the side. Orzo means barley or grain in Italian, and that's what it resembles. I love the way it slides across the tongue. I have to make extra servings of this for dear family friend Ben Zamora. He's really the son we never had, and always hungry.

1 cup uncooked orzo pasta

2 teaspoons olive oil

½ cup (4 ounces) heavy cream

¼ cup (4 ounces) truffle butter or ¼ cup unsalted butter with 2 teaspoons truffle juice

1 ½ tablespoons mascarpone cheese

1½ tablespoons grated mozzarella cheese

1½ tablespoons grated Gruyère cheese

2 teaspoons truffle oil

Kosher salt and ground white pepper

Extra-virgin olive oil

Minced fresh chives, basil, or other compatible herb

TO PREPARE THE ORZO

1. Bring a large saucepan of salted water to a rolling boil.

2. Add the orzo and par-cook it for 5–7 minutes, until still somewhat firm at the center.

3. Drain the orzo and toss it with the olive oil. It can sit at room temperature for up to an hour before you finish the dish.

PUTTING IT ALL TOGETHER

1. Combine the cooked orzo in a saucepan with the cream, butter, and three cheeses. Bring to a simmer over medium heat, stirring to release more of the starch from the orzo and thicken the sauce.

2. When the orzo is tender and the sauce is creamy, stir in the truffle oil, season with salt and pepper, and spoon into 1 large serving bowl or 4 (or more) individual bowls. Dribble a bit of the extra-virgin olive oil over the top and garnish with chives. Serve right away.

poultry

SLOW-ROASTED WHOLE CHICKEN WITH WATERCRESS-APPLE SALAD AND CITRUS PAN SAUCE

SERVES 4

I grew up eating all kinds of poultry dishes in Guadalajara, often stews made by my mother to extend a main ingredient so that it fed the whole family. My dad, brothers, and I hunted for pigeons, and I learned to love the dark, lightly gamey meat. When I cook a nice plump chicken at home, I'm the one who grabs for the juicier thigh and leg portions. This whole chicken is often our family's Sunday night supper—it's one of the few exceptions to the mainly vegetarian tastes of the ladies in the family. All the citrus juices steam the chicken while it cooks, adding their fragrance as well as keeping the bird moist, but the skin does crisp because of the butter and oil lavished on it.

POSSIBLE DO-AHEAD STEPS

- Make the Dark Chicken Stock up to 1 week ahead.

FOR THE CHICKEN

1 large orange, sliced

2 large lemons, sliced

1 large lime, sliced

1 large sprig fresh tarragon

4 bacon slices, preferably applewood-smoked, chopped

3½-pound whole chicken, neck and giblets removed

2 tablespoons (1 ounce) olive oil

2 tablespoons (1 ounce) unsalted butter, softened

Kosher salt and ground white pepper

16–20 whole garlic cloves

4 cups (1 quart) Dark Chicken Stock (see page xxviii)

FOR THE WATERCRESS-APPLE SALAD

8 ounces watercress

2 Granny Smith apples, cut into matchsticks

2 celery stalks, shaved lengthwise with a vegetable peeler

2 ounces salted roasted cashews

2 tablespoons (1 ounce) olive oil

1 tablespoon fresh lemon juice

1 teaspoon grated orange zest

1 teaspoon grated lemon zest

2 tablespoons chopped fresh chives

Kosher salt and ground white pepper

TO PREPARE THE CHICKEN

1. Preheat the oven to 325°F.

2. Combine the sliced citrus, tarragon, and bacon in a roasting pan not much larger than the chicken.

3. Arrange the chicken over the bed of citrus, rub the oil and butter all over it, and season with salt and pepper. Roast for 45 minutes.

4. Remove the chicken from the oven, and using a spoon, baste it thoroughly with the pan juices. Add the garlic cloves to the roasting pan. Turn up the oven temperature to 375°F and return the chicken to the oven.

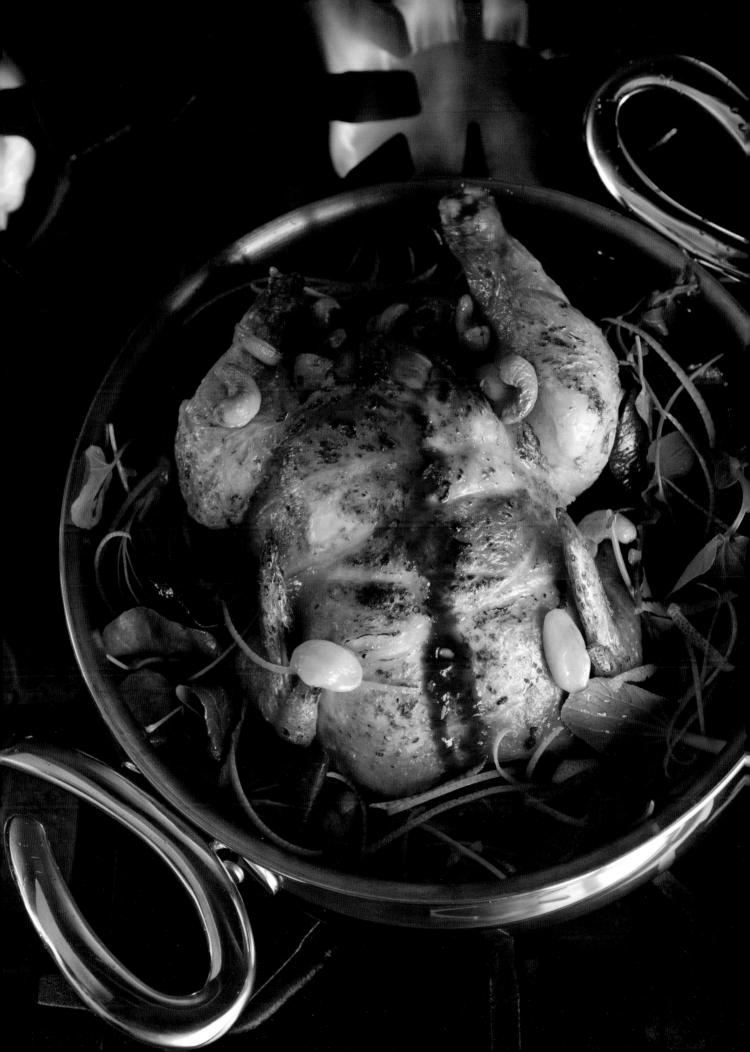

5. Continue cooking until the chicken is golden-brown and the juices run clear (160°F–165°F on an instant-read thermometer), 20–25 minutes more.

6. Lift the chicken, draining the juices back into the roasting pan. Transfer the chicken to a platter or shallow baking dish and tent with foil.

7. With a slotted spoon, remove the garlic cloves from the roasting pan and reserve them. Spoon and pour everything else from the pan into a large saucepan—pan juices, fruit, bacon, and all. Scrape out any browned bits too. If they are sticking, pour a few tablespoons of the stock into the roasting pan, scraping up from the bottom, and then pour out the browned bits into the saucepan.

8. Pour all the remaining stock into the pan. Simmer the mixture over medium-high heat to reduce the liquid by half, about 10 minutes.

9. Pour the mixture through a fine-mesh strainer, into a gravy boat or small serving bowl. Discard the solids.

TO PREPARE THE SALAD

Combine the watercress, apples, celery, and cashews in a bowl. Just before serving, toss with the oil, lemon juice, orange and lemon zests, and chives. Season with salt and pepper.

PUTTING IT ALL TOGETHER

Arrange the salad around the chicken. Some of the greens should wilt slightly from the warmth of the chicken. Scatter the garlic cloves over the chicken and salad. Serve the chicken whole at the table, accompanied by the pan sauce.

restaurant embellishments

Instead of adding the garlic cloves to the roasting pan as the chicken is cooking, at the restaurant I make a Garlic Confit in a separate step and place it on the chicken and salad prior to serving. If you want to try it at home, here's how.

GARLIC CONFIT

> 16–20 whole garlic cloves
> 2 cups (1 pint) olive oil
> 1 sprig fresh thyme
> 2 dried bay leaves

Combine garlic, oil, thyme, and bay leaves in a broad saucepan or small roasting pan. Cover the pan (use aluminum foil for a roasting pan), and cook on the stovetop over very low heat for 30–40 minutes or until the garlic is tender and very lightly colored. Remove the garlic cloves with a slotted spoon. Cool the oil, strain out the solids, and save it for salads or other dishes that can benefit from a mild garlicky taste.

SEARED CHICKEN BREASTS WITH GLAZED CIPOLLINI ONIONS AND CHARRED OAXACAN CHICHILO SAUCE

SERVES 4

I was thinking about creating a chile sauce for chicken, something deeply flavored like a Mexican black mole, but not so overpowering for the poultry. I also wanted the sauce to have good chile flavor without searing heat. I didn't remember chichilo sauce from my childhood in Mexico, but I stumbled onto it while doing research. It sounded like it could be the inspiration I was after. I mentioned it to my mother, who still makes wonderful moles, including a version of the legendary achiote-and-charred fruit mole called manchamanteles or "table-stainer" sauce. She smiled and told me she knew the sauce from many years ago back in Guadalajara because some other cooks at the main market made something similar. It seemed a good omen for the dish, which I top with some glazed small onions. In a home kitchen, I would make the chichilo sauce a day ahead of the planned timing for the meal, to give it a chance to fully absorb its complex flavors and to relax the preparation time.

POSSIBLE DO-AHEAD STEPS

- Make the Dark Chicken Stock up to 1 week ahead.
- Make the chichilo sauce and blanch and peel the cipollini onions up to 1 day ahead.

FOR THE CHICHILO SAUCE

1 large red tomato, cut in quarters

½ medium onion, cut in half through the stem end

2 large tomatillos

Canola or vegetable oil for pan frying

2 dried ancho chiles, seeded

1 dried mulatto or pasado chile, seeded

1 dried pasilla chile, seeded

2 corn tortillas

1 cup (8 ounces) canola or vegetable oil

2 garlic cloves

8 allspice berries

2 whole cloves

¼ teaspoon cumin seeds

2 cups (1 pint) Dark Chicken Stock (see page xxviii)

Kosher salt and ground white pepper

FOR THE GLAZED ONIONS

4 cups water

Kosher salt

16 whole cipollini onions, root ends sliced off

½ cup (4 ounces) apple cider

1 tablespoon unsalted butter

1 large sprig of fresh thyme

Ground white pepper

FOR THE CHICKEN

4 boneless, skin-on individual chicken breasts, about 6 ounces each

Kosher salt and ground white pepper

Canola or vegetable oil for sautéing

FOR THE FINISHED DISH

Baby arugula and rainbow amaranth, or other small salad greens

Thin-sliced radishes or Granny Smith apple, optional

TO PREPARE THE CHICHILO SAUCE

1. Char the tomato and onion chunks in a dry heavy skillet over high heat, blackening them on all sides. Expect this to take about 10 minutes. Once charred, scrape the tomato and onion chunks and any blackened bits from the skillet into a large bowl.

2. Char the whole tomatillos on an asador or directly over a stove burner until soft and very blackened. (I char the tomatillos whole because I want a strong contrast between the surface and the acidic interior.) Add them to the bowl of tomato and onion chunks.

3. Pour 1 inch of oil into a high-sided skillet or other pot and warm it until the oil ripples. Fry each whole chile briefly, just until a bit puffy, a few seconds each. Don't hesitate in pulling them out, because they burn quickly and become bitter. Add them to the bowl.

4. Fry each tortilla in the oil until it turns stiff and medium brown, a matter of seconds. Add them to the bowl.

5. Warm the 1 cup of oil in a large saucepan over medium-high heat to 350°F–360°F. Carefully, using tongs or a long-handled spoon, add the contents of the bowl to the oil. Watch out for splatters when the moist ingredients come in contact with the oil.

6. Add the garlic, allspice berries, cloves, and cumin to the saucepan, and cook the mixture for 5 minutes.

7. Pour in the stock carefully, and reduce the heat to maintain a simmer. Cook for 10 minutes more.

8. Pour about half of the sauce mixture into a blender. (Do not overfill a blender with hot ingredients or you may be scraping charred vegetables off the kitchen ceiling). Puree.

9. Strain the mixture through a fine-mesh sieve into a bowl, pushing on the solids. Repeat with the remaining sauce mixture. Season with salt and pepper. Cover and refrigerate until needed.

TO PREPARE THE GLAZED ONIONS

1. Make an ice bath.

2. Bring water to a boil in a saucepan. Salt it generously. Dunk the onions into the water to blanch them for about 1 full minute. Remove the onions with a slotted spoon and plunge them into the ice bath.

3. When cool enough to handle, peel the onions, trimming off the stem ends.

4. Combine the onions in a small saucepan with the cider, butter, thyme, and pepper. Simmer over medium-high heat, stirring, until the liquid evaporates and cider glazes the onions, about 3 minutes.

5. Put the onions in a bowl, cover, and reserve at room temperature.

TO PREPARE THE CHICKEN

1. Preheat the oven to 350°F.

2. Pound the chicken breasts to an even ½-inch thickness. Season them with salt and pepper.

3. Warm a 10- or 12-inch ovenproof skillet on the stovetop over medium-high heat. Add a thin film of oil to the skillet.

4. Arrange the chicken breasts in the skillet skin-side down and sear them for about 2½ minutes on each side until evenly browned.

5. Transfer the skillet with the chicken skin-side up to the oven and bake until juices run clear (160°F–165°F on an instant-read thermometer), about 6 minutes.

PUTTING IT ALL TOGETHER

1. Let the chicken breasts rest about 3 minutes, then cut each into 4 equal slices.

2. Reheat the chichilo sauce.

3. Spoon ¼ cup of the warm sauce on each of 4 plates, pooling it to one side of the plate and then brushing it across the center of the plate.

4. Arrange one slice of the chicken above the sauce and another slice below it. In between, arrange the 2 other slices. Top each of the center slices with an onion, then arrange 2 other onions on the plate, to either side of the chicken. Repeat with the remaining ingredients and plates. Tuck arugula and amaranth leaves and optional garnishes in and around the chicken and onions and serve right away.

restaurant embellishments

Instead of a standard chicken breast we use a cut known in the restaurant world as an "airline breast." It's similar in most respects to any other skin-on breast except that it has a protruding drummette bone. Your butcher may know the cut as a frenched chicken breast. We roll it into a chicken "log" as in the following recipe and cook it in the same manner as these breasts. We do the extra work required mainly for presentation value instead of flavor enhancement.

Kitchen Notes

If you have any sauce left, it's wonderful with pork belly tacos, or shredded pork, beef, or chicken tacos, and also mixed into or spooned on top of meatloaf.

LOBSTER-STUFFED CHICKEN THIGHS WITH SHERRY-BRAISED SHALLOTS

SERVES 4

I was invited, along with a half-dozen other chefs, to serve as a "Celebrated Chef" for the National Pork Board. At a special dinner in Chicago, all the pork dishes were quite good, but the one that stuck with me was a mixed grill served to us later that paired a grilled chicken breast alongside a lobster-and-shrimp sausage. Until that time, I thought about surf-and-turf pretty much in the classic way of seafood with beef or pork. Back in my own kitchen the idea evolved into this dish, complemented with slow-cooked shallots.

POSSIBLE DO-AHEAD STEPS

- Make the Sherry-Braised Shallots up to 1 day ahead.
- Form the chicken "logs" and poach them up to 4 hours ahead.

FOR THE LOBSTER FILLING

6 ounces medium shrimp, shelled

¼ cup (2 ounces) ice water

1 tablespoon Dijon mustard

8 ounces lobster, coarsely chopped

1 teaspoon chopped fresh tarragon

½ teaspoon chopped fresh chives

Kosher salt and ground white pepper

FOR THE CHICKEN LOGS

4 (4-ounce) skin-on boneless chicken thighs

Kosher salt and ground white pepper

FOR THE SHALLOTS

7 or 8 medium shallots, sliced thin

¼ cup plus 2 tablespoons (3 ounces) oloroso or cream sherry

2 tablespoons (1 ounce) water, or more if needed

2 tablespoons (1 ounce) olive oil

1 large sprig of fresh thyme

1 tablespoon champagne vinegar

FOR THE FINISHED DISH

Kosher salt and ground white pepper

Canola or vegetable oil

Small nasturtium leaves, beet greens, red amaranth leaves, coriander or fennel blossoms, or small salad greens

TO PREPARE THE LOBSTER FILLING

1. Make an ice bath.
2. Place the shrimp, ice water, and mustard in a food processor and puree.
3. Transfer the mixture to a medium bowl and place over the ice bath.
4. Fold in the lobster and herbs and season with salt and pepper. If you are not using the filling within 30 minutes, cover the bowl and refrigerate until needed.

TO PREPARE THE CHICKEN LOGS

1. Pound each thigh to an even ¼ inch.

2. Arrange a thigh in the middle of a 12-inch-square of plastic wrap.

3. Season the top of the chicken with salt and pepper.

4. Spoon ¼ of the lobster filling in a line down the center of the thigh. Fold the thigh up over the filling, using the plastic wrap to help enclose the filling. Twist the plastic wrap on the sides up against the outer edges of the breast. Holding the plastic wrap by the side "handles," start rolling the chicken back and forth on the work surface.

5. You are creating a plump little "log" of chicken, about 6 inches long and no thicker than 2 inches in diameter. Repeat with the remaining chicken thighs. Refrigerate the chicken logs in their plastic wraps in a sealed gallon zipper-lock bag for at least 30 minutes and up to 4 hours.

TO PREPARE THE SHALLOTS

Combine all the ingredients in a small saucepan and bring to a simmer over medium heat. Cook the mixture until it becomes tender and jammy in consistency, with little liquid remaining, about 15 minutes. Add a few more tablespoons of water if the mixture becomes dry before the shallots are tender. Spoon the mixture into a bowl, cover, and refrigerate until needed.

TO POACH THE CHICKEN LOGS

1. Unseal the zipper-lock plastic bag. Bring a stockpot half full of water to just below a simmer, approximately 200°F. Lower the open bag into the hot water, watching out for your fingers. The water squeezes the air out of the bag. Seal the bag when the water is within ¼ inch of the zipper seal.

2. Poach the chicken logs in the water, maintaining the cooking temperature at 195°F–200°F for 15 minutes.

3. While the logs poach, make an ice bath.

4. Remove the bag from the water and chill the chicken in the ice bath. When cold, remove the chicken logs from the plastic bag. Transfer the plastic-wrapped chicken to a plate and refrigerate until needed.

5. See Kitchen Notes on page 164 about the alternative option of *sous vide* cooking.

TO FINISH THE CHICKEN LOGS

1. Preheat the oven to 350°F.

2. Unwrap the chicken and discard the plastic. With kitchen twine, tie each log near both ends and in the middle. Make the ties firm but don't squeeze the thighs. Sprinkle with salt and pepper.

3. Warm a 10- or 12-inch ovenproof skillet on the stovetop over medium-high heat. Add a thin film of oil to the skillet. Arrange the chicken thighs in the skillet and sear them for about 4 minutes, turning to brown on all sides.

4. Transfer the skillet with the chicken to the oven and bake for 6–8 minutes, until the filling is heated through. Slice into the center of a log to check.

PUTTING IT ALL TOGETHER

1. Let the chicken thighs rest for about 3 minutes, then cut off the twine and slice each in half.

2. Reheat the shallots.

3. On 4 plates, arrange 2 chicken thigh halves leaning into each other. Place a spoonful of the warm shallots next to the chicken. Tuck leaves and blossoms around the chicken and serve.

Kitchen Notes

- If you are equipped for *sous vide* cooking, seal the chicken thighs in a *sous vide* bag under medium pressure, rather than simply placing them in a zipper-lock bag. Instead of poaching them in the pot, pre-cook them in a 142°F water bath in an immersion circulator for 1 hour. This is how we poach the thighs in the restaurant kitchen.

- An important lesson I learned from Chef David Burke was how to make a seafood mousse containing shrimp. He maintained correctly that it was not at all necessary to add cream or egg to a mixture to make it light and, in fact, that those ingredients simply take away from the intensity of the seafood's flavor. The ice water in the filling helps the shrimp get the right consistency without toughening, as does the ice bath.

restaurant embellishments

I've loved eggplant ever since my wife Jennifer made me her famous-in-our-family New Jersey–style eggplant parmigiana back in our dating days. I knew I wanted to stay with anyone who could make eggplant taste that memorable. The restaurant kitchen often makes a Caramelized Eggplant to accompany these thighs.

CARAMELIZED EGGPLANT

> 2 cups (1 pint) water
> 4½ tablespoons granulated sugar
> 1 tablespoon plus 1 teaspoon kosher salt
> Oblong white or purple eggplant, cut into planks, about 5 x 2 inches
> Additional kosher salt and ground white pepper
> Canola or vegetable oil, for pan frying

1. In a medium saucepan, heat water to a boil. Add sugar and salt and cook, stirring, until both are dissolved.

2. Place the eggplant planks in the mixture and arrange a plate over the pan to keep them submerged. Remove the pan from the heat and let the planks cool in the mixture for 15 minutes before removing them. Pat dry with paper towels.

3. To finish the preparation, salt and pepper the eggplant. Warm a thin film of oil in a skillet over medium heat. Add the eggplant and sauté it until browned and caramelized on the surface but creamy in the center, 5–8 minutes.

Another frequent accompaniment at the restaurant is a Gorgonzola and Pear Puree.

GORGONZOLA AND PEAR PUREE

> 2 ripe Anjou pears, cored and chopped
> 1 small shallot, chopped
> 1 garlic clove
> 1 cup (8 ounces) Light Chicken Stock (see page xxviii)
> 3 ounces Gorgonzola cheese
> 2 ounces mascarpone cheese
> Kosher salt and ground white pepper

1. Combine pears, shallot, and garlic in a saucepan, cooking and stirring the mixture over medium heat until it turns a light amber, about 10 minutes.

2. Add stock, Gorgonzola and mascarpone cheeses, and reduce the liquid by half.

3. Puree the mixture in a blender and season with salt and pepper before serving warm.

PAN-ROASTED DUCK BREAST WITH BLACK OLIVE-MEDJOOL DATE PUREE AND CHANTERELLES

SERVES 4

My first-ever work experience was in a Santa Fe restaurant called Fresco. I washed dishes there on an occasional basis after I finished my high school classes, scoring the job with the help of my older brother Eduardo, a cook at the restaurant. Fresco unfortunately only lasted a short time. Looking back on it, the chef-owner was way ahead of the era. He was offering simple Mediterranean-influenced live-fire-cooked foods, both wood-grilled and roasted. Now people flock to places like this, especially for pizza, but thirty-five years ago some customers thought our very thin, lightly topped, true Italian-style pies were stingy. I had grown up eating stewed wild duck with my mom's mole, but at Fresco I tasted farm-raised duck breasts, seared crispy on the grill and served on a salad or with a light sauce on the side. It was a whole different bird and I was instantly in love. To this day, I would rather eat duck than just about any other fowl or meat. In this recipe, I pair it with the flavors of the Mediterranean that I first learned about as that kid dishwasher. The olive-and-date puree brings together salty, tangy, sweet, and meaty in every bite.

POSSIBLE DO-AHEAD STEPS
- Make the Black Olive-Medjool Date Puree up to 2 hours ahead.

FOR THE PUREE

1 cup pitted dried Medjool dates

½ cup pitted black Kalamata olives

2 cups (1 pint) dry red wine

2 tablespoons (1 ounce) red wine vinegar

Peel of 1 medium orange, removed in several pieces

Peel of 1 medium lemon, removed in several pieces

1 tablespoon Dijon mustard

Kosher salt and ground white pepper

FOR THE SAUTÉED CHANTERELLES

2 tablespoons (1 ounce) olive oil

8–10 medium chanterelle mushrooms, cut in 1-inch pieces

Leaves from 1 sprig of fresh tarragon

Kosher salt and ground white pepper

FOR THE DUCK

4 (5- to 6-ounce) skin-on individual duck breasts

Kosher salt and ground white pepper

1 tablespoon canola or vegetable oil

FOR THE FINISHED DISH

Tarragon or chervil leaves or sprigs, or other small herbs or salad greens

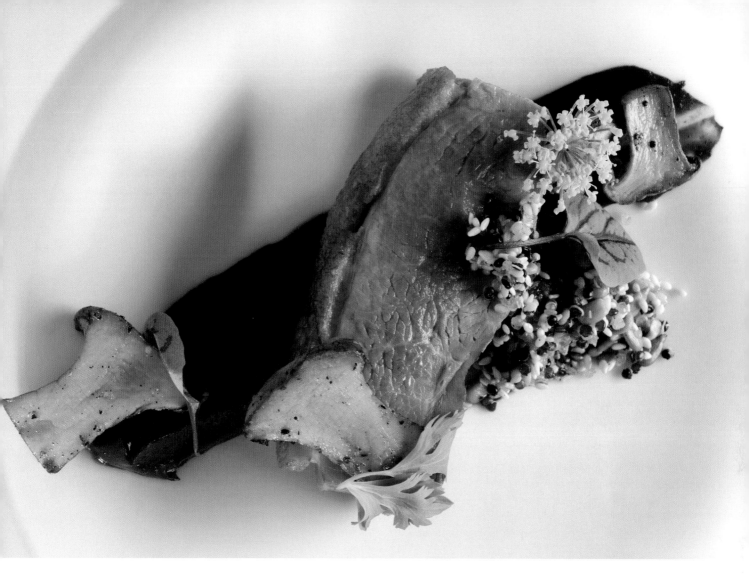

TO PREPARE THE OLIVE-DATE PUREE

1. Heat all the ingredients together in a saucepan and bring to a quick boil. Reduce the heat to a simmer and reduce the liquid by half, 5–10 minutes.

2. Transfer to a blender and puree. Season with salt and pepper. Spoon into a bowl, cover, and refrigerate until needed.

TO PREPARE THE CHANTERELLES

Warm the oil in a small skillet over medium heat, add the mushrooms, and sauté until tender and golden brown, 5–7 minutes. Remove from the heat, add the tarragon leaves, and season with salt and pepper. Reserve at room temperature.

TO COOK THE DUCK BREASTS

1. Score the skin-side of the duck breasts in a 1-inch diamond or crosshatch pattern. Make crisscross cuts, about ½ inch apart, through the skin but not into the flesh. This promotes gradual and easy rendering of fat, and gives more surfaces for the seasonings to flavor. Sprinkle with salt and pepper.

2. Warm a sauté pan over high heat until it just starts to smoke. Turn the heat down to medium, and pour in the oil, swirling it around quickly. Place the duck breasts in the

pan, skin-sides down. Sauté until the skin renders some fat and becomes richly brown and crisp, at least 4 minutes. (The browning may take twice this long, depending on the thickness of the skin and the exact heat level.) If the skin is browning before a good bit of fat is rendered, reduce the heat.

3. Turn the duck breasts over and sear for about 4 minutes on the other side for rare to medium-rare doneness, an internal temperature of 130°F–135°F. Let the duck breasts rest on a cutting board for 2–3 minutes.

PUTTING IT ALL TOGETHER

Reheat the olive-date puree. Spoon about ¼ cup of the warm puree into the center of the first plate. I spoon it into a long line but do what you wish. Cut the duck breasts in half the long way and place the 2 halves on top of the puree, overlapping a bit so you see their ruby centers. Spoon ¼ of the chanterelles around the duck. Repeat with the remaining ingredients on the other 3 plates. Garnish all the plates with greens and herb leaves. Serve any additional olive-date puree in small bowls on the side if you wish.

restaurant embellishments

I like to serve this dish with Toasted Grains and Seeds scattered on top just before serving.

TOASTED GRAINS AND SEEDS

3 cups (1½ pints) canola or vegetable oil
½ cup cooked tri-colored quinoa
½ cup salted, roasted sunflower seed kernels
¼ cup sesame seeds
½ teaspoon grated lemon zest
¼ teaspoon *piment d'Espelette*
Kosher salt and ground white pepper

1. In a medium saucepan, warm oil to 350°F–355°F, arranging several thicknesses of paper towels and having a spider strainer close by.

2. Spoon quinoa, sunflower seed kernels, and sesame seeds into the oil and fry for 20 seconds or until they develop just a touch more color.

3. Quickly scoop the grains and seeds out of the oil with the spider and dump them on the paper towels to drain and cool. When they are cool, scatter lemon zest and *piment d'Espelette* over the mixture and season with salt and pepper.

CURED AND ROASTED DUCK BREAST "HAM" WITH COCO BEAN PUREE, CHARRED ONION BROTH, AND GREENS

SERVES 4

I didn't start out trying to improvise on the southern idea of ham, beans, greens, and gravy, but that's where this recipe landed. It takes an international detour on its way there, since the charring technique for the onion comes from the Mexican roasting or charring of ingredients for salsas and sauces. I love creamy haricots cocos, *white French coco (not cocoa!) beans, especially when you puree them with bacon and a bit of butter. Because the cured duck breast feels heartier, I only serve half of a large breast for each guest. You need to soak the beans overnight for the creamiest texture, so plan accordingly.*

POSSIBLE DO-AHEAD STEPS

- Make the Light Chicken Stock up to 1 week ahead.
- Cure the duck breasts, make the Coco Bean Puree, and make the Charred Onion Broth up to 2 days ahead.

FOR THE DUCK BREASTS

¼ cup plus 1 ½ teaspoons packed brown sugar

2 tablespoons kosher salt

2 cups (1 pint) water

1 large sprig of fresh thyme

1 large sprig of fresh rosemary

2 (7- to 8-ounce) skin-on individual duck breasts

FOR THE PUREE

1 cup dried coco beans, soaked overnight

8 cups (2 quarts) Light Chicken Stock
   (see page xxviii)

2 bacon slices, preferably applewood-smoked

2 whole garlic cloves

1 whole medium shallot

1 dried bay leaf

4 tablespoons (2 ounces) unsalted butter

Kosher salt and ground white pepper

FOR THE ONION BROTH

2 small onions, halved

2 crushed garlic cloves

1 tablespoon dried bonito flakes (katsuobushi)

2 tablespoons (1 ounce) ponzu sauce

¼ cup plus 2 tablespoons (3 ounces) oloroso
   or cream sherry

4 cups (1 quart) Light Chicken Stock
   (see page xxviii)

FOR THE FINISHED DISH

Canola oil or vegetable oil for sautéing

Lamb's quarters (quelites), rainbow amaranth, lemon
   balm, purslane, small nasturtium leaves or sprigs,
   or baby spinach

TO CURE THE DUCK BREASTS

1. Whisk together the sugar, salt, water, and herbs until the sugar and salt dissolve in a medium bowl. Dunk the duck breasts into the cure liquid and refrigerate covered for 30 minutes.

2. Remove the duck from the cure, discarding the liquid. Rinse the breast and pat it dry with a paper towel. The breasts will be somewhat firmer than when raw.

3. Score the skin of the duck breasts in a 1-inch diamond or crosshatch pattern. Make crisscross cuts through the skin but not into the flesh. This promotes gradual and easy rendering of fat. Refrigerate covered until needed.

TO PREPARE THE COCO BEANS

1. Combine the beans, stock, bacon, garlic, shallot, and bay leaf in a medium saucepan and simmer until the beans become tender. (If the liquid level gets within 1 inch of the beans before the beans are ready, add enough water or additional stock to bring it up to that level.)

2. Transfer the beans and half their liquid to a blender and add the butter. Puree, adding a bit more bean liquid if needed to get a thin but smooth mixture. Season with salt and pepper. Scrape into a bowl, cover, and refrigerate until needed.

TO PREPARE THE ONION BROTH

1. Place the onion halves over a stove burner and cook until blackened and charred all over, 10–15 minutes.

2. Transfer the onions to a medium saucepan. Add the rest of the ingredients and reduce by half.

3. Strain the broth through a fine-mesh sieve lined with cheesecloth. Do not press on the solids so that the broth stays clear. Return the broth to the saucepan and keep warm on low heat.

TO COOK THE DUCK

1. Preheat the oven to 350°F.

2. Warm a sauté pan over high heat until it just starts to smoke. Turn the heat down to medium, and pour in enough oil to coat the pan lightly, swirling it around quickly.

3. Place the duck breasts in the pan, skin-sides down. Sauté until the skin renders some fat, and becomes golden, 2–3 minutes. If the skin is browning before some fat is rendered, reduce the heat.

4. Turn over the duck breasts and cook for about 2 minutes skin-sides up.

5. Transfer the skillet to the oven and roast for about 4 minutes, or until the skin is crispy and the duck is cooked to rare to medium-rare, an internal temperature of 130°F–135°F. Let the duck breasts rest on a cutting board for 2–3 minutes.

PUTTING IT ALL TOGETHER

1. Reheat the bean puree.

2. Spoon a mound of the warm puree in the center of each of 4 plates. Slice the duck breasts thinly across the grain. Lay half a duck breast over the puree on each plate. Pour equal portions of the broth over and around the duck. Garnish the dish with assorted greens and serve.

restaurant embellishments

In the restaurant we serve this with a Crispy Black Barley accompaniment. In 4 cups (1 quart) of water, we simmer ½ cup of the barley with a garlic clove until the grain is tender, about 35–45 minutes. After draining the liquid and patting the barley dry with paper towels, we warm 3 cups of canola oil in a saucepan to 325°F–330°F. Using a spider, we lower the barley into the oil and deep-fry it for 15 seconds, draining the grain on paper towels and sprinkling it with a teaspoon of kosher salt. Right before serving, we scatter the crispy barley over the dish.

Kitchen Notes

I choose my garnishing herbs for flavor and aroma as well as looks. In this dish I like the peppery notes of nasturtium leaves and lamb's quarters. Lemon balm and purslane both have citrus notes good with these flavors too.

SMOKY LEMON-GLAZED DUCK BREAST WITH PICKLED PLUMS AND PEA PODS

SERVES 4

Chinese dishes such as tea-smoked duck were on my mind when I put together this fairly simple combination. Smoky Chinese lapsang souchang tea always seems somewhat exotic and mysterious. The smoldering pine wood embers that the tea leaves dry over during processing leave behind an alluring and heady scent that perfumes the light finishing sauce. Zesty lemon and a sweet-and-sour plum compote offset the rich meat and smoke.

POSSIBLE DO-AHEAD STEPS

- Make the Dark Chicken Stock up to 1 week ahead.
- Make the Pickled Plum Compote up to 3 days ahead.
- Make the Lapsang Souchang Tea Sauce up to 1 day ahead.

FOR THE COMPOTE

8 medium-size fresh black plums or other fresh plums, sliced into 6 segments each

½ cup (4 ounces) dry red wine

1 tablespoon red wine vinegar

⅓ cup granulated sugar

1 dried bay leaf

2-inch sprig of fresh rosemary

FOR THE TEA SAUCE

2 medium shallots, chopped

4 garlic cloves, chopped

1 small sprig of fresh thyme

4 cups (1 quart) Dark Chicken Stock (see page xxviii)

1 tablespoon loose lapsang souchang tea

1 tablespoon minced fresh ginger

Kosher salt and ground white pepper

FOR THE DUCK

4 (5- or 6-ounce) skin-on individual duck breasts

Kosher salt and ground white pepper

2 tablespoons (1 ounce) mild-flavored honey, such as orange blossom

½ teaspoon grated lemon zest

¼ cup (2 ounces) Dark Chicken Stock (see page xxviii)

2 tablespoons (1 ounce) plus 1 teaspoon olive oil (divided use)

2 dozen sugar snap pea pods

Tiny lettuce leaves, mint or thyme leaves or sprigs, or sugar snap pea shoots

TO PREPARE THE PLUM COMPOTE

Place all the ingredients in a small saucepan and bring to a boil. Set aside to steep until cool, then spoon into a bowl, cover, and refrigerate until needed.

TO PREPARE THE TEA SAUCE

1. Combine the shallots, garlic, and thyme in a small saucepan and cook over medium heat, stirring occasionally, until the mixture turns amber.

2. Stir in the stock, tea, and ginger, and cook until the liquid reduces to about 1 cup.

3. Strain through a fine-mesh sieve and season with salt and pepper.

4. Return the sauce to the saucepan and keep warm over low heat.

TO COOK THE DUCK

1. Score the skins of the duck breasts in a 1-inch crosshatch pattern, cutting down to the meat but not into it. This promotes gradual and easy rendering of fat, and gives more surfaces for the seasonings to flavor.

2. Season the duck breasts with salt and pepper.

3. Stir the honey, lemon zest, and stock together in a small bowl.

4. Warm 1 teaspoon of oil in a large heavy skillet over medium-high heat. Stir in the pea pods and toss them until they have just begun to soften, 1–2 minutes. You still want them to have some crunch. Spoon the pea pods onto paper towels to drain.

5. Add the rest of the oil to the skillet and turn the heat down to medium.

6. Place the duck breasts in the skillet skin-side-down and cook until the skin has browned richly and is crisp, at least 4 minutes. (The browning may take twice this long, depending on the thickness of the skin and the exact heat level.) It will also have rendered a good bit of fat.

7. Turn over the duck breasts and cook the second side for 2 more minutes.

8. Spoon portions of the lemon-scented honey mixture equally over each breast. Turn up the heat to high and cook for another couple of minutes to an internal temperature of 130°F–135°F for rare to medium-rare doneness. The breasts should be nicely glazed with the honey mixture.

9. Drain skin-side-up on paper towels, and let rest for 2–3 minutes.

PUTTING IT ALL TOGETHER

Slice each duck breast in half lengthwise and position the portions leaning against each other, cut-sides-up, on 4 plates. Spoon the chilled plum compote and juice around the duck. Arrange a half-dozen pea pods around the plate. Drizzle the tea sauce over and around the duck. Garnish with the greens and serve right away.

restaurant embellishments

Black Forbidden Rice lends its own rather mysterious air to this duck dish. Give it a try sometime.

BLACK FORBIDDEN RICE

> 1 cup black rice
> 3 cups (1½ pints) Light Chicken Stock (see page xxviii)
> 2 dried bay leaves
> Pinch of kosher salt

1. Combine rice, stock, bay leaves, and salt in a medium saucepan.

2. Bring to a boil over high heat. Reduce the heat to medium-low and cook until the rice is tender, 45–50 minutes.

3. Cover the rice and let it sit for at least 10 minutes.

4. Serve it mounded across the center of the plate with duck breast slices leaning up against it.

For the elaborated version of the plum compote we make in the restaurant, consider this if you have the vacuum sealer associated with *sous vide* cooking. Place the same ingredients in a small *sous vide* plastic bag, arranging the plums side-by-side and pouring the rest of the ingredients around them. Seal with medium pressure and then refrigerate the mixture until needed. The pressure infuses the fruit with even more of the pickling mixture and makes the plums as smooth as silk.

Kitchen Notes

The fresh plums and sugar snap peas are summery items in this preparation. The dish is easy to make at other times of the year by using dried plums in the compote and substituting another green vegetable for the peas.

PAN-SEARED QUAIL WITH FRENCH LENTILS, HUCKLEBERRIES, AND COGNAC-SCENTED APPLES

While I was working in Vonnas, France, my French landlord invited me to go pheasant hunting with him on some of my days off. As a retired park ranger, monsieur knew where to go, and we always came home with our limit. My conversational French was about 40 percent proficient, but we could always understand each other when it came to food. He and his wife turned some of our bounty into a scrumptious rustic pheasant stew. I was thinking about the ingredients they used when I conceived this dish: The mildly gamey meat, smoky bacon, lentils, and apples are perfect for fall and winter. If you want to streamline the process, you can cut the apples into chunks rather than scoop them out into spheres.

POSSIBLE DO-AHEAD STEPS

- Make the Light Chicken Stock up to 1 week ahead.
- Make the Lentil Stew up to 1 day ahead.

FOR THE BEGINNING OF THE LENTIL STEW

1 cup French green lentils Du Puy

1 small onion, quartered

1 celery stalk, cut in 4 chunks

2 garlic cloves, bruised

3 bacon slices, preferably applewood-smoked

1 dried bay leaf

2 curry leaves, optional

1 cinnamon stick

Chunk of fresh ginger the size of a small walnut

2 star anise

1 small sprig of fresh thyme

4 cups (1 quart) Light Chicken Stock
(see page xxviii)

FOR THE APPLES

2 tablespoons (1 ounce) olive oil

1 tablespoon unsalted butter

1 tablespoon granulated sugar

1 tablespoon fresh lemon juice

1 tablespoon cognac

Peel of ¼ medium orange (in 1 or 2 pieces)

2 Honey Crisp apples, peeled and scooped into approximately 10 balls each with a melon baller

FOR THE REST OF THE STEW

1 bacon slice, preferably applewood-smoked,
chopped fine

1 small shallot, minced

3 heaping tablespoons fresh huckleberries, blackberries, or blueberries

Kosher salt and ground white pepper

FOR THE QUAIL

4 semi-boneless quail (about 5 ounces each), wing
tips cut off

Kosher salt and ground white pepper

Canola or vegetable oil for sautéing

FOR THE FINISHED DISH

Fresh chervil or oregano sprigs, fennel fronds, or
other herb sprigs or salad greens

TO BEGIN THE LENTIL STEW

1. Combine the lentils in a medium saucepan with the remaining stew ingredients. Bring to a boil over high heat. Reduce the heat as needed to maintain a simmer and cook until the lentils are tender, 20–25 minutes.

2. Strain the lentils and cooking liquid into a bowl, removing and discarding the pieces of onion, celery, garlic, bacon, herbs, and spices. Cover and refrigerate until needed.

TO PREPARE THE APPLES

1. Make an ice bath.

2. Stand a quart zipper-lock plastic bag up in a small high-sided bowl.

3. Combine the oil, butter, sugar, lemon juice, cognac, and orange peel in a small saucepan. Warm over medium heat. Once the mixture comes to a simmer, cook it for 1 minute.

4. Stir in the apples and cook for 2–3 more minutes, until the apple balls have softened slightly.

5. Pour the apples and liquid into the plastic bag and zip shut. Place the closed bag in the ice bath and let cool until needed.

TO CONTINUE THE STEW

1. Remove the lentil stew from the refrigerator and finish the preparation.

2. Fry the chopped bacon in a medium saucepan until almost brown and crisp.

3. Add the shallot and cook until soft, about 5 minutes.

4. Add the lentils, their cooking liquid, and the berries. Bring to a quick simmer and cook for about 3 minutes, just until the berries soften slightly. Season with salt and pepper.

TO COOK THE QUAIL

1. Season the quail with salt and pepper.

2. Pour a good ¼ inch of oil into a large skillet and warm over medium heat.

3. Sauté the quail about 4 minutes per side, or until golden brown all over. The breast meat should still be somewhat rosy with the legs cooked through.

4. Drain. Carve each quail into four pieces, first down through the breastbone and backbone to halve, and then between the wing and leg to quarter.

PUTTING IT ALL TOGETHER

Spoon a mound of the lentil stew in the center of each of 4 plates. Place 4 quail parts leaning against each other over the lentils. Divide the apple balls among the plates. Garnish with herbs and serve.

restaurant embellishments

In the restaurant I make Lemon Gel to accompany this dish. Agar agar, as discussed in the chapter "Bringing the Restaurant Home," is a powdered seaweed-based thickener, available in supermarket baking and spice aisles. It turns liquid into gel, and holds that consistency whether hot or chilled, which is perfect for this warm gel.

LEMON GEL

1 cup (8 ounces) Light Chicken Stock
(see page xxviii)

4 tablespoons (2 ounces) Meyer lemon
juice or other lemon juice

2 tablespoons (1 ounce) rice vinegar

2 tablespoons packed brown sugar

1 tablespoon soy sauce

¼ teaspoon sriracha, sambal oelek, or
other Asian red chile sauce

1 teaspoon agar agar

Kosher salt and ground white pepper

1. In a small saucepan, combine the stock, lemon juice, vinegar, sugar, soy sauce, and red chile sauce.

2. Bring the mixture to a boil and simmer for 5 minutes.

3. Transfer it to a blender, add agar agar. Puree. Season with salt and pepper.

I also like to add drizzles of Fennel Oil to the plate. I make sure I have leftovers of the bright, beautiful green oil to use on salads, sprinkle over grilled vegetables, or toss with pasta.

FENNEL OIL

1 whole fennel bulb with at least several
inches of very green tops

1 small garlic clove

1 small shallot

2 cups (1 pint) olive oil

Kosher salt and ground white pepper

1. Prepare an ice bath.

2. Place whole fennel, garlic, and shallot in a blender.

3. In a saucepan, warm olive oil just to the point when a bit of fennel dunked into the oil results in happy bubbles around it.

4. Pour the warm oil into the blender and puree.

5. Transfer the mixture to a bowl and placed it over the ice bath to prevent discoloration.

6. Season the puree with salt and pepper and let it cool.

7. Once chilled, the fennel will separate from the slightly more viscous oil. Strain it through a fine-mesh strainer into a bowl or jar. Cover and refrigerate for up to a week.

In the restaurant we prepare the apples with *sous vide* techniques. If you are equipped for *sous vide* cooking, seal the apples in a *sous vide* bag under high pressure, rather than sautéing them and placing them in a zipper-lock bag. Instead of poaching them in the pot, we cook them in a 130°F water bath in an immersion circulator for 30 minutes.

PAN-SEARED BUTTER-BASTED QUAIL WITH STONE-GROUND SEMOLINA, CRUNCHY SUNCHOKES, AND PICKLED BLACKBERRIES

SERVES 4

Coffee-marinated quail served over a pool of buttery grits was the starting inspiration here. I love the little background bitterness the coffee brings to the quail, balanced here with ginger and honey in the marinade and with a tangy-sweet blackberry puree. In place of corn grits, I like the surprise of the semolina, the coarse-ground wheat flour used for pasta, which can make a similar creamy rich base for the little birds. The sunchokes (also known as Jerusalem artichokes), fry up to make nice vegetable chips.

POSSIBLE DO-AHEAD STEPS
- Make the Light Chicken Stock up to 1 week ahead.
- Make the Pickled Blackberry Puree up to 3 days ahead.

FOR THE QUAIL
½ cup (4 ounces) cold strong coffee

½ cup (4 ounces) olive oil

1 small shallot, minced

2 garlic cloves, minced

2 tablespoons minced fresh ginger

2 teaspoons medium-flavored honey, such as wildflower

4 (approximately 5-ounce) semi-boneless quail, wing tips cut off

FOR THE PUREE
1 pint fresh blackberries

½ cup (4 ounces) Light Chicken Stock (see page xxviii)

2 tablespoons packed brown sugar

2 tablespoons (1 ounce) rice vinegar

2 tablespoons (1 ounce) hoisin sauce

1 tablespoon soy sauce

2 teaspoons minced fresh ginger

1 teaspoon agar agar

Kosher salt and ground white pepper

FOR THE SUNCHOKE CHIPS
2 medium (about 4 ounces each) sunchokes

4 cups (1 quart) canola or vegetable oil

Kosher salt

FOR THE SEMOLINA
1 cup (8 ounces) whole milk

1 cup (8 ounces) Light Chicken Stock (see page xxviii)

2 tablespoons freshly grated Parmesan cheese

4 tablespoons (2 ounces) unsalted butter

½ cup stone-ground semolina flour

Kosher salt and ground white pepper

FOR THE QUAIL
Kosher salt and ground white pepper

Olive oil for sautéing

2 tablespoons (1 ounce) unsalted butter

1 large sprig of fresh thyme

FOR THE FINISHED DISH
Small sprigs of fresh chervil, or mustard flowers, or small Orach "spinach" leaves, or other small greens

TO MARINATE THE QUAIL

Combine in a shallow dish the coffee, olive oil, shallot, garlic, ginger, and honey. Place the quail in the marinade, cover, and refrigerate for 1–2 hours.

TO PREPARE THE PICKLED BLACKBERRY PUREE

1. Combine the blackberries, stock, brown sugar, vinegar, hoisin sauce, soy sauce, and ginger in a small saucepan.

2. Bring the mixture to a boil, reduce the heat to a simmer, and cook until the blackberries have softened and partially disintegrated, 5–7 minutes.

3. Whisk in the agar agar. Transfer the mixture to a blender and puree.

4. Return the puree to the saucepan, and bring it back to a boil, whisking again.

5. While the puree is coming to a boil, make an ice bath. Place the pan over the ice bath and cool the mixture down. The agar agar will gel the mixture within a few minutes. When it has set up lightly, puree the mixture one more time. Strain the puree through a fine-mesh sieve into a bowl, then reserve covered at room temperature.

TO PREPARE THE SUNCHOKE CHIPS

1. Line a baking sheet with a couple thicknesses of paper towels.

2. Scrub the sunchokes in cold water, but do not peel them.

3. Using a mandoline, slice the sunchokes thinly, more or less in a long direction.

4. Warm the oil in a large saucepan to 300°F. Fry the sunchoke slices, in batches if needed, until lightly golden and crisp, 5–7 minutes. Drain the chips on the paper towels, seasoning with salt while they are still warm.

TO PREPARE THE SEMOLINA

1. Combine the milk, stock, Parmesan, and butter in a large saucepan (because the mixture will bubble up).

2. Bring to a boil over high heat, then pour in the semolina flour slowly, whisking to combine it with the liquid.

3. Reduce the heat to a simmer and cook until thickened and creamy, about 10 minutes. Whisk the mixture constantly to prevent it from burning.

4. Season with salt and pepper, cover, and keep warm on low heat.

TO COOK THE QUAIL

1. Season the quail with salt and pepper. Warm a good ¼ inch of olive oil in a large skillet over medium heat.

2. Add the quail, breast-side-down, and cook for about 4 minutes per side, until golden brown all over.

3. Turn off the heat and add the butter and thyme sprig to the skillet. As the butter melts, baste the quail with the buttery pan juices for about 30 seconds.

4. The quail are ready when the breasts are still somewhat rosy, but the legs are cooked through. Drain and let sit for 2 minutes. Carve each quail into four pieces, first down through the breastbone and backbone to halve, and then between the wing and leg to quarter.

PUTTING IT ALL TOGETHER

Place a mound of the semolina on each of 4 plates. Place 4 quail pieces, leaning against each other, over the semolina. Pile sunchoke chips over the top of each quail. Spoon the blackberry puree around the edge of each plate. Scatter a few herbs or greens over the plates and serve.

restaurant embellishments

We usually serve this quail with Sautéed Shiitake Mushrooms as an accompaniment. I'm a bit obsessive about the look of the mushrooms, so I cut 1- and 2-inch circles out of the caps, reserving the trimmings for another dish. This means that I start with a little more of the shiitakes than I actually need, about 4 ounces. In a medium sauté pan I warm 2 tablespoons (1 ounce) of olive oil over medium heat, add the mushrooms, and cook until they are tender and browned a bit, about 5 minutes. I pour in 2 tablespoons (1 ounce) of brandy, allowing the alcohol to evaporate, then stir in 1 tablespoon of unsalted butter, a sprig of fresh thyme, and a large sprig of fresh mint, and cook for another minute, basting the mushrooms with the buttery sauce. After seasoning with salt and pepper, I drain the mushrooms and serve them warm alongside the quail.

SAUTÉED SQUAB WITH DRIED FRUIT COMPOTE AND MAYAN COCOA SAUCE

SERVES 4

As you've seen throughout this chapter, I love sweet-sour fruity flavors with game birds such as quail and squab. Young squab may be my favorite game bird of all, dark and juicy, bold but not livery, as can be the case with the pigeon so beloved by the French. As a kid in Mexico, I ate some pigeons that we hunted, which is where I was first intrigued with dark-meat birds. It was during my time at Georges Blanc, though, that my love and respect for squab became full-blown. My initial job in the restaurant kitchen was to check in all the fowl—chickens, pheasants, guinea hens, quail, partridge, pheasants, squab, and more—delivered to us from farmers, hunters, and commercial suppliers. I tasted them all in search of the best.

POSSIBLE DO-AHEAD STEPS

- Make the Dark Chicken Stock up to 1 week ahead.
- Poach the squabs and make the Dried Fruit Compote and Mayan Cocoa Sauce up to 1 day ahead.

FOR THE SQUABS

2 (about 1-pound) whole squabs

4 tablespoons (2 ounces) unsalted butter

2 garlic cloves, bruised

1 large sprig of fresh thyme

FOR THE COMPOTE

4 ounces dried black Mission figs

1 ounce dried plums

1 ounce dried cherries

¼ cup plus 2 tablespoons (3 ounces) dry red wine

2 tablespoons (1 ounce) aged red wine vinegar

Kosher salt and ground white pepper

FOR THE COCOA SAUCE

1 tablespoon olive oil

½ small onion, chopped

1 ounce sliced prosciutto, chopped

1 garlic clove

1 tablespoon Mayan cocoa powder

2 cups (1 pint) Dark Chicken Stock (see page xxviii)

FOR COOKING THE SQUAB

Kosher salt and ground white pepper

Olive oil for sautéing

FOR THE FINISHED DISH

Micro-greens, small nasturtium leaves, or small sprigs of thyme

Thinly sliced baby carrots

TO POACH THE SQUABS

1. First place the squabs, butter, garlic, and thyme in a gallon zipper-lock plastic bag but don't zip the bag shut.

2. Bring a stockpot half full of water to just below a simmer, approximately 200°F.

3. Lower the open bag into the hot water, watching out for your fingers. The water squeezes the air out of the bag. Seal the bag when the water is within ¼ inch of the zipper seal.

4. Poach the squabs in the water, maintaining the cooking temperature at 195°F–200°F for 20 minutes.

5. While the squabs poach, make an ice bath.

6. Remove the bag from the water and chill in the ice bath until completely cold, then refrigerate sealed until needed.

TO MAKE THE DRIED FRUIT COMPOTE

1. Combine the dried figs, plums, cherries, wine, and wine vinegar in a small saucepan, and bring to a boil.

2. Transfer the mixture to a blender and puree.

3. Season with salt and pepper. Spoon the compote into a bowl, cover, and refrigerate until needed.

TO MAKE THE COCOA SAUCE

1. Warm the oil in a small saucepan over medium-high heat. Stir in the onion, prosciutto, and garlic. Cook until golden brown, about 5 minutes.

2. Stir in the cocoa and cook for about 1 minute, until you smell the toasted aroma.

3. Pour in the chicken stock, stir, and reduce the mixture by half. Strain through a fine-mesh sieve, discarding the solids. Keep the sauce warm on low heat if using shortly. If you are making it ahead, refrigerate covered until needed.

TO COOK THE SQUAB

1. Remove the squabs from the plastic bag and dry with paper towels. Season with salt and pepper. With a chef's knife or cleaver, slice the squabs in half lengthwise, cutting down through the breastbone and backbone of each.

2. Warm a good ¼ inch of oil in a 10- or 12-inch skillet over medium heat.

3. Add the squab halves, a skin-side down, and sauté until the skin is nicely browned, 2–3 minutes. Turn the pieces over and cook an additional 2–3 minutes. The breast meat should still be rosy.

4. Remove the squabs from the pan and let them rest for a minute. Slice each squab half into 2 pieces, one with the breast and wing section, one with the leg section.

PUTTING IT ALL TOGETHER

Place a spoonful of fruit compote in the center of each of 4 plates and top with 2 pieces of squab, a breast and a leg section. Spoon cocoa sauce around the plates. Garnish with greens and serve.

restaurant embellishments

I like to serve squab with a Parsnip and Manchego Cheese Puree.

PARSNIP AND MANCHEGO CHEESE PUREE

> 2 medium parsnips (about 8 ounces total), peeled and chopped
> 1 Granny Smith apple, chopped
> 1 medium shallot, chopped
> 4 cups (1 quart) Light Chicken Stock (see page xxviii)
> 4 tablespoons (2 ounces) unsalted butter
> ¼ cup grated manchego cheese
> Kosher salt and ground white pepper

1. Combine parsnips, apple, shallot, stock, and butter in a saucepan. Cook the mixture over medium heat until it is almost dry, with just a bit of very thick liquid binding everything.

2. Transfer the mixture to a blender, and add manchego cheese. Puree.

3. Season with salt and pepper and strain the mixture through a fine-mesh sieve. Serve it warm alongside the squab halves.

If you are equipped for *sous vide* cooking, poach the squabs like we do in the kitchen. Seal them in a *sous vide* bag under high pressure rather than placing them in a zipper-lock bag. Instead of poaching them in the pot, cook them in a 142°F water bath in an immersion circulator for 25 minutes.

Kitchen Notes

- You may have to order squabs ahead from a butcher shop. You can substitute Cornish game hens, if necessary, but they are less flavorful to me.

- Mayan cocoa powder is a blend of cocoa with a bit of cinnamon and chile. I pick it up at Santa Fe's Savory Spice Shop, which offers mail order through savoryspiceshop.com. You can make something similar by starting with 1 tablespoon of good cocoa powder and adding ¼ teaspoon ground cinnamon and ⅛ teaspoon ground dried New Mexican red or ancho chile.

fish and seafood main dishes

SEARED YELLOWFIN TUNA WITH DUCK-FAT ROASTED CARROTS AND CARROT-COCONUT PUREE

SERVES 4

My fish supplier, Above Sea Level, says that some weeks Restaurant Martín goes through more fish than any other restaurant they service. We pay meticulous attention to it. I really think you can tell the intentions of a restaurant by how it handles and prepares seafood. In our kitchen, every other element of a dish will be ready before any accompanying seafood comes out of the refrigerator. Over the years, I may have made more versions of tuna dishes than anything else on my menus. We've crusted it with ground nori seaweed mixed with wasabi, with our own dehydrated onions, with ground porcinis from the mountains around us. We even made what the kitchen staff lightheartedly referred to as a tuna enchilada, where we sandwiched a New Mexican green chile in the middle of a tuna loin, then wrapped it in wonton wrappers and fried it. Yes, it looked like an enchilada and tasted superb. This is even better, and developed from a more conventional preparation with a Southeast Asian twist.

POSSIBLE DO-AHEAD STEPS

- Make the Carrot-Coconut Puree up to 1 day ahead.

FOR THE CARROTS

8 young purple carrots, with tops

8 young yellow or white carrots, with tops

8 young orange carrots, with tops

½ cup (4 ounces) duck fat

Kosher salt and ground white pepper

2 tablespoons (1 ounce) unsalted butter

FOR THE PUREE

4 tablespoons (2 ounces) unsalted butter

¾ pound carrots, peeled and sliced thin

½ cup (4 ounces) heavy cream

½ cup (4 ounces) canned coconut milk (with the can's milk and cream mixed together)

1 cup (8 ounces) water

½ teaspoon *piment d'Espelette,* or ground dried mild or medium New Mexican red chile

Kosher salt and ground white pepper

FOR THE TUNA

Olive oil for sautéing

4 (4-ounce) sections of tuna loin, at least 1 inch in thickness

4 tablespoons (2 ounces) unsalted butter

2 tablespoons (1 ounce) fresh lemon juice

Kosher salt and ground white pepper

FOR THE FINISHED DISH

Pok choi leaves, carrot leaves, or small radish leaves, or a combination

TO PREPARE THE ROASTED CARROTS

1. Preheat the oven to 350°F.

2. Scrub the carrots and their tops. Trim the greens to a 3-inch length. Reserve a handful of the best-looking trimmings and discard the rest.

3. Spoon the duck fat into a roasting pan and place on a stovetop burner over high heat. When the fat is melted, add the carrots and cook for 2 minutes, stirring them around in the pan to coat them in the fat.

4. Sprinkle the carrots with salt and pepper and transfer the pan to the oven. Cook for 5 minutes, remove the pan from the oven, add the butter, and mix it around with the carrots.

5. Return the pan to the oven. Continue cooking until the carrots are lightly browned and tender, about 10 more minutes depending on the size of the carrots.

TO PREPARE THE PUREE

1. While the carrots are roasting, prepare the carrot-coconut puree. Warm the butter in a medium saucepan over medium-low heat. Add the carrots and cook for 5 minutes.

2. Add the cream, coconut milk, and water. Cook for about 15 minutes or until very tender.

3. Transfer the mixture to a blender, add the *piment d'Espelette*, and puree. Season with salt and pepper.

TO PREPARE THE TUNA

1. Warm a large heavy skillet over high heat almost to the smoking point. Pour in just enough oil to cover the bottom. Add the tuna and sear well on all sides. You want it to stay rare at the center. It only takes about 20 seconds on each side, so work quickly.

2. Turn off the heat and add the butter and lemon juice to the skillet. As the butter melts, baste the tuna right away with the pan juices for about 20 seconds. Tilt the skillet as needed to have enough buttery pan juices to spoon.

3. Remove the tuna from the skillet and drain on paper towels. Sprinkle with salt and pepper.

4. Pour the pan juices into a small bowl and reserve.

PUTTING IT ALL TOGETHER

Slice each tuna loin into 3 pieces. Make 2 swipes of carrot-coconut puree across 4 plates at different angles. Place the 3 pieces of tuna, a cut side up, on each plate. Arrange the roasted carrots playfully around the tuna. Drizzle a bit of the lemony pan juices over the tuna. Garnish with leaves and serve.

restaurant embellishments

After I've cooked the tuna, turned off the heat, and removed the fish and the pan juices from the skillet, I throw a handful of pok choi stems into the skillet and let them soften for about 2 minutes. I serve them on the plate tossed alongside the roasted carrots and use their lovely dark-green leaves for a garnish. I also add to a restaurant plate a Buttermilk-Miso Puree.

BUTTERMILK-MISO PUREE

1 cup (8 ounces) buttermilk

½ cup (4 ounces) heavy cream

1 tablespoon yellow miso

½ teaspoon agar agar

¼ teaspoon xanthan gum

1 teaspoon grated lemon zest

1. Combine the buttermilk, cream, and miso in a medium saucepan. Bring the mixture to a boil and reduce it by half.

2. Pour the mixture into a blender, add agar agar, xanthan gum, and lemon zest. Blend for 2 minutes.

3. Put the combined mixture into a clean small saucepan, place the pan back on the heat, and bring the temperature up to just below boiling, then cook for 2 minutes.

4. Pour the mixture through a fine-mesh sieve into a bowl, then cool it over an ice bath.

5. Once the mixture has gelled, spoon it back into the blender and puree. In the puree, the agar agar helps set the mixture. The xanthan gum adds body, shine, and a sense of creaminess. The heating, and back and forth to the blender, activate them and combine them fully in the dish. It's a little involved but creates a special look and feel to the puree.

Kitchen Notes

- We cook plenty of ducks to provide us with the bonus of duck fat. However, the silken fat is sold in many supermarkets and gourmet stores today, often in the frozen food section.

- Piment d'Espelette is the only chile with a long history in French cooking. It developed from a chile taken to France from the New World centuries ago. It grows traditionally in the Basque country, near the village of Espelette. Houses in the village have long strings of the dried mild red chile peppers for decoration and for cooking, just like houses here in Santa Fe hang out strings of our local chiles. Look for piment d'Espelette in specialty food stores or order from zingermans.com.

KING SALMON WITH PROSCIUTTO, KOSHIHIKARI RICE, AND LEMON SABAYON

SERVES 4

This dish evolved from the pairing of salmon, especially the lusciously rich king salmon, with crispy pork belly. The flavors are so good together that I began thinking of other ways to team up salmon with something porcine, and settled eventually on prosciutto. I love the way prosciutto wraps around a salmon fillet, lends the salmon a little of its savoriness, and crisps in the skillet. Some sushi rice mixed with toasty sesame adds a nutty tone. I like to use Koshihikari, a top quality sushi rice, which is in many Asian groceries, some supermarkets, and—of course—on amazon.com; other kinds of sushi rice can be used too. A frothy lemon sauce adds a light, bright note of citrus.

FOR THE SALMON

4 (4-ounce) fillets king salmon, or other wild Alaskan salmon

8 thin slices prosciutto (3–4 ounces total)

Kosher salt

FOR THE RICE

1 ½ cups Koshihikari rice or other short-grained sushi rice

1 cup plus 2 tablespoons (9 ounces) water (add 2 more tablespoons of water if cooking at Santa Fe's 7,000-foot altitude)

½ cup (4 ounces) sake, or additional water

¼ cup (2 ounces) rice vinegar

2 tablespoons (1 ounce) mirin

1 quarter-size slice fresh ginger

1 fresh lemongrass stalk, crushed lightly

1 teaspoon kosher salt

2–3 tablespoons Eden brand Shake (a mixture of sesame seeds and nori seaweed), or 1 tablespoon toasted sesame seeds and 2 tablespoons nori, cut in small bits

FOR THE LEMON SABAYON

3 large egg yolks

¼ cup (2 ounces) apple cider

6 tablespoons (3 ounces) unsalted butter, melted

Grated zest and juice of 1 lemon

Kosher salt and ground white pepper

FOR THE SALMON LOGS

¼ cup (2 ounces) olive oil

2 tablespoons (1 ounce) unsalted butter

Large sprigs of fresh thyme and rosemary

FOR THE FINISHED DISH

Tarragon leaves and pea shoots, or radish sprouts, purple or green basil sprigs, pok choi leaves, or some combination of these

Chopped fresh chives

TO START THE SALMON PREPARATION

1. Place a 12-inch square of plastic wrap on a working surface.

2. Lay out 2 slightly overlapping slices of the prosciutto on the plastic. The width of the 2 slices should be nearly the same as your salmon fillet.

3. Place a fillet at one of the narrow ends of the prosciutto, salt it very lightly (since the prosciutto is salty too), and roll the prosciutto up around it snugly.

4. Tightly wrap in the plastic wrap, rolling it back and forth to make a log. Repeat with the same ingredients. Refrigerate the logs about 30 minutes.

TO PREPARE THE RICE

1. Combine the rice, water, sake, rice vinegar, mirin, ginger, lemongrass, and salt together in a medium saucepan. Bring to a boil, then cover and reduce the heat to low and cook for 14–16 minutes, or until no steam is escaping from under the lid.

2. Remove the pan from the heat and let the rice sit covered for another 5–10 minutes. Alternatively, combine the same ingredients in a rice cooker, and cook according to the rice cooker's directions.

3. Lightly mix in the sesame seeds and nori. Cover the pan again to keep the rice warm. Remove the ginger slice and lemongrass before serving.

TO PREPARE THE SABAYON

1. While the rice is cooking, prepare the sabayon. Combine the egg yolks and cider in the top of the double boiler. Place the top over the simmering pan of water and whisk the yolks and cider for 1½ minutes, until just warmed through, frothy, and several shades lighter yellow.

2. Take the top off the heat, and begin to whisk in the melted butter slowly and steadily until the mixture becomes light and fluffy.

3. Pour in the lemon juice slowly, while still whisking, and add the lemon zest, salt, and pepper. Reserve at room temperature.

TO COOK THE SALMON LOGS

1. Warm the olive oil in a medium sauté pan or skillet over medium heat. Sauté the salmon logs on all sides, cooking for 6– 7 minutes total, until the prosciutto is crisp and just a bit of translucence remains at the center of each fillet. (You can make a small cut with a thin knife to check.)

2. Turn off the heat, add the butter, thyme, and rosemary to the pan and, as the butter melts, baste the salmon with the pan juices for 20 seconds. Tilt the pan as needed to have enough buttery pan juices to spoon. Transfer the fish to paper towels and drain.

PUTTING IT ALL TOGETHER

To one side of each of 4 plates, spoon out rice in something of a line. Cut each salmon fillet in half, trimming off the ends too, just a bit, if uneven. Stand the salmon pieces alongside the rice. Spoon a portion of the sabayon around each plate, pooling some of it in the center of each. Serve right away.

restaurant embellishments

When we plate the salmon in the restaurant kitchen, we like to add our version of an Oyster Pan Roast, made in this case with tangy crème fraîche.

OYSTER PAN ROAST

1 tablespoon olive oil

1 garlic clove, thinly sliced

2 medium shallots, thinly sliced

½ cup (4 ounces) dry white wine

8 small to medium Blue Point oysters, their liquid reserved

3 tablespoons crème fraîche

Kosher salt and ground white pepper

½ teaspoon minced tarragon leaves

1. Warm olive oil in a small saucepan over medium heat.

2. Add garlic and shallots, covering the pan to sweat the mixture for 5 minutes until soft.

3. Uncover the pan and add wine. Reduce the mixture by half, then add oysters and their liquid.

4. Cook them about 1 minute, just enough to lightly poach and curl the edges of the oysters.

5. Add crème fraîche, salt, pepper, and tarragon.

6. At the restaurant, we arrange a line of the oyster pan roast on the opposite side of the plate from the rice.

Kitchen Notes

- In the restaurant kitchen, I use the *sous vide* technique to par-cook the salmon. If you are equipped for *sous vide* cooking, place the wrapped logs of salmon in a vacuum bag and seal to medium pressure. Place in a 115°F circulating water bath and cook for 10 minutes. Remove from the bag shortly before time to sear the salmon logs, and pat dry. Sauté them over high heat for just a couple of minutes, just enough to crisp the prosciutto.

- Koshihikari rice is a short-grain variety, but with lower starch and higher natural sugar content than most. Because of the lower starch content, it's not necessary to rinse and soak this rice before cooking it. "Koshi" rice still has enough starch to stick together lightly after cooking, like other sushi rice. Sushi chefs typically mix rice vinegar and sometimes other flavorings into the rice as it cools. Here, we simply mix that and other seasonings into the rice before cooking, so that the flavors are absorbed fully by the rice.

PAN-SEARED ALASKAN HALIBUT WITH HEIRLOOM TOMATO MARMALADE, TEMPURA SHIITAKES, AND SHELLFISH BORDELAISE

SERVES 4

My personal favorite among the fish we serve at the restaurant is halibut. I always look forward to the March opening of the eight-month Alaska halibut season with great anticipation. This is one of my later summer into fall preparations for the firm but flaky white fish. My customers definitely love halibut too. On a recent Saturday night, we had 142 patrons for dinner; 46 of them ordered halibut from our selection of eight entrees. This recipe has more elements than most of my dishes in the book, including some last-minute frying, but I promise you it's a stellar combination.

POSSIBLE DO-AHEAD STEPS

- Make the Light Chicken Stock up to 1 week ahead.
- Make the Shellfish Bordelaise Sauce up to 1 day ahead.
- Make the Heirloom Tomato Marmalade up to 4 hours ahead.

FOR THE BORDELAISE SAUCE

1 medium onion, peeled, halved, and charred over a stove burner

1 celery stalk, chopped roughly

2 garlic cloves, bruised with the side of a chef's knife

1 large sprig of fresh thyme

2 tablespoons black peppercorns

1 tablespoon green peppercorns

2 plum (roma) tomatoes, chopped

1 cup (8 ounces) dry red wine

½ cup (4 ounces) red wine vinegar

2 teaspoons granulated sugar

2 cups (1 pint) shellfish or seafood stock, made with shrimp or lobster shells, or bottled clam juice

FOR THE TOMATO MARMALADE

3 heirloom tomatoes, about 8 ounces each, red and yellow or orange if available

½ cup (4 ounces) orange juice

2 tablespoons (1 ounce) red wine vinegar

1 cup (8 ounces) Light Chicken Stock (see page xxviii)

1 tablespoon packed brown sugar

Pinch ground dried mild or medium New Mexican red or ancho chile powder

1 medium shallot, minced

1 tablespoon minced peeled fresh ginger

2 teaspoons grated lemon zest

FOR THE TEMPURA BATTER

1 cup (8 ounces) seltzer water or club soda

1 large egg yolk

½ cup unbleached all-purpose flour

¼ cup cornstarch

Scant ¾ teaspoon baking powder (use ½ teaspoon at Santa Fe's 7,000-foot altitude)

FOR THE FISH FILLETS

4 (4-ounce) halibut fillets

Kosher salt and ground white pepper

2 tablespoons (1 ounce) olive oil

2 tablespoons (1 ounce) unsalted butter

Large sprig of fresh thyme

FOR THE MUSHROOMS

2 cups (1 pint) canola or vegetable oil

8 medium shiitake mushrooms, stems removed

FOR THE FINISHED DISH

Tiny salad greens, or rainbow or red amaranth leaves

TO PREPARE THE BORDELAISE SAUCE

1. Combine the charred onion, celery, garlic, thyme, black and green peppercorns, and tomatoes. Cook down over medium heat for a few minutes, until the tomatoes release their liquid and the celery and garlic get some amber edges.

2. Add the wine, vinegar, and sugar, raise the heat to medium-high, and reduce until only about ¼ cup of liquid remains, about 5 minutes.

3. Pour in the stock and reduce the liquid by approximately half, to a thin sauce-like consistency, about 5 more minutes.

4. Strain the sauce through a fine-mesh sieve into a bowl. Don't press on the solids. Cool briefly, cover, and refrigerate.

TO PREPARE THE TOMATO MARMALADE

1. Peel the tomatoes by first plunging them into a pan of simmering water for 1 minute. Make a small incision at the base of each tomato with the tip of a small knife to loosen the skin. Pull off the skin in pieces.

2. Quarter the tomatoes and squeeze out the watery seeds. Discard the skins and seeds. Cut the tomatoes into fine dice, transfer them to a saucepan, add the remaining ingredients.

3. Cook the mixture down over medium heat to marmalade consistency, about 20 minutes. Season with salt and pepper and reserve at room temperature.

TO PREPARE THE TEMPURA BATTER

Whisk together in a small bowl the seltzer water and egg yolk. Whisk in the remaining ingredients, stopping as soon as the batter is smooth. It should be thin. Cover and refrigerate.

TO COOK THE FISH

1. Season the halibut fillets with salt and pepper.

2. Warm a 10- or 12-inch skillet to almost smoking.

3. Pour in the olive oil and reduce the heat to medium. Sear the halibut on all sides, and cook just until white and flaky throughout, 6–7 minutes. Remove the skillet from the heat and add the butter and thyme. As the butter melts, baste the fish with the pan juices for 30 seconds. Tilt the pan as needed to have enough buttery pan juices to spoon. Transfer the fillets to paper towels to drain.

TO PREPARE THE SHIITAKE MUSHROOMS

Heat the canola oil in a saucepan to 325°F–330°F. Dip the mushrooms in the chilled tempura batter and fry several minutes, until crispy and lightly colored. Drain over paper towels.

PUTTING IT ALL TOGETHER

1. Reheat the bordelaise sauce.

2. Place a halibut fillet in the middle of each of 4 plates. Add a big spoonful of tomato marmalade to one side. Place a tempura shiitake on top of each fillet and another leaning against it. Spoon the sauce around the fillets. Garnish lightly with the greens and serve.

restaurant embellishments

I like to make a French-style salad of celery-root to accompany this halibut.

CELERY ROOT SALAD

6 ounces peeled celery root

2 tablespoons mayonnaise

1 teaspoon Dijon mustard

½ teaspoon grated lemon zest

1 teaspoon chopped fresh chives

Pinch of kosher salt

1. Bring a medium saucepan of water to a boil over high heat. While it's reaching a boil, cut celery root as needed to fit in a food processor's feed tube, and use the julienne or large grating disk to shred it.

2. Blanch the celery root in the boiling water for 2 minutes, then shock it in ice water.

3. When it's cool, drain the celery root, dry it with paper towels, and transfer it to a bowl.

4. Mix in mayonnaise, mustard, lemon zest, chives, and salt. Chill for at least 30 minutes, then serve spooned beside the halibut.

Kitchen Notes

Because halibut is meaty, I add a couple of elements here that might be seen with meat, mushrooms and a bordelaise sauce. I keep them lighter, though, by adding ethereal crispy tempura batter to the mushrooms and a seafood stock rather than veal demi-glace to the sauce. I also use a smaller quantity of wine than is typical. I always have shells from shrimp and lobster around to make stock, but you can buy and use packaged seafood stock or clam juice for this.

SERVES 4

I developed this when thinking about the number of ways I could use onions to add flavor, color, and texture to a dish while keeping it balanced and harmonious. The result is not at all strong like you might think, and is actually fairly subtle. The halibut fillets are wrapped in scallion tops, and I use a touch of squid ink to darken a leek emulsion. You can get squid ink in many seafood departments, at gourmet groceries, and online from spanishtable.com. However, you can leave out the small amount if you wish.

POSSIBLE DO-AHEAD STEPS

- Make the Pickled Cipollinis up to 4 days ahead.
- Wrap the halibut in scallion tops and refrigerate, char 1 onion and 1 leek for the Charred Leek Emulsion up to 4 hours ahead.

FOR THE CIPOLLINIS

2 cups (1 pint) water

¼ cup (2 ounces) sherry vinegar

3 tablespoons raw turbinado sugar, or packed brown sugar

1 teaspoon white peppercorns

½ teaspoon fennel seeds

½ teaspoon mustard seeds

½ teaspoon coriander seeds

6 juniper berries

1 star anise

Pinch of kosher salt

16 cipollini onions

FOR THE HALIBUT

Green tops from 2 large bunches of scallions or other green onions

4 (4-ounce) halibut fillets

Kosher salt and ground white pepper

FOR THE LEEK EMULSION

1 medium leek, greens trimmed to about 3 inches

½ medium onion

2 large egg yolks

½ teaspoon roasted garlic puree

¼ teaspoon squid ink, optional

½ cup olive oil

Kosher salt and ground white pepper

FOR THE FINISHED DISH

Tiny beet greens, chard or pok choi leaves, mustard leaves, or small salad greens

Borage or chive blossoms, optional

Smoked coarse-ground or flaky sea salt, such as Maldon, optional

TO PREPARE THE CIPOLLINI ONIONS

1. Combine the water, vinegar, sugar, peppercorns, fennel, mustard and coriander seeds, juniper berries, star anise, and salt in a medium saucepan. Bring to a boil over high heat, then simmer for 5 minutes.

2. Add the onions and cook 1 minute. Turn off the heat and let the onions sit until cool. If making them well ahead, spoon into a lidded jar with the pickling liquid and refrigerate them until needed.

TO START THE HALIBUT

1. Prepare an ice bath.

2. Blanch the scallion tops in boiling water for about 30 seconds. Immediately shock them in the ice bath.

3. Cut the tops just over 4 inches long.

4. Lay a 12-inch square of plastic wrap on a work surface.

5. Lay out ¼ of the scallion tops on the plastic wrap slightly overlapping and just longer than a portion of the halibut.

6. Season the fish with salt and pepper.

7. Center a fillet over the scallion tops and roll them together into a tight tube, occasionally poking the plastic wrap with a cake tester or toothpick to let out excess air.

8. Tie off each end of the tube with kitchen string and refrigerate until shortly before cooking. Repeat with more plastic wrap and the remaining halibut and scallion tops.

TO PREPARE THE CHARRED LEEK EMULSION

1. Char the outside of the leek and onion over a stovetop burner on high heat, 8–10 minutes.

2. Place the leek, onion, egg yolks, garlic, and the optional squid ink in a blender. Puree.

3. Once you have a smooth mixture, add the oil in a slow steady stream until the mixture emulsifies.

4. Strain through a fine-mesh sieve into a bowl and season with salt and pepper. Cover and refrigerate.

PUTTING IT ALL TOGETHER

1. Place an Asian bamboo steamer or metal vegetable steamer over simmering water. Place the plastic-wrapped halibut pieces in the steamer. Cook through, about 8 minutes. Remove one halibut fillet and unwrap it to check that it is flaky at the center, using a small knife blade. If not, return to the steamer for an additional 1–2 minutes.

2. Meanwhile, warm the pickled cipollinis and charred leek emulsion. Spread the leek emulsion, with an offset spatula or spoon, across the center of each of 4 plates.

3. When the halibut is ready, use a sharp knife to cut a thin slice off of each end of the plastic-wrapped fish. Unroll each halibut section from the plastic, so that you have 4 very pretty green wrapped white fillets. Place a fillet on the leek emulsion on each plate, then scatter with cipollinis. Garnish with greens and maybe a blossom or 2 or a few grains of smoked sea salt. Serve right away.

restaurant embellishments

We usually add a Roasted Onion-Tomato Bouillon to this dish. Another common accompaniment at the restaurant is Fennel Pudding.

ROASTED ONION-TOMATO BOUILLON

1 medium-size onion

6 cups (1½ quarts) water

6 medium plum (roma) tomatoes

1 sprig of fresh basil

1 sprig of fresh thyme

2 teaspoons granulated sugar

Pinch of kosher salt

1. Place a piece of cheesecloth in a fine-mesh stieve over a bowl.

2. Char the onion over a burner, then chop it. Place the pieces in a saucepan with water, tomatoes, basil and thyme, sugar, and salt.

3. Cook the mixture over medium heat for about 10 minutes, spoon it into the cloth-lined strainer, and let it drain without pressure on the solids for about 30 minutes.

4. Discard the solids and pour the bouillon around the halibut.

FENNEL PUDDING

¼ cup (2 ounces) olive oil

1 medium head of fennel

1 small shallot

1 garlic clove

2 cups (1 pint) whole milk

1 teaspoon iota carrageenan (a tasteless natural substitute for gelatin)

Kosher salt and ground white pepper.

1. Warm oil in a medium saucepan over medium heat.

2. Add fennel, shallot, and garlic and lightly sauté for about 3 minutes.

3. As the ingredients begin releasing their moisture, pour in milk and continue cooking until the vegetables are tender, about 15 minutes.

4. Transfer the warm fennel mixture to a blender and puree.

5. Add iota carrageenan and season the pudding with salt and pepper. Serve spoonfuls beside the halibut.

Kitchen Notes

- In the restaurant kitchen, I use the *sous vide* technique to quickly pickle the cipollini onions. If you are equipped for *sous vide* cooking, place the ingredients in a medium vacuum bag and seal on high pressure. Place in a 181°F circulating water bath and cook for 45 minutes. Reserve the onions in their liquid in the refrigerator until needed.

- Smoked salts are pretty easy to find these days. The Maldon variety is in many supermarkets and other versions are common in spice markets and gourmet stores.

SAUTÉED GROUPER WITH TANDOORI PUMPKIN SEED GRANOLA AND CURRY FLAVORS

SERVES 4

This dish actually started with the granola rather than the grouper. I've always been drawn to dishes that mix nuts, seeds, and dried spices, like my mother's mole back in Mexico. I was thinking more at the time, though, about the tastes connected to countries that surround the Arabian Sea. I tend to stick with classic flavor profiles so, for example, I wouldn't throw something like Jamaican jerk seasoning into a dish like this even though there's a bit of overlap in some of the spices. I wanted a meaty fish to stand up to the spice and texture of the granola, so I chose grouper. The curry flavors are just that, in a brothy sauce.

POSSIBLE DO-AHEAD STEPS

- Make the Light Chicken Stock up to 1 week ahead.
- Make the Tandoori Pumpkin Seed Granola up to 4 days ahead.
- Make the Curry Flavors Broth up to several hours ahead.

FOR THE GRANOLA

½ cup pepitas (shelled pumpkin seeds)

¼ cup plus 2 tablespoons sliced almonds

¼ cup pecan pieces

¼ cup cashew pieces

1 tablespoon old-fashioned rolled oats

4 tablespoons (2 ounces) unsalted butter, melted

2 tablespoons (1 ounce) mild-flavored honey, such as orange blossom

1 teaspoon store-bought tandoori or masala spice blend

1 teaspoon ground dried mild or medium red chile, such as New Mexican or ancho

Kosher salt and ground white pepper

FOR THE BROTH

1 teaspoon canola or vegetable oil

⅔ cup chopped onion

½ cup chopped carrot

¼ cup chopped fennel

2 garlic cloves, chopped

1 tablespoon fresh curry leaves or 2 teaspoons grated lime zest

¾ teaspoon fenugreek seeds

¾ teaspoon whole cumin seeds, toasted in a dry skillet and ground

¾ teaspoon dry mustard powder

4 whole cloves

Pinch of fresh-ground nutmeg

4 cups (1 quart) Light Chicken Stock (see page xxviii)

½ teaspoon minced fresh chives

FOR THE GROUPER

4 (4-ounce) grouper fillets, about ¾ inch thick, or another mild but meaty white fish such as mahi-mahi

Kosher salt and ground white pepper

2 tablespoons (1 ounce) canola or vegetable oil

4 tablespoons (2 ounces) unsalted butter

FOR THE FINISHED DISH

Small mint leaves, amaranth leaves, or radish sprouts, or small salad greens

TO PREPARE THE GRANOLA

1. Preheat the oven to 325°F.

2. Line a baking sheet with a non-stick mat or lightly oiled parchment paper.

3. Combine all the ingredients in a medium bowl and mix well. Spoon the mixture out onto the baking sheet. Bake for about 20 minutes, stirring twice to toast evenly. Set aside to cool.

TO PREPARE THE CURRY FLAVORS BROTH

1. Warm the oil in a medium saucepan over medium heat. Stir in the onion, carrot, and fennel. Let the vegetables soften and release some of their water, about 3 minutes.

2. Add the garlic, curry leaves, fenugreek, cumin, mustard, cloves, and nutmeg, and cook several minutes more until the mixture has browned.

3. Pour in the stock and continue to cook as needed to reduce by three-quarters, about 10 minutes.

4. Strain the liquid through a fine-mesh sieve into a small saucepan, stir in the chives, and keep warm on low heat.

TO COOK THE GROUPER

1. Season the grouper fillets with salt and pepper.

2. Warm a large skillet over high heat. When very hot, pour in the oil, and swirl to coat the skillet. Add the fillets to the pan and cook them until golden brown, about 3 minutes per side, until just beginning to flake.

3. Turn the heat off and add the butter to the skillet. As the butter melts, baste the fillets for 30 seconds with the pan juices, tilting the skillet as needed to spoon up the buttery pan juices. Let the fillets rest in the pan for 30 seconds more. Transfer the fillets to paper towels to drain.

PUTTING IT ALL TOGETHER

If you have 4 large shallow bowls, use them to plate the dish. Arrange a grouper fillet in the center of each bowl. Spoon 2–3 heaping tablespoons of the granola over each piece of fish. Some of it will fall to the side. Spoon the curry flavors broth over and around each bowl. Garnish each with leaves or greens as you wish. Serve immediately.

PAN-SEARED WHITE SEA BASS WITH CRAB AND LEMON BALM COURT BOUILLON AND DAIKON RADISH, OKRA, AND CAULIFLOWER

SERVES 4

When I was nine years old, we lived for about half a year in the Mexican state of Baja California. My father found some autobody work near Ensenada. My brother Danny and I weren't in school, so we just up and moved there with Dad and Mom. We found an adequate place to live, with the bonus that it was very close to the rocky coast. Danny and I would play along the water and learned to scavenge the various sea creatures of the area. We'd get lots of mussels and even a few abalone off the rocks, and dig for clams when we could see their air holes in the sand as the tide went out. Catching octopus, though, was the biggest thrill for us. I really don't remember them seeming especially scary, which amazes my daughters now. We'd wait until about sunset and find them near the rocks. When we had a bunch of seafood, we'd take it home to Mom and she'd cook a big seafood cazuela. Other times Dad might buy a piece of fish that we'd cook on a rudimentary grill over wood we collected. We didn't have a lot, but we nearly always ate well. What we didn't have was anything quite like this, which is one part France, one part New Orleans, and one part me.

POSSIBLE DO-AHEAD STEPS
- Make the Crab and Lemon Balm Court Bouillon up to 1 day ahead.

FOR THE BOUILLON

2 tablespoons (1 ounce) olive oil

1 small onion, chopped

2 celery stalks, chopped

2 carrots, chopped

2 tablespoons chopped fresh ginger

1 pound cracked crab shells, or shrimp shells

2 tablespoons tomato paste

2 plum (roma) tomatoes, chopped

1 large bunch lemon balm

1 cup (8 ounces) sake

4 cups (1 quart) water

Kosher salt and ground white pepper

FOR THE DAIKON RADISH, OKRA, AND CAULIFLOWER

1 medium daikon radish, cut into 8 lengthwise ¼-inch-thick slices on a mandoline

8 ounces large cauliflower florets, sliced about ⅓ inch thick, so they look like flat trees

4 medium to large okra pods

2 tablespoons (1 ounce) extra-virgin olive oil

2 tablespoons olive oil

1 teaspoon minced fresh chives

½ teaspoon grated lemon zest

1 tablespoon unsalted butter

Kosher salt and ground white pepper

FOR THE SEA BASS

4 (4-ounce) skin-on white California sea bass fillets, or other skin-on white fish fillets

Kosher salt and ground white pepper

2 tablespoons (1 ounce) olive oil

2 tablespoons (1 ounce) unsalted butter

1 large sprig of fresh thyme

FOR THE FINISHED DISH

Small nasturtium leaves, amaranth leaves, or small salad greens

Smoked coarse-ground or flaky sea salt, optional

TO PREPARE THE COURT BOUILLON

1. Warm the oil in a medium stockpot over medium-high heat. Add the onion, celery, carrots, ginger, and crab shells. Allow the ingredients to cook to a golden brown, to deepen their flavor, stirring occasionally.

2. Add the tomato paste, tomatoes, and lemon balm. Continue cooking for another 5 minutes, until the mixture starts getting rather sticky.

3. Pour in the sake and reduce the mixture by half, about 3 more minutes.

4. Pour in the water, reduce the heat to a simmer, and reduce the liquid to about 2 cups, another 10 or so minutes.

5. Line a fine-mesh sieve with a piece of cheesecloth and place it over a bowl. Strain the court bouillon through the sieve. Season with salt and pepper, cover, and refrigerate until needed.

TO PREPARE THE DAIKON RADISH, OKRA, AND CAULIFLOWER

1. Prepare an ice bath.

2. Bring a large saucepan of water to a boil. Blanch the radish slices for about 30 seconds, remove them with a spider, and then shock them in the ice water.

3. Blanch the cauliflower slices for 1 minute, remove them with a spider, and then add them to the ice water.

4. Blanch the okra pods for 1 minute, remove them with a spider, and then add them to the ice water.

5. When the vegetables are cool, drain them.

6. Place the daikon in a small bowl. To it, add 2 tablespoons extra-virgin olive oil, chives, and lemon zest, and season with salt and pepper.

7. Slice the okra pods lengthwise. Warm the other 2 tablespoons olive oil in a sauté pan over medium heat.

8. Place the okra pods in the skillet, cut side down. Cook until the okra has developed some color, then remove with tongs and drain on paper towels.

9. Add the cauliflower to the same sauté pan, in batches if needed. Get some golden brown spots on the cauliflower.

10. Remove from the heat, and add the butter to the pan. As the butter melts, baste the cauliflower with the pan juices for 10 seconds. Tilt the pan a bit to be able to spoon up the buttery pan juices. Season with salt and pepper, and drain on paper towels.

TO COOK THE SEA BASS

1. On each sea bass fillet, cut 3 parallel slashes into the skin so the fillets don't curl while cooking. Sprinkle with salt and pepper,

2. Warm a 10- or 12-inch skillet over high heat.

3. Pour in the oil. Add the fillets, skin-side up first, and sear them for about 3 minutes on each side. The flesh side should be golden and the skin side brown and crisp.

4. Turn off the heat and add the butter and thyme to the skillet. As the butter melts, use a spoon to baste the fillets for 20 seconds with the pan juices. Tilt the skillet a bit to be able to spoon the buttery pan juices. Transfer the bass to paper towels to drain.

PUTTING IT ALL TOGETHER

1. If you have 4 large shallow bowls, use them here to plate the dish. Rimmed plates are certainly fine though.

2. Reheat the court bouillon.

3. Lay 2 slices of radish crossways on a bowl. Place a sea bass fillet on the daikon. Curl the daikon up and over the fish on at least one side. Arrange okra and cauliflower trees around each fish fillet. Curl some of the daikon up around either a piece of okra or cauliflower. Pour the court bouillon around each fillet. Garnish with leaves and, if you wish, with smoked salt, and serve.

Kitchen Notes

- Generally a court bouillion (pronounced "coo boo yon") is a liquid used to poach fish, mildly seasoned in French classic style on its home turf and jazzed up in a more lively fashion in New Orleans, where it found a home too. I really just use it as a sauce here. Sea bass doesn't have too much natural oil in it, so having a brothy sauce makes it feel more moist in your mouth.

- The restaurant always has loads of shellfish shells to use in making this sauce. Ask your seafood counter for the crab or shrimp shells needed. They might have lobster shells that would work too.

- I love the peppery, minty, and even basil-y notes of lemon balm and lemon verbena. I use them much more than lemongrass, for example, because their complexity is more appealing to me.

WILD STRIPED BASS FILLETS WITH YUZU TAPIOCA PEARLS AND EDAMAME PUREE

SERVES 4

I like light Asian flavors with robust wild striped bass. Wild-caught stripers are actually a somewhat different fish than their farm-raised cousins, which are a milder-tasting hybrid of white bass and striped bass. Either can work in this dish, depending on what's available and freshest at your favorite fish counter. The yuzu tapioca pudding is savory rather than sweet. It surprises our guests initially, but then they love it.

POSSIBLE DO-AHEAD STEPS

- Make the Light Chicken Stock up to 1 week ahead.
- Make the Edamame Puree and the Savory Yuzu Tapioca Pudding up to 1 day ahead.

FOR THE PUDDING

½ cup (4 ounces) small pearl tapioca, soaked in water for 30 minutes, then drained

1 ¾ cups (14 ounces) whole milk

1 (14-ounce) can unsweetened coconut milk

1 cup (8 ounces) Light Chicken Stock (see page xxviii)

Pinch of kosher salt

2 large egg yolks

½ teaspoon yuzu juice or more to taste

1 tablespoon grated lime zest

Big pinch of curry powder

Kosher salt and ground white pepper

FOR THE PUREE

1 cup shelled edamame (soy beans)

¼ cup fresh Italian parsley

¼ teaspoon roasted garlic puree

½ cup (4 ounces) ice water

1 tablespoon olive oil

Kosher salt and ground white pepper

FOR THE BASS

4 (4-ounce) skin-on wild striped bass fillets, preferably, or farmed striped bass fillets

Kosher salt and ground white pepper

2 tablespoons (1 ounce) olive oil

2 tablespoons (1 ounce) unsalted butter

Small sprig of fresh thyme

Small sprig of fresh tarragon or another small sprig of fresh thyme

FOR THE FINISHED DISH

Grated lime zest

Tarragon sprigs, radish sprouts, or small salad greens

TO PREPARE THE PUDDING

1. Combine the tapioca, milk, coconut milk, chicken stock, and pinch of salt in a heavy large saucepan.

2. Bring the mixture to a simmer over medium heat and cook, stirring occasionally, until the tapioca is translucent and tender, about 20 minutes. Don't let the mixture boil.

3. Meanwhile whisk together the egg yolks in a small bowl. When the tapioca is tender, spoon out about ¼ cup of the warm mixture and whisk it into the egg yolks in a steady stream. Whisk the egg yolk mixture back into the saucepan. Continue to cook the pudding over medium heat, stirring frequently, until it has thickened and coats the back of a spoon or rubber spatula, about 5 minutes.

4. Whisk in yuzu juice, lime zest, and curry powder. Remove from the heat and season with salt and pepper. Taste and add a bit more yuzu juice if the pudding doesn't yet have a mild citrus flavor. Some versions are more concentrated or stronger tasting than others. Keep warm on low heat. (If you made the pudding a day ahead, reheat it very slowly before serving.)

TO PREPARE THE EDAMAME PUREE

1. Make an ice bath.

2. Bring a large saucepan of water to a boil. Blanch the edamame for about 30 seconds, remove them with a spider, and then shock them in the ice bath.

3. Blanch the parsley in the water for 10 seconds, remove it with a spider, and then add it to the ice water.

4. Drain the edamame and parsley and place them in a blender with the garlic, ice water, and oil. Puree. Season with salt and pepper. Reserve at room temperature.

TO COOK THE BASS

1. On each striped bass fillet, cut 3 parallel slashes into the skin so that the fillets don't curl while cooking. Season the fillets with salt and pepper. Warm a 10- or 12-inch skillet over high heat. Pour in the oil. Add the fillets, skin-side up first, and sear them about 3 minutes on each side until well browned.

2. Turn the heat off and add the butter, thyme, and tarragon to the skillet. As the butter melts, use a spoon to baste the fillets for 20 seconds with the pan juices. Tilt the skillet a bit to be able to spoon the buttery pan juices. Transfer the fillets to paper towels to drain.

PUTTING IT ALL TOGETHER

Spoon warm tapioca pudding on the center of each of 4 plates. Place a piece of bass over the pudding. Spoon on splashes of edamame puree. Scatter a bit of lime zest over each plate and tuck in a few herbs. Serve right away.

restaurant embellishments

I think that a contrasting crunchy taste makes a nice foil here, and came up with Kohlrabi and Daikon Radish Rounds as an accompaniment. We slice the two vegetables on a mandoline into ⅛-inch-thick rounds. Fellow cooks in the restaurant kitchen call me crazy, but I use a small biscuit cutter to make all the rounds the same size. In 2 tablespoons (1 ounce) of olive oil, we sauté the rounds for about 2 minutes or until heated through, drain them on paper towels, and serve alongside the fish.

SOFT-SHELL CRABS WITH PRETZEL CRUST, AVOCADO PUREE, AND SMOKY TAMARIND SAUCE

SERVES 4

Yes, we celebrate soft-shell crab season here in the Rockies. I get them shipped in fresh from the East Coast each weekend of their summer season, and we prepare them in a different style every week. Some folks come back each Saturday or Sunday to see what we've dreamed up. This is one of the most popular and recent versions. It was inspired by the California roll, the sushi with crab and avocado. The pretzels make an especially crunchy crust.

POSSIBLE DO-AHEAD STEPS

- Make the Smoky Tamarind Sauce up to 1 day ahead.
- Dredge the crabs in the pretzel crumb mixture and keep them in the refrigerator up to 1 hour ahead.

FOR THE SAUCE

2 tablespoons (1 ounce) olive oil

½ cup tamarind paste

¼ cup (2 ounces) honey

2 bacon slices, preferably applewood-smoked, chopped

2 plum (roma) tomatoes, quartered

1 tablespoon coriander seeds

1 teaspoon minced fresh ginger

1 cup (8 ounces) water

Kosher salt and ground white pepper

FOR THE PUREE

1 large ripe avocado

1 tablespoon minced peeled fresh ginger

1 teaspoon minced fresh or pickled jalapeño

¼ cup chopped cilantro leaves

Juice of 1 medium lime

2 teaspoons olive oil

½ cup (4 ounces) ice water

Pinch of xanthan gum (see Kitchen Notes page 215)

Kosher salt and ground white pepper

FOR THE CRABS

2 large eggs

2 tablespoons (1 ounce) Dijon mustard

2 tablespoons (1 ounce) water

4 cups salted pretzel crumbs (ground in a food processor)

4 large soft-shell crabs

Olive oil for pan frying

FOR THE FINISHED DISH

Fresh mint leaves, small frisée leaves, or other small salad greens

TO PREPARE THE TAMARIND SAUCE

1. Warm the oil in a medium saucepan over medium-high heat. Add the tamarind paste, honey, bacon, tomatoes, coriander, and ginger, and cook until thick and caramelized, 10–15 minutes, stirring up from the bottom frequently.

2. Pour in the water and simmer for 10 minutes.

3. Strain the mixture through a fine-mesh sieve into a bowl and discard the solids. Return the sauce to the pan. Continue simmering the sauce to a maple syrup consistency, probably another 5–10 minutes. Season with salt and pepper.

TO PREPARE THE AVOCADO PUREE

Combine the ingredients in a blender and puree. Scrape the puree out into a bowl, cover, and refrigerate until needed.

TO PREPARE THE SOFT-SHELL CRABS

1. Whisk the eggs, mustard, and water together in a broad shallow bowl.

2. Place the pretzel crumbs in another broad shallow bowl or on a plate.

3. Dip the crabs first in the egg mixture and soak them for about 1 minute. Then dip each crab into the pretzel crumbs and press to coat them well.

4. Pour a good 1½ inches of oil into a large heavy skillet to fry the crabs, in batches, if necessary. Heat the oil to 325°F–335°F.

5. Fry the crabs to golden brown and crunchy, about 2 minutes per side. The crabs contain a good bit of moisture, so watch out for popping oil. Drain the crabs on paper towels. Slice each crab in half, down through the center of the body.

PUTTING IT ALL TOGETHER

Spread a mound of avocado puree in the center of each of 4 plates. Arrange 2 crab halves standing on their cut sides, so that the legs are squiggling upward. Drizzle generously with the tamarind sauce, garnish with herbs or greens, and serve immediately.

restaurant embellishments

If you happen to be, like me, a big fan of dim sum Shrimp Dumplings, you should consider making these as an accompaniment, as we do in the restaurant. They require some effort, but you will want to reward me with a kiss.

SHRIMP DUMPLINGS

4 large shrimp, shelled and deveined

1 tablespoon Dijon mustard

½ teaspoon sriracha, sambal oelek, or other Asian red chile sauce

2 tablespoons (1 ounce) ice water

1 tablespoon heavy cream

1 teaspoon chopped fresh mint

Kosher aalt and ground white pepper

About ½ cup cooked sushi rice at room temperature

1. Prepare the filling first. Turn on your food processor and drop the shrimp, mustard, chile sauce, ice water, and heavy cream into it. Process briefly to a coarse consistency.

2. Scrape into a small bowl, and fold in mint. Season with salt and pepper.

3. Lay a 6-inch piece of plastic wrap on a work surface. Place 2 generous tablespoons of sushi rice in the center of the plastic and, with wet fingers, press it into about a 2-inch square. Patch any holes with a bit more rice.

4. Place a mound of the shrimp mixture in the center of the rice and, using the plastic for support, fold the rice up around the shrimp filling. Push in the corners to form a golf-ball-size dumpling with the filling enclosed.

5. Wrap snugly in the plastic. Repeat to make 4 plump dumplings.

6. Refrigerate for at least 30 minutes.

7. When the plastic-wrapped dumplings are chilled, place them in a bamboo steamer or vegetable steamer and steam over simmering water for 5 minutes.

8. Turn off the heat and let them rest for a couple of minutes. Unwrap from the plastic and serve 1 each alongside the crab.

Kitchen Notes

- Tamarind paste is a luscious cooked down, and very sticky, version of the tamarind fruit. It's used in Asian dishes, perhaps most famously pad thai, and in Mexican cooking. Look for it in a Southeast Asian, Indian, or Mexican market. Avoid suggested online substitutes like lime juice mixed with brown sugar. Look for the real thing.

- The xanthan gum helps the creamy avocado puree bind together. If you don't have it, though, you can leave it out.

MAINE SEA SCALLOPS WITH BUTTERY POTATOES AND KING TRUMPET MUSHROOMS

SERVES 4

La Ratte potatoes are an extra-buttery, somewhat waxy fingerling potato that French chefs love. I first worked with this potato in the kitchen at Georges Blanc, but it was Chef Joel Robuchon who really made it famous worldwide when he said it was the secret behind his ethereal potato purees. I love it with silky sea scallops and elegant large mushrooms like king trumpets. Look for La Ratte potatoes at a farmers' market. You can use Yukon golds, though, if no one in your area is growing La Rattes. I get king trumpet mushrooms from my neighborhood Asian market, Ta Lin, but portobellos will work too.

POSSIBLE DO-AHEAD STEPS

- Make the Vegetable or Light Chicken Stock up to 1 week ahead.
- Make the brown butter to use in the Buttery Potatoes up to 4 days ahead.

FOR THE MUSHROOMS

1 tablespoon olive oil

4 king trumpet mushrooms, halved or quartered lengthwise, depending on size

2 medium shallots, thinly sliced

2 tablespoons (1 ounce) unsalted butter

2 large sprigs of fresh thyme

Kosher salt and ground white pepper

FOR THE POTATOES

1 stick (4 ounces) unsalted butter

2 small shallots, chopped

1 pound La Ratte potatoes, or Yukon Gold potatoes, peeled, and cut in 1-inch chunks

¼ cup plus 2 tablespoons (3 ounces) whole milk

¼ cup plus 2 tablespoons (3 ounces) Vegetable Stock (see page xxvii) or Light Chicken Stock (see page xxviii)

Kosher salt and ground white pepper

FOR THE SCALLOPS

12 medium sea scallops

Kosher salt and ground white pepper

¼ cup (2 ounces) olive oil

1 tablespoon unsalted butter

Large sprig of fresh thyme

FOR THE FINISHED DISH

Small watercress, basil, or amaranth leaves, or tiny sprouts

TO PREPARE THE MUSHROOMS

1. In a medium sauté pan or skillet, warm the oil over medium heat.

2. Add the mushrooms and sauté until golden brown and tender.

3. Stir in the shallots and cook an additional minute.

4. Turn off the heat, and add the butter and thyme. As the butter melts, baste the mushrooms for 15 seconds. Tilt the pan as needed to spoon up the buttery pan juices. Transfer the mushrooms to paper towels to drain. Season lightly with salt and pepper. Reserve at room temperature.

TO PREPARE THE POTATOES

1. Brown the butter to start. Cook the butter over medium heat in a small pan (preferably with a light-colored bottom so that you can easily see the butter change color). When the butter foams, swirl it around in the pan a few times, and watch it carefully as it turns from golden to nutty brown. The butter's aroma will become nutty too.

2. Pour the butter into a medium saucepan and let it cool briefly before turning the heat to medium.

3. Add the shallots and sauté for 3 minutes, just enough to soften them. Stir in the potatoes, milk, and stock.

4. Lower the heat and cook at just below a simmer for 5–10 minutes, until the potato chunks are tender.

5. Transfer the mixture to a blender and puree.

6. Strain through a fine-mesh sieve into a bowl. Season with salt and pepper. Reserve at room temperature.

TO COOK THE SCALLOPS

1. Season the scallops with salt and pepper on both sides.

2. Warm a 10- or 12-inch skillet over high heat until very hot. Add the oil to the skillet and reduce the heat to medium.

3. Place the scallops in the skillet and cook about 2 minutes per side, until brown on the surface and just translucent throughout.

4. Turn off the heat and add the butter and thyme to the skillet. As the butter melts, baste the scallops for 20 seconds with the buttery pan juices. Remove the scallops from the skillet immediately, so as not to overcook them, and drain them on paper towels.

PUTTING IT ALL TOGETHER

If you have 4 deep plates or large shallow bowls, use them here. Any plates will work though. Spoon potatoes in the center of the serving dishes. Arrange 3 scallops over each portion of potatoes. Place mushroom halves over or alongside the scallops. Garnish with leaves or sprouts and serve right away.

restaurant embellishments

- I add an element to this in the restaurant that I call a Turnip Veil. I use the mandoline to cut 8 paper-thin slices from a large turnip. I cook the slices in simmering water just until they become tender, then drain and toss them with about 1 tablespoon of extra-virgin olive oil, enough to coat the turnips, then sprinkle them with kosher salt and ground white pepper. Two go partially over the scallops on each plate. It's a little culinary fun and adds a bit of pepperiness to the dish.

- I also plate the dish with long, thin slices of an English cucumber, a more substantial accompaniment since they bring a refreshing contrast to the richer flavors. For 4 servings, I slice a single English cucumber lengthwise and let the pieces bathe at room temperature in a shallow bowl with 2 tablespoons (1 ounce) of extra-virgin olive oil, ¼ teaspoon of grated lime zest, and kosher salt and ground white pepper. When serving, I roll up the slices loosely and tuck them between the scallops and mushrooms.

Kitchen Notes

In the restaurant, we use an iSi cream whipper (with one N_2O cartridge) to froth the potatoes as we plate them. It makes a fluffy almost whipped-cream-like cloud of potatoes. If you want to experiment with one of these, home versions are sold at Williams-Sonoma and other high-end kitchen shops. You can make mousses, frostings, and all kinds of froths and foams with the whipper and its accompanying gas cartridges. It can keep ingredients at hot or cold temperatures for long periods.

MAINE LOBSTER TAILS POACHED IN CULTURED BUTTER WITH PIQUILLO PEPPER PUREE AND ARUGULA COULIS

SERVES 4

This is a visual knockout, the crimson-tinged lobster meat sitting over a stop sign–red pepper puree and bright green arugula sauce. We start with whole lobsters, using the tails for this and other portions of them in stock and salads, but you can just buy tails to start. Do look for real Maine lobster tails, not the much less desirable rock lobster tails that are really from oversize crawfish. Cultured butter has a little extra tang to it, from lactic acid cultures that make crème fraîche. I swear by the version from Vermont Creamery, available at Whole Foods, Wegman's, and many other supermarkets, but you can use any kind of butter you wish.

POSSIBLE DO-AHEAD STEPS

- Make the Light Chicken Stock up to 1 week ahead.
- Make the Piquillo Pepper Puree up to 1 day ahead.

FOR THE PUREE

2 tablespoons (1 ounce) olive oil

1 large shallot

2 small garlic cloves

6 ounces Spanish piquillo peppers (half of a 12-ounce jar)

½ cup (4 ounces) orange juice

1 teaspoon tomato paste

⅛ teaspoon smoked Spanish paprika

⅓ cup (approximately 2½ ounces) Light Chicken Stock (see page xxviii)

½ teaspoon grated lemon zest

Kosher salt and ground white pepper

FOR THE ARUGULA COULIS

2 packed cups arugula

1 bunch fresh Italian parsley

1 garlic clove

1 teaspoon minced peeled fresh ginger

1 cup (8 ounces) ice water

¼ cup (2 ounces) olive oil

Kosher salt and ground white pepper

FOR THE LOBSTER TAILS

Two 8-ounce Maine lobster tails

1–2 pounds unsalted cultured butter or other unsalted butter

Small (187.5 milliliter) split of "demi-sec" champagne, Prosecco, cava, or other sparkling wine

Large sprig of fresh thyme

Kosher salt and ground white pepper

FOR THE FINISHED DISH

Pea shoots or small arugula leaves

TO PREPARE THE PIQUILLO PEPPER PUREE

1. Warm the oil in a small saucepan over medium heat. Add the shallots and garlic, and cook until tender, about 5 minutes.

2. Add the peppers (no need to chop them), orange juice, tomato paste, paprika, and stock, and reduce until just a bit of liquid remains, about 10 minutes.

3. Transfer to a blender and puree. Mix in the lemon zest and season with salt and pepper. Spoon into a bowl, cover, and refrigerate until needed.

TO PREPARE THE ARUGULA COULIS

1. Make an ice bath.

2. Bring a medium saucepan of water to a boil. Blanch the arugula for about 20 seconds, remove it with a spider, and then shock it in ice water.

3. Blanch the parsley for 10 seconds, remove it with a spider, and add it to the ice water.

4. When cool, drain and squeeze out extra liquid with your hands. Place arugula and parsley in a blender with the garlic, ginger, and ice water, and puree.

5. Stir in the oil, season well with salt and pepper, and reserve at room temperature.

TO PREPARE THE LOBSTER TAILS

1. Pry the lobster meat carefully from the shells. The shells can be saved for stock or discarded. Cut each tail in half lengthwise.

2. Reheat the piquillo pepper puree.

3. Select a pan in which the 4 lobster tail sections can be poached side-by-side. You can save on the amount of butter used if you have a fairly close fit. Warm 1 pound of butter and the champagne together over low heat. When the butter is melted, add the lobster tail sections, the thyme, and a big pinch each of salt and pepper. If the lobster is not fully covered, you will need to add more butter until the tails disappear in the butter sea.

4. Raise the temperature to just under a simmer, about 190°F–195°F. Poach the lobster until tender, opaque, and just cooked through, 10–12 minutes. Transfer it to paper towels to drain. Slice each lobster tail section crosswise into 2 pieces.

PUTTING IT ALL TOGETHER

Spread a portion of the pepper puree across each of 4 plates. Spoon arugula coulis across the other side of the plate. Arrange 2 pieces of lobster on each plate where the red and green meet in the center. Garnish with shoots or leaves and serve.

restaurant embellishments

- I have another element I like to add to these plates at the restaurant, some Charred Spring Onion "Petals." I first blanch 4 large spring onions, sometimes referred to as baby bulb onions, the kind popular on Mexican grill dishes. Once soft, I shock them in ice water. When cold, I cut the onion in half through its stem and root ends and peel apart the layers or petals. Just before serving, I heat them in a dry skillet over high heat to char them slightly, add just a dribble or 2 of olive oil and a little salt and pepper, and arrange them on the plates.

- I also frequently add Chickpea Crackers for a texture contrast. Here's my recipe if you'd like to do the same.

CHICKPEA CRACKERS

¾ cup (4 ounces) cooked garbanzo beans
¼ cup (2 ounces) water
2 teaspoons tahini paste
1 teaspoon fresh lemon juice
½ teaspoon tapioca powder
Pinch of xanthan gum

1. Preheat the oven to 225°F. Line a baking sheet with a non-stick mat and spray it with vegetable oil.

2. In a food processor, puree garbanzo beans, water, tahini paste, and lemon juice.

3. Transfer this mixture to a small saucepan and heat slowly until the mixture boils.

4. Stir in tapioca powder and a pinch of xanthan gum, and remove the pan from the heat.

5. Spread the mixture on the prepared baking sheet, preferably using an offset handled spatula, like one you might use for frosting cakes.

6. Bake it for 35–40 minutes, or until it is dry and crackly, and breaks easily along the fissures that develop during baking. I serve several of the crackers on each plate, often leaning against the lobster.

Kitchen Notes

The butter and champagne mixture can be reused, if you happen to want to make more of this in the next few nights. Otherwise you can refrigerate the mixture, and when the butter separates from the liquid, you can pour away the champagne. That will leave you with butter that you can use for other seafood dishes. It can be frozen for up to several weeks if you wish.

beef, pork, lamb, and venison

SPICE-RUBBED BEEF SHORT RIBS WITH BLACK PLUMS, GLAZED PORCINIS, AND POTATOES

SERVES 4

I love braised dishes, coaxing deep savor out of tough cuts of meat like short ribs. As with any braise or stew, this can be an extra flavorful dish made a day ahead of when you want to serve it. Chef Gray Kunz, who was an influential force in modern French cooking in New York in the 1990s, inspired this preparation with beer and spice and everything nice. While chef at L'Espinasse, Chef Gray came to demonstrate his cooking techniques to my class at the CIA. To this day I remember the fish and beef short rib preparations, so bold and complex, layered with South American and Caribbean flavors, but still grounded in solid French technique.

POSSIBLE DO-AHEAD STEPS

- Make the Light Chicken Stock and Veal Demi-Glace up to 1 week ahead.
- Make the Dry Spice Rub, apply it to the short ribs, and bake the meat up to 2 days ahead.

FOR THE DRY SPICE RUB AND BRAISING LIQUID

2 medium dried ancho chiles or 1 tablespoon dried ancho chile powder

1 tablespoon black peppercorns

2 teaspoons coriander seeds

1 teaspoon allspice berries

1 teaspoon cumin seeds

3 whole star anise

1 tablespoon packed brown sugar

1 teaspoon ground cinnamon

2 teaspoons kosher salt

2 (1¼ or 1½-pound) or 4 (7- or 8-ounce) boneless beef short ribs

2 tablespoons (1 ounce) olive oil

1 celery stalk, chopped

½ small onion, sliced

2 ounces fresh ginger, sliced thin

3 garlic cloves

3 ounces tamarind paste

2 plum (roma) tomatoes, chopped

1 cup (8 ounces) dry red wine

2 teaspoons soy sauce

12-ounce bottle or can dark beer, such as Santa Fe Brewing Company Nut Brown Ale

4 cups (1 quart) Light Chicken Stock (see page xxviii)

1 cup (8 ounces) Veal Demi-Glace (see page xxviii)

FOR THE PORCINIS AND POTATOES

4 medium size russet potatoes

¼ cup (2 ounces) olive oil

8 ounces porcini mushrooms, or other wild mushrooms, sliced or cut in equal-size chunks

12 cipollini onions, blanched and peeled

1 teaspoon chopped fresh tarragon

Kosher salt and ground white pepper

FOR THE PLUMS

1 teaspoon olive oil

1 teaspoon unsalted butter

2 large black plums, or other plums, halved

Kosher salt and ground white pepper

FOR THE FINISHED DISH

2 teaspoons fresh grated horseradish or more to taste

Tarragon leaves, small arugula leaves, or tiny salad greens

TO PREPARE THE SPICE RUB AND RIBS

1. Combine the chiles, peppercorns, coriander, allspice, cumin, and star anise in a small sauté pan. Warm over medium heat until lightly toasted and fragrant.

2. Transfer to a spice grinder or clean coffee grinder and process to a coarse texture. Mix in the brown sugar, cinnamon, and salt.

3. Rub the short ribs with the spice mixture and place the meat in a large zipper-lock bag or in a shallow dish covered with plastic wrap. Refrigerate at least 1 hour and up to 8 hours.

4. Warm a heavy medium-size roasting pan on the stovetop over high heat. When the pan is very hot, add the oil and quickly swirl it around.

5. Add the short ribs and sear until richly brown on all sides, 5–6 minutes. With tongs, remove the beef and place it on a plate.

6. Add the celery, onion, ginger, and garlic to the pan. Lower the heat to medium and cook for 5 minutes, then add the tamarind and tomatoes, and sear until the ingredients are deeply browned, almost black.

7. Pour in the wine, soy sauce, and beer. Scrape up the mixture from the bottom, and reduce the liquid by half.

8. Return the short ribs to the pan, add the stock and demi-glace, cover the pan and bake until the meat is quite tender but short of falling apart, 2 ½–3 hours.

9. Remove the short ribs from the pan and wrap in foil to keep them warm if you will be serving them within 1 hour. If you have cooked them ahead, let them cool a little and then refrigerate.

10. Degrease the braising liquid and keep it warm over low heat.

TO PREPARE THE PORCINIS AND POTATOES

1. Pare off about half of the potato peels, leaving them striped, more or less, from top to bottom. Cut the potatoes in 1-inch cylinders or, more simply, into 1-inch cubes.

2. Warm the oil in a medium saucepan over medium-high heat. Add the potatoes and brown them on all sides over several minutes.

3. Stir in the mushrooms and onions, and sear them all around briefly.

4. Add 1 inch of the braising liquid to the pan (reserving the rest), adjust the heat to medium-low, and cook until the vegetables are tender. Stir and scrape the vegetables up a few times to cook them evenly. If liquid still remains, turn the heat up to high to evaporate it and glaze the vegetables. (If the vegetables aren't yet tender when the mixture is drying out, just add a little water.)

5. Stir in the tarragon. Taste and add salt and pepper as needed.

TO PREPARE THE PLUMS

1. Warm the oil and butter in a small skillet over medium heat.

2. Add the plums, cut-side down. Sauté on that one side until softened with a few caramelized spots, a couple of minutes. Season with salt and pepper.

PUTTING IT ALL TOGETHER

If needed, reheat the short ribs and remaining braising liquid. Divide the ribs equally among 4 plates. Drizzle each with a few tablespoons of the braising liquid. Spoon vegetables around the meat, getting a few potatoes, porcinis, and onions on each plate. Add the plums, leaning them against the meat. Scatter horseradish over each plate, garnish with leaves, and serve.

ROASTED BEEF TENDERLOIN WITH TOASTED HORSERADISH QUINOA, BLACK GARLIC SAUCE, AND RED WINE DRIZZLE

SERVES 4

Some of our diners are just dedicated beef people. A regular visitor from Texas comes in and asks for two orders of this tenderloin, but hold everything else other than the beef. It's a superb tenderloin, Black Angus Top Choice from Utah, like all our beef, but he sure misses out on some other great flavors.

POSSIBLE DO-AHEAD STEPS

- Make the Veal Demi-Glace and Light Chicken Stock up to 1 week ahead.
- Make the Red Wine Drizzle and the Black Garlic Sauce up to 1 day ahead.

FOR THE WINE DRIZZLE

2 tablespoons (1 ounce) olive oil

1 small onion, chopped

1 small carrot, chopped

4 ounces button mushrooms, or mushroom stems

1 teaspoon green peppercorns

Small sprig of fresh thyme

1 cup (8 ounces) dry red wine

2 cups (1 pint) Veal Demi-Glace (see page xxviii)

Kosher salt and ground white pepper

FOR THE QUINOA

2 teaspoons olive oil

½ cup uncooked quinoa

1 cup (8 ounces) Light Chicken Stock (see page xxviii)

1 dried bay leaf

Small sprig of fresh thyme

1 teaspoon grated fresh horseradish

Kosher salt and ground white pepper

FOR THE GARLIC SAUCE

10–12 fermented black garlic cloves (see Kitchen Notes page 231)

1 small shallot, sliced

½ cup (4 ounces) dry red wine

1 cup (8 ounces) Light Chicken Stock (see page xxviii)

Kosher salt and ground white pepper

FOR THE TENDERLOIN

1½ pounds center-cut beef tenderloin

Kosher salt and ground white pepper

¼ cup plus 2 tablespoons (3 ounces) olive oil

4 tablespoons (2 ounces) unsalted butter

1 large shallot, sliced

2 garlic cloves

Small sprig of fresh thyme

Small sprig of fresh rosemary

TO PREPARE THE WINE DRIZZLE

1. Warm a small saucepan over high heat. Pour in the oil and then add the onion, carrot, mushrooms, peppercorns, and thyme. Sauté about 5 minutes to a deep golden brown, then add the wine and reduce the liquid by half, just a few minutes.

2. Pour in the demi-glace, reduce the heat to medium-low, and simmer until the liquid again reduces by half, another 5–8 minutes.

3. Strain the mixture through a fine-mesh sieve into a bowl, return the liquid to the pan, and keep warm on low heat.

TO PREPARE THE QUINOA

1. While the wine drizzle cooks, prepare the quinoa. Warm the oil in a medium saucepan over medium heat and stir in the quinoa. Cook several minutes, stirring, until the quinoa turns golden and takes on a toasty aroma.

2. Add the stock, bay leaf, and thyme, turn the heat to low, cover and cook for 10–15 minutes, until the liquid evaporates and the quinoa is tender.

3. Turn off the heat, stir in the horseradish, salt, and pepper, and cover again. Let the quinoa sit 5 more minutes to steam.

TO PREPARE THE GARLIC SAUCE

1. Combine the garlic cloves, shallot, red wine, and chicken stock in a small saucepan. Bring to a boil, then reduce the heat to a simmer, and reduce the mixture by half.

2. Transfer the mixture to a blender and puree. Season with salt and pepper.

TO COOK THE TENDERLOIN

1. Preheat the oven to 350°F. Season the tenderloin with salt and pepper.

2. Warm a large, heavy, ovenproof skillet, such as cast-iron, over high heat to nearly smoking.

3. Pour the oil into the skillet, add the tenderloin, and sear on all sides until deeply brown, about 6 minutes.

4. Add the butter, shallots, garlic, and herb sprigs to the skillet.

5. Transfer the skillet with the beef to the oven and roast for 6–8 more minutes, or until the beef reaches an internal temperature of about 125°F on an instant-read thermometer. The meat's temperature will rise a few more degrees to medium-rare while it sits.

6. Remove the skillet from the oven and then baste the beef with the pan juices for 30 seconds. Transfer the beef to paper towels and let it rest for several minutes.

PUTTING IT ALL TOGETHER

Spoon a line of quinoa down the center of each of 4 plates. Cut the tenderloin into 8 slices, resting 2 on each plate to either side of the quinoa. Spoon the wine drizzle over the beef and quinoa on each plate and serve.

restaurant embellishments

It's not too much effort to add my Young Carrots and Pan-Grilled Figs to the dish, and they enhance the main event with different colors, tastes, and textures. Take 8 young slim carrots and slice them in half lengthwise. If they remain thicker than ¼ inch, slice them again lengthwise. Then slice 4 plump mission figs in half. Warm a film of olive oil in a skillet or on a griddle over medium heat. Sauté the carrots briefly until they become tender, then add the figs to the skillet and sear until they soften and caramelize a bit. Season both with salt and white pepper, arrange the carrots at angles over the beef and quinoa, and lean a couple of fig halves against the beef.

Kitchen Notes

- In the restaurant kitchen, we use mushroom caps in our dish and save the less tender stems to cook down in sauces.

- Black garlic is called fermented, but the process to make it is more like caramelization. Long low heat turns it a funky brown-black, but it is also sweet, mild, and almost jammy. You can find it at Trader Joe's, Asian markets, and at online retailers.

SEARED BEEF STRIP LOIN WITH EGGPLANT-TOMATO WRAP AND BROWN ALE REDUCTION

SERVES 4

Our lunch menu offers fare that's much simpler than our dinner offerings, featuring soups, salads, tacos, a burger, and sandwiches. That works better for the state capitol office workers and other business folks who don't have a lot of time to eat multiple courses in a leisurely fashion. When we don't sell as much beef at dinner as I expect, we put some amazing quality trimmings into burgers or steak sandwiches. During New Mexico's winter legislative session, we keep the steak sandwich on the menu every day. A lot of business gets done here over that meal. You can always tell the day the legislators head home because the demand for beef at both meals falls by about 50 percent. This summery preparation also sells out, even without those politicians in town from all over the state. The eggplant wrap takes the flavors of a Provençal tian or gratin but in an atypical form. The beery sauce evolved as a refinement from a barbecue sauce I used to make twenty years ago for flank steak, and it still makes a good mate for a simple grilled flank.

POSSIBLE DO-AHEAD STEPS

- Make the Veal Demi-Glace up to 1 week ahead.
- Form the Eggplant-Tomato Wrap and make the Brown Ale Reduction up to 4 hours ahead.

FOR THE EGGPLANT-TOMATO WRAP

1-pound purple eggplant, peeled and sliced lengthwise ⅛ inch thick

¼ cup plus 2 tablespoons (3 ounces) olive oil

2 large red-ripe tomatoes, sliced as thinly as you can manage

Kosher salt and ground white pepper

1 small bunch of fresh basil leaves

2 teaspoons fresh thyme leaves

2 tablespoons minced black Kalamata olives

2 tablespoons freshly grated Parmesan cheese

FOR THE BROWN ALE REDUCTION

12-ounce bottle or can dark beer, such as Santa Fe Brewing Company's Nut Brown Ale

½ cup (4 ounces) strong coffee

½ cup (4 ounces) dry red wine

2 tablespoons (1 ounce) maple syrup

1 tablespoon Dijon mustard

1 small shallot, chopped

2 garlic cloves

Two 4- to 5-inch sprigs of fresh tarragon

Small sprig of fresh thyme

1½ cups (12 ounces) Veal Demi-Glace (see page xxviii)

1 tablespoon chopped fresh tarragon

Kosher salt and ground white pepper

FOR THE BEEF STRIP LOIN

1¼ pounds trimmed well-marbled beef strip loin

Kosher salt and ground white pepper

¼ cup (2 ounces) olive oil

6 tablespoons (3 ounces) unsalted butter

2 medium shallots, sliced thin

3 garlic cloves

Small sprig of fresh thyme

Small sprig of fresh oregano or an additional small sprig of fresh thyme

FOR THE FINISHED DISH

Small basil leaves, thyme leaves, beet greens, or small salad greens

TO PREPARE THE EGGPLANT-TOMATO WRAP

1. Preheat the oven to 350°F.

2. Place a 12-inch square piece of plastic wrap on a work surface.

3. Brush 6–8 of the best-looking eggplant slices on both sides with several tablespoons of the oil.

4. Warm a griddle or large sauté pan over medium heat and lay out the eggplant slices, in batches if needed. Cook on each side for a couple of minutes, until the eggplant is limp and golden in spots.

5. Lay the eggplant slices side-by-side on the plastic wrap, long sides slightly overlapping. Over the eggplant, lay the tomatoes, covering the surface as completely as possible. Season with salt and pepper, and scatter the surface with basil, thyme, olives, and Parmesan.

6. Using the plastic wrap for support, roll the eggplant snugly into 1 long tube 11–12 inches in length. Transfer carefully to a rimmed baking sheet. Season the eggplant itself with a bit more salt and pepper if you wish.

7. Spoon the remaining oil evenly over the top of the eggplant wrap. (The eggplant can be prepared to this point up to 4 hours ahead of when you plan to bake it.)

8. Bake for 12–15 minutes, until the eggplant is tender and the wrap is heated through so that the cheese has melted. Transfer the baking sheet to a baking rack. Leave the oven on.

TO PREPARE THE ALE REDUCTION

1. While the eggplant is baking, prepare the ale reduction sauce. Combine the beer, coffee, wine, maple syrup, mustard, shallot, garlic cloves, and the sprigs of tarragon and thyme in a medium saucepan. Bring to a boil, then reduce the heat to a simmer, and reduce the mixture by half, about 10–15 minutes.

2. Stir in the demi-glace and continue simmering until the sauce is reduced by about two-thirds to a rich sauce consistency.

3. Strain through a fine-mesh sieve, pushing on the solids to release all their juices. Return the sauce to the pan, stir in the chopped tarragon, season with salt and pepper, and keep warm on low heat.

TO COOK THE BEEF LOIN

1. Warm a large heavy ovenproof skillet, such as cast-iron, over high heat to nearly smoking.

2. Season the strip loin with salt and pepper.

3. Pour the oil into the skillet, add the beef, and sear on all sides until deeply brown, about 6 minutes.

4. Add the butter, shallots, garlic, and herb sprigs to the skillet.

5. Transfer the skillet with the meat to the oven and roast for 8–12 more minutes, until the beef reaches an internal temperature of about 125°F on an instant-read thermometer. The temperature will rise a few more degrees while the meat sits.

6. Remove the strip loin from the oven and then baste with the pan juices for 30 seconds. Let the meat rest on paper towels for several minutes.

PUTTING IT ALL TOGETHER

With a sharp knife, slice the eggplant-tomato wrap into 8 equal pieces and place 2 pieces on each of 4 plates, one to each side. Slice the strip loin into 8 slices and arrange 2 slices on each plate leaning into the eggplant. Spoon the sauce over the beef and let it pool around the slices. Tuck herbs or greens around each plate and serve right away.

restaurant embellishments

In August and September, the time that Santa Fe gardens are bursting with tomatoes and eggplant, we get fresh chanterelles from foragers who find them around the Santa Fe ski area above the city. I can extend that season by having the mushrooms flown in fresh from Oregon as well. We end up with enough of them to dry some for use into the winter. Nothing's better as a steak accompaniment, including in this dish. If you'd like to add chanterelles to your preparation, warm a sauté pan over high heat, add 1 ounce of olive oil, and then 4 ounces of small fresh chanterelles. Sear quickly to a deep golden brown, reduce the heat to medium-low, add 1 tablespoon of unsalted butter, and stir and cook for about 30 seconds more. Pour in 2 tablespoons of brandy and cook until it's evaporated. Season with salt and white pepper and serve.

I also like to add Glazed Salsify to servings of strip loin. Here's the recipe I use.

GLAZED SALSIFY

4 medium salsify roots, peeled and cut into 1½-inch lengths

4 cups water

Juice of 1 lemon

3 small sprigs fresh thyme

1 teaspoon coriander seeds

1 dried bay leaf

2 ounces extra-virgin olive oil

2 tablespoons (1 ounce) unsalted butter

2 tablespoons (1 ounce) Veal Demi-glace (see page xxviii) or Light Chicken Stock (see page xxviii)

Kosher salt and ground white pepper

2 teaspoons minced fresh chives

1. Place the salsify roots in a saucepan and cover with water. Add the lemon juice, thyme, coriander seeds, and bay leaf.

2. Bring the liquid to a boil over high heat, then reduce the heat to medium and cook until the salsify is tender, which may take as long as 20 minutes because it is quite dense. If the liquid runs low before it is soft, add some hot water to the pan.

3. Once the salsify is tender, warm olive oil in a sauté pan over medium heat. Stir in the salsify, and cook it until it turns several shades darker than its usual creamy white.

4. Add butter and demi-glace or stock and season salt and pepper. Cook briefly until the salsify is glazed and the liquid has evaporated.

5. Sprinkle with chives before serving the salsify alongside the steak.

CINNAMON-ANCHO BRINED HERITAGE PORK CHOP WITH WHEATBERRY-FARRO SAUTÉ, PICKLED PEACHES, AND SUGAR SNAP PEAS

SERVES 4

For pork chops, I love the heritage breed called Duroc. The meat has a rich flavor and juiciness, but it has few of the knobby pockets of fat that people have to eat around in some other good chops. We cut our chops from the pork loin, leaving the hefty rib bone in place for a primal caveman appeal. Since the meat has plenty of its own moisture, we brine mainly for extra flavor. The richness of the pork balances well with the tang of the pickled peaches. The wheatberry-farro sauté evolved originally from an early cautiousness about costs when Jennifer and I opened our own place. Grains are inexpensive and shelf-stable, but they've gained a greater role on the menu over time because they taste so good and add all kinds of interesting textures to a plate.

POSSIBLE DO-AHEAD STEPS

- Make the Veal Demi-Glace and Light Chicken Stock up to a week ahead.
- The Wheatberry-Farro Sauté starts with pre-cooked wheatberries and farro, so you might want to make big batches of both. You can double or triple the sauté to have leftovers of it for later meals, perhaps as ingredients to add heft to salads or to be combined together in a breakfast cereal. It can be made a few days ahead of when you want to use it.
- Make the Pork Chop Brine and Pickled Golden Peaches up to 1 day ahead.
- Brine the pork chops up to 4 hours ahead.

FOR THE BRINE

2 dried ancho chiles, stemmed and seeded

4 cups (1 quart) water

2 tablespoons (1 ounce) champagne vinegar

½ cup granulated sugar

1 tablespoon kosher salt

1 small onion, chopped

1 small carrot, chopped

2 cinnamon sticks

4 (approximately 1-inch-thick) bone-in pork chops

FOR THE PEACHES

1 cup (8 ounces) water

½ cup (4 ounces) apple cider

2 tablespoons (1 ounce) apple cider vinegar

2 tablespoons granulated sugar

1 tablespoon chopped fresh ginger

Peel of ½ lemon, sliced off in 1 or several pieces

Peel of ½ orange, sliced off in 1 or several pieces

2 sprigs of fresh thyme

1 dried bay leaf

1 whole star anise

2 large peaches, unpeeled, cut into ½- or ¾-inch cubes

FOR THE WHEATBERRY-FARRO SAUTÉ

4 tablespoons (2 ounces) unsalted butter

2 tablespoons (1 ounce) olive oil

½ cup chopped walnuts

1 small shallot, minced

1 thin slice prosciutto, chopped
   (about 2 tablespoons)

1 cup cooked farro

½ cup cooked wheatberries

3 tablespoons chopped dried tart cherries

½ cup (4 ounces) Veal Demi-Glace (see page xxviii)

1 tablespoon minced fresh chives

Kosher salt and ground white pepper

TO COOK THE PORK

¼ cup (2 ounces) olive oil

FOR THE PEAS

2 tablespoons (1 ounce) olive oil

1 tablespoon unsalted butter

8 ounces sugar snap peas, tipped and tailed

¼ cup (2 ounces) Light Chicken Stock
   (see page xxviii)

Kosher salt and ground white pepper

FOR THE FINISHED DISH

2 tablespoons (1 ounce) unsalted butter

Small sprig of fresh thyme

1 garlic clove

½ cup (4 ounces) Veal Demi-Glace (see page xxviii)

TO PREPARE THE PORK CHOP BRINE

1. Warm a medium saucepan over medium heat. Add the ancho chiles to the dry pan and toast them on both sides for a couple of minutes, just until fragrant. Immediately pour in the water, vinegar, sugar, and salt and bring to a boil, stirring to dissolve the sugar and salt.

2. Add the onion, carrot, and cinnamon, and simmer for 3 minutes.

3. Transfer to a shallow dish that can hold the liquid and the 4 pork chops, and let the brine cool to room temperature. You can speed along the process, if you like, by placing the dish over an ice bath.

4. Submerge the pork chops in the brine, cover, and refrigerate for at least 2 hours and up to 4 hours.

TO PICKLE THE PEACHES

1. Warm the water, cider, cider vinegar, sugar, ginger, citrus peels, thyme, bay leaf, and star anise in a medium saucepan over medium heat. Bring to a boil, then reduce the heat to a simmer and cook for about 10 minutes.

2. Gently stir in the peach cubes and remove the pan from the heat. Let the peaches sit in the pickling liquid at room temperature, placing a plate over them if they float.

TO PREPARE THE WHEATBERRY-FARRO SAUTÉ

1. Warm the butter and oil in a medium saucepan over medium heat. Stir in the walnuts, shallot, and prosciutto, and cook several minutes until fragrant and lightly colored.

2. Add the farro, wheatberries, cherries, and demi-glace, and simmer about 3 minutes, until the liquid is absorbed.

3. Stir in the chives, remove from the heat, and season with salt and pepper. Cover to keep warm.

TO COOK THE CHOPS

1. Preheat the oven to 350°F. Remove the chops from the brine, rinse them, and pat them dry with paper towels.

2. Warm a 12-inch ovenproof skillet, such as cast-iron, over high heat. Add the oil, swirl it around, and reduce the heat to medium.

3. Add the pork chops. Sear until deeply golden brown, about 3 minutes per side.

4. Transfer the skillet to the oven and roast the pork another 8–10 minutes, or until the temperature on an instant-read thermometer stuck horizontally into a chop registers 140°F–145°F for medium doneness.

TO PREPARE THE SUGAR SNAP PEAS

1. Prepare the peas while the chops are in the oven. Warm the oil and butter in a small saucepan over medium-high heat.

2. Stir in the peas and sauté for 1 minute.

3. Pour in the stock, reduce the heat to medium-low and cook several minutes until the liquid has evaporated and the peas are glazed and tender. Season with salt and pepper.

1. Remove the skillet from the oven and add to it the butter, thyme, and garlic. As the butter melts, baste the chops for 30 seconds with the pan juices. Transfer the chops to a cutting board and let them rest for a minute.

2. Add the demi-glace to the pan juices and heat the mixture through, scraping up any browned bits from the bottom.

3. Spoon 2 mounds of wheatberry-farro sauté on each of 4 plates. Halve each pork chop and stand up both portions in the middle of the plate, bone upward. Add several cubes of peach to each plate and top with peas. Spoon pan juices around each plate and serve.

restaurant embellishments

I love Crusted Cheesy Polenta with these chops and it can be made a day ahead. It needs to be firm for use anyway.

CRUSTED CHEESY POLENTA

1½ cups Light Chicken Stock (see page xxviii)

1½ cups whole milk

3 ounces mascarpone cheese

1 cup quick-cooking (not instant) stone-ground polenta cornmeal, such as Roland's

1 ounce grated smoked cheddar or another medium-to-sharp cheddar cheese

½ teaspoon ground white pepper

1 teaspoon of chopped fresh oregano (optional, but don't substitute dried oregano, which is too different in flavor here)

1. Combine stock, milk, and mascarpone cheese in a large saucepan. When the mixture is simmering, gradually stir in cornmeal. Once combined, turn the heat down to low and cook for 5–7 minutes, until the grains are soft and excess liquid has evaporated.

2. Stir in cheddar cheese, pepper, and oregano.

3. Pour the warm polenta into a greased 8-inch-square dish and set aside to cool. When it's cool, cover and refrigerate the polenta.

4. Just before serving, cut half of the polenta into approximately 1-inch blocks. (You can save the rest for another couple of days.)

5. Coat a griddle or heavy skillet with canola or vegetable oil and sear the polenta blocks over medium-high heat until they are nicely browned on all sides, about 5 minutes total.

6. Or you can cook the polenta to crispness, as I prefer to do in the restaurant kitchen, by heating 2 cups of canola or vegetable oil to 335°F–340°F and deep-frying the polenta cubes for a couple of minutes until they are richly golden brown.

PORK TENDERLOIN MEDALLIONS WITH SUNCHOKE PUREE, PEAR-ALMOND CAKE, AND BOURBON-MUSTARD SAUCE

SERVES 4

The inspiration for this preparation was dead simple: biscuits and gravy with pork. The biscuit developed over time into a buttery French financier-style cake, and the gravy became a combination of bourbon-mustard sauce and sunchoke puree. I make a full cake, more than you need for the dish, because it's nice to have leftovers around for a snack or to toast for breakfast.

POSSIBLE DO-AHEAD STEPS

- Make Light Chicken Stock and Veal Demi-Glace up to 1 week ahead.
- Make the brown butter for the cake, the Sunchoke Puree, and the Bourbon-Mustard Sauce up to 1 day ahead.
- Make the Pear-almond Cake up to 8 hours ahead.

FOR THE CAKE

1 cup (8 ounces) unsalted butter

1 scant cup unbleached all-purpose flour

1 scant cup almond flour

½ cup confectioners' sugar

7 ounces (7 or 8 large eggs) egg whites

6-ounce ripe pear, preferably Anjou, skin-on, cut in ½-inch dice

½ teaspoon grated orange zest

⅛ teaspoon ground allspice

⅛ teaspoon ancho chile powder

Kosher salt and ground white pepper

FOR THE PUREE

1 tablespoon olive oil

1 pound sunchokes (Jerusalem artichokes), peeled and thinly sliced

1 small (about 6 ounces) parsnip, peeled and thinly sliced

2 garlic cloves

1 small shallot, chunked

2 cups (1 pint) Light Chicken Stock (see page xxviii)

4 tablespoons (2 ounces) unsalted butter

Juice of 1 lemon

Kosher salt and ground white pepper

FOR THE BOURBON-MUSTARD SAUCE

1 tablespoon olive oil

2 garlic cloves

1 large shallot, sliced

½ teaspoon white peppercorns

1 teaspoon yellow mustard seed

Large sprig of fresh thyme

Large sprig of fresh rosemary

½ cup (4 ounces) olorosa or cream sherry

1 tablespoon sherry vinegar

1 tablespoon packed brown sugar

1 tablespoon Dijon mustard

2 cups (1 pint) Veal Demi-Glace (see page xviii)

2 tablespoons (1 ounce) bourbon

Kosher salt and ground white pepper

FOR THE MEDALLIONS

4 (6-ounce) sections pork tenderloin

Kosher salt and ground white pepper

¼ cup (2 ounces) olive oil

2 tablespoons (1 ounce) unsalted butter

2 garlic cloves

Small sprig of fresh thyme

FOR THE FINISHED DISH

Mint, thyme, or celery leaves, or mustard leaves

TO PREPARE THE CAKE

1. Preheat the oven to 375°F.

2. Cook the butter over medium heat in a small pan (preferably with a light-colored bottom so that you can easily see the butter change color). When the butter foams, swirl it around in the pan a few times, and watch it carefully as it turns from golden to nutty brown. The butter's aroma will become nutty too. Pour the butter into a heatproof bowl to stop its cooking.

3. In a stand mixer fitted with the paddle attachment, mix together on low speed the flour and almond flour with the confectioners' sugar.

4. Add the egg whites and increase the mixer speed to medium-high.

5. When well blended, begin to mix in the brown butter. Add it about 1 ounce at a time, turning the mixer speed down to low while adding each portion of butter, then turning the speed back up to medium-high until the butter disappears into the batter.

6. By hand, mix in the pear, orange zest, allspice, chile powder, and pinches of salt and pepper. Scrape the batter into an 8-inch square pan.

7. Bake the cake for 10 minutes. Reduce the heat to 350°F, then turn the cake around in the oven to ensure it cooks evenly, and bake for 8–10 more minutes until golden brown and fairly firm. Cool the cake on a baking rack.

TO PREPARE THE SUNCHOKE PUREE

1. While the cake is baking, prepare the puree. Warm the oil in a medium saucepan over medium heat.

2. Add the sunchokes, parsnips, garlic, and shallots and cook 5–7 minutes, until the vegetables begin to soften and have some lightly browned edges.

3. Pour in the stock, and simmer until the vegetables are tender and only about ¼ cup of liquid remains.

4. Transfer the mixture to a blender, add the butter and lemon juice, and puree. Season with salt and pepper.

TO PREPARE THE BOURBON-MUSTARD SAUCE

1. Warm the olive oil in a medium saucepan over high heat. Stir in the garlic, shallot, white peppercorns, mustard seed, thyme, and rosemary. Cook for 5 minutes, until the garlic and shallots are golden.

2. Add the sherry, sherry vinegar, brown sugar, mustard, and reduce by half, about 5 minutes.

3. Pour in the demi-glace and reduce the heat to medium. Simmer to reduce by about half, about 10 minutes.

4. Stir in the bourbon and remove the sauce from the heat. Strain the sauce through a fine-mesh sieve into a smaller pan, season with salt and pepper, and keep warm on low heat.

TO COOK THE PORK MEDALLIONS

1. Preheat the oven to 350°F. Season the pork medallions with salt and pepper.

2. Warm a 10- or 12-inch ovenproof skillet over high heat. Pour in the oil, swirl to coat evenly, and add the pork medallions. Sear to deeply golden on all sides, about 8 minutes total. Transfer the skillet to the oven and roast 8–10 minutes, until the temperature on an instant-read thermometer registers 140°F–145°F for medium doneness.

3. Remove the skillet from the oven and add the butter, garlic, and thyme. As the butter melts, baste the pork for another 30 seconds with the pan juices. Transfer the pork to paper towels and let it rest for a minute.

PUTTING IT ALL TOGETHER

Cut the cake into 1½-inch squares. Place 2 cake squares on opposite sides of each of 4 plates, then several spoonfuls of sunchoke puree between them. Slice the pork medallions in half and arrange a pair of medallions over the puree. Drizzle the bourbon-mustard sauce around the plates. Tuck herbs, leaves, or blossoms in and around each plate and serve right away.

restaurant embellishments

- When preparing the cake at the restaurant, I first sauté the pear in about 2 teaspoons of olive oil before mixing it into the cake batter. It softens the texture and gives it a bit of savoriness to balance the sweetness.

- In the kitchen, we like to garnish this with Charred Asparagus and Scallions. Blanch a dozen thin asparagus spears and a dozen scallions. Warm 1 tablespoon of oil in a skillet over medium-high heat, add the asparagus to the skillet, and place another pan over it to press it down. Cook it for a couple of minutes until the asparagus is browned, then flip the asparagus over, cover again with the second pan, and cook an additional couple of minutes until browned. Repeat with the scallions.

Kitchen Notes

The cake batter is essentially the blend used for the French confection financiers. The key to the right texture is getting the butter emulsified into the mixture so that it looks almost like mayonnaise. Go slowly as you drizzle it in. You'll be rewarded with a very buttery golden cake when it's baked.

BRAISED PORK BELLY WITH GUINNESS-MARCONA ALMOND MOUSSELINE, OLIVE-OIL POACHED TOMATOES, AND PEPPERED CRUMBS

Pork belly is the meat that can be cured for bacon. Berkshire pork belly, my favorite, certainly makes superlative bacon, but I use it fresh here, first brined and then braised to succulence. I like it balanced with a creamy nut sauce with bit of bitterness from deeply flavored Guinness beer, then brightened with small warm tomatoes and crunchy breadcrumbs.

POSSIBLE DO-AHEAD STEPS

- The stock and demi-glace can be made up to 1 week ahead.
- Brine the pork belly up to 2 days ahead. Be sure to rinse it immediately, then refrigerate until needed.
- Braise the pork belly up to 1 day ahead and reduce the braising liquid to a sauce.
- The mousseline can be made up to 4 hours ahead and warmed over a double boiler.

FOR THE PORK BELLY BRINE

1 quart (4 cups) water

1 tablespoon soy sauce

⅓ cup packed brown sugar

2 tablespoons kosher salt

2 cinnamon sticks

1 dried ancho chile

2 teaspoons mustard seeds

2 teaspoons caraway seeds

2½-pound section pork belly

FOR THE PORK BELLY BRAISING LIQUID

2 tablespoons (1 ounce) olive oil

3 slices apple-wood smoked bacon

1 small onion, chopped

1 small carrot, chopped

10 ounces mushroom stems or chopped button mushrooms

2 large sprigs fresh tarragon

2 teaspoons Dijon mustard

1 cup sherry, preferably fino or oloroso

6 cups Dark Chicken Stock (see page xxviii)

1 cup Veal Demi-Glace (see page xxviii)

FOR THE OLIVE-OIL POACHED TOMATOES

1 to 2 cups olive oil

2 garlic cloves

1 teaspoon black peppercorns

1 teaspoon kosher salt

Sprig fresh thyme

Sprig fresh rosemary

12 petite heirloom tomatoes

FOR THE PEPPERED CRUMBS

1 teaspoon olive oil

1 slice apple-wood smoked bacon, minced

8 ounces dry brioche crumbs or other dry breadcrumbs

2 teaspoons mixed peppercorns (black, green, and pink), toasted in a dry skillet and crushed

2 tablespoons freshly grated pecorino toscano or pecorino romano cheese

FOR THE GUINNESS-MARCONA ALMOND MOUSSELINE

2 tablespoons (1 ounce) unsalted butter

8 ounces marcona almonds

1 small shallot, sliced

2 whole garlic cloves

1 cup chicken stock

½ cup Guinness Stout or other stout beer

Kosher salt and ground white pepper

Olive oil for pan frying

Arugula leaves or microgreens

TO BRINE THE PORK BELLY

1. Combine all of the ingredients, except the pork belly, in a medium sauce pan. Bring the mixture to a boil, stirring to dissolve the salt. Chill the brine over an ice bath.

2. Place the pork belly in a shallow dish large enough to hold it flat. Pour the brine over it. Weight it down with a plate and refrigerate for 3–4 hours.

3. Remove the belly from the brine and rinse it well. Discard the brine.

TO BRAISE THE PORK BELLY

1. Preheat the oven to 300°F.

2. Combine the oil and bacon in a medium to large roasting pan. Warm the mixture over medium heat on the stovetop until the bacon becomes translucent. Scoot the bacon slice to the edge of the pan and add the pork belly. Sear the belly well on both sides, about 8 minutes total. With tongs, transfer the belly to a plate. Add the vegetables, tarragon, and mustard, and saute until the vegetables are golden brown and limp. The bacon should be well-browned.

3. Pour the sherry into the pan and reduce until almost dry. Pour in the stock and demi-glace and bring to boil. Return the pork belly to the pan. Cover the pan and place in the oven to braise for about 2 hours, until quite tender. With tongs, transfer the belly to a plate again. Degrease the pan liquid. Place the pan back on a stove burner over medium heat. Reduce the liquid by approximately one-half, to a sauce consistency. Discard the bacon.

TO PREPARE THE TOMATOES

In a small to medium sauce pan, combine enough oil to cover the tomatoes with the garlic, pepper, salt, and herbs. Warm the oil 125°F–130°F. Gently drop in the tomatoes and poach them for 5–7 minutes, until soft with lightly wrinkled skins. With a spider, transfer the tomatoes from the oil to paper towels.

TO PREPARE THE CRUMBS

Warm the oil in a small saute pan over medium heat. Add the bacon and cook briefly until it is brown and crisp. Stir in the brioche crumbs and peppercorns and cook another couple of minutes until the crumbs are toasted and crisp. Set aside to cool, then fold in the cheese.

TO PREPARE THE MOUSSELINE

1. Combine in a small sauce pan the butter, almonds, shallot, and garlic. Warm over medium heat until the shallot and garlic have softened and almonds have colored a shade darker, about 5 minutes. Add the stock and stout and reduce by one-half, about 5 more minutes.

2. Transfer the mixture to a blender and puree until smooth.

1. Cut the pork belly into 8 equal pieces. Season it with salt and pepper. Warm a large skillet pan with the olive oil over high heat until almost smoking. Sear the pork belly for 2 minutes on each side or until well-browned. Pour in the sauce made from the braising liquid, and reduce the heat to medium.

2. Arrange 2 pieces of belly on each plate, place 3 tomatoes on each plate, then sprinkle the crumbs evenly over each portion of tomatoes. Spoon on 1 or 2 mounds of mousseline on each plate, garnish with arugula leaves, and serve.

restaurant embellishments

Peppery turnips cut through the richness of pork belly and also echo the pepper in the bread crumbs. I use small white Tokyo turnips and braise them to tenderness. Combine in a small roasting pan 1 pound of small turnips, 2 tablespoons of olive oil, 1 cup each of orange juice and Light Chicken Stock (see page xxviii), and a sprinkle of thyme, orange zest, crushed red pepper flakes, and kosher salt. Bring the mixture to a boil on the stovetop, then cover and finish in a 325°F oven until tender, about 30 minutes for 1-inch turnips.

BRAISED PORK CHEEKS WITH LITTLE NECK CLAMS, SAVORY SWEET CORN AND RYE BREAD PUDDING, AND ENDIVE-RADISH SALAD

SERVES 4

We braise halibut and lamb cheeks as well as pork cheeks, but the latter are usually the easiest for a home cook to find. The meat is always succulent and pulls apart into shreds like beef chuck roast. I've paired pork cheeks with shrimp, scallops, and tempura oysters, but love it most with clams, my favorite among shellfish. Clams—and mussels—remind me of the carefree days I spent as a kid plucking them from sand and rocks on the coast of Baja California, using a trusty piece of re-bar as my only tool. I pair the surf-and-turf duo here with a bread pudding made from rye bread that we get from the excellent Sage Bakehouse, just around the corner from the restaurant, though any light rye will work. A little salad adds a contrasting spark of tang and brightness to the dish.

POSSIBLE DO-AHEAD STEPS

- Make the Light Chicken Stock and Veal Demi-Glace up to 1 week ahead.
- Make the Braised Pork Cheeks up to 1 day ahead.
- Make the bread pudding mixture up to 1 day ahead, but don't bake it until shortly before you plan to serve it.

FOR THE PORK CHEEKS

2 pounds pork cheeks, trimmed of any surface sinew or fat

Kosher salt and ground white pepper

2 tablespoons (1 ounce) olive oil

1 bacon slice, preferably applewood-smoked

½ small onion, chopped

1 small carrot, chopped

5 ounces sliced button mushrooms or mushroom stems

1 large sprig of fresh tarragon

½ cup (4 ounces) honey

2 teaspoons (1 ounce) Dijon mustard

¼ cup (2 ounces) olorosa or cream sherry

4 cups (1 quart) Light Chicken Stock (see page xxviii)

1 cup (8 ounces) Veal Demi-Glace (see page xxviii)

FOR THE PUDDING

1½ cups (12 ounces) Light Chicken Stock (see page xxviii)

6 ounces light rye bread (likely about 4 slices), cut or torn in 1-inch pieces, toasted

½ cup corn kernels, chopped (to release more of their milk and starch)

1 cooked bacon slice, preferably applewood-smoked, minced

4 tablespoons (2 ounces) unsalted butter, melted

2 large eggs, whisked together

1 teaspoon minced shallots

¼ teaspoon roasted garlic puree, optional

1 teaspoon chopped fresh rosemary leaves or ½ teaspoon dried rosemary

Pinch of freshly ground nutmeg

Kosher salt and ground white pepper

FOR THE ENDIVE-RADISH SALAD

1 large head Belgian endive, julienned

½ watermelon radish, peeled and julienned

½ teaspoon grated lemon zest

Kosher salt and ground white pepper

1 teaspoon chopped fresh chives

FOR THE CLAMS

8 littleneck or cherrystone clams

½ cup (4 ounces) Light Chicken Stock (see page xxviii)

¼ cup (2 ounces) sparkling white wine, or dry white wine

1 tablespoon unsalted butter

1 small shallot, thinly sliced

2 garlic cloves, thinly sliced

Pinch dried red chile flakes

1 teaspoon chopped fresh tarragon

Kosher salt and ground white pepper

FOR THE FINISHED DISH

Baby chard leaves, cilantro leaves, or small salad greens

TO PREPARE THE PORK CHEEKS

1. Preheat the oven to 300°F. Season the pork cheeks with salt and pepper.

2. Place a Dutch oven or medium roasting pan on the stovetop and add the oil and bacon. Cook over medium heat until the bacon becomes translucent.

3. Add the pork cheeks, and sear them until nicely brown, about 2 minutes per side. Remove the cheeks from the pan, placing them on a plate.

4. Add the vegetables, tarragon, honey, and mustard to the pan. Continue cooking until the mixture is golden brown and the water has evaporated from the honey.

5. Pour in the sherry and cook briefly until the mixture is almost dry.

6. Add the stock and demi-glace and bring to a boil. Add the pork cheeks back into the pan, cover, and transfer to the oven. Bake 2½–3 hours, until the cheek meat shreds apart easily.

7. Remove the cheeks from the pan, placing the meat on another plate. Put the pan back on the stovetop and simmer the braising liquid to a medium-bodied sauce consistency. Degrease the sauce. Return the cheeks to the sauce and cover to keep warm.

TO PREPARE THE BREAD PUDDING

1. While the pork cheeks bake, prepare the bread pudding. Stir together the ingredients in a large bowl, then let the mixture sit for about 15 minutes for more of the liquid to absorb into the bread.

2. Give the mixture another good stir and spoon into four 8-ounce ramekins, mounding the pudding up in the center of each.

3. When the pork cheeks are finished cooking, raise the oven temperature to 350°F. Bake the bread puddings for 25–30 minutes, or until the tops are brown and crisp. Let them sit for several minutes, then remove the pudding from the ramekins.

TO PREPARE THE ENDIVE-RADISH SALAD

Combine the ingredients in a small bowl.

TO STEAM THE CLAMS

In a medium saucepan, combine the clams, stock, wine, butter, shallot, garlic, and chile flakes. Cover and cook over medium heat about 6–10 minutes, until the clams pop open. Discard any clams that haven't opened after 10 minutes. Stir in the tarragon and taste the broth. Add salt and pepper as you wish.

PUTTING IT ALL TOGETHER

Place 3–4 pieces of the braised cheeks on each of 4 plates. Add a bread pudding to one side of the meat. Drizzle the cheeks' braising sauce over the cheeks and the bread pudding. Spoon a pair of clams in the shell over the cheeks. Add the salad to the plates, garnish with leaves, and serve right away.

restaurant embellishments

- Instead of baking the bread pudding in individual ramekins, I turn it into a roulade that is steamed, sliced, and then crisped in a skillet just before serving. It makes the pudding's interior texture a touch creamier and the exterior crunchier. To prepare the bread pudding in this style, spoon half of the un-baked pudding mixture out on a 12-inch square of plastic wrap in a mound about 6 inches long. Using the plastic, roll the pudding mixture into a log 2–2½ inches in diameter. With a knife tip, poke 4 small holes along the length of the roulade. Repeat with a second piece of plastic and the remaining pudding. Steam the roulades in a large vegetable or bamboo steamer over simmering heat. They are done when an instant-read thermometer inserted into the end of a roulade registers 170°F. Unwrap and slice each roulade into 4 equal portions. Fry in a skillet with a thin film of olive oil over medium heat until richly brown and crisp. Add 2 pieces to each plate.

- I add flecks of a chilled Basil-Shallot Gel to the restaurant plates. I combine ½ cup of water, 1 sliced small shallot, and ¼ teaspoon of xanthan gum in a blender. Then I blend in ½ cup of blanched basil and ½ cup of blanched spinach and season with salt and pepper before refrigerating the gel briefly until set.

Kitchen Notes

- Our pork cheeks come from Beeler's in La Mars, Iowa, from their Heluka pork. Heluka is raised without antibiotics or growth stimulants on a vegetarian diet. Sows have their babies in private, bedded areas rather than in farrowing crates. Once they are weaned they are moved to another area with other babies, where they can play outside and in deeply bedded indoor areas. The size of the cheeks can vary a little. After braising, you can pull a larger one into smaller sections if you wish.

- It's always good with clams to buy a few more than you think you will need. If one or two don't open, you still have plenty. If they all open, you have a cook's treat and should enjoy the extras in the kitchen.

ROASTED LAMB LOIN WITH TOMATO-OLIVE SOFRITO, SHEEP'S MILK YOGURT, AND MINT-AND-LEMON THYME SAUCE

SERVES 4

Beef and pork probably are the most popular meats at most American restaurants today, but lamb reigns supreme with our guests. Maybe that reflects my own passion for it and its frequent appearance on the menu. I occasionally ate stewed or braised lamb growing up, and then learned to enjoy the finer cuts when I began working in restaurant kitchens. It was the time I spent in France, though, that taught me a full appreciation for all the parts. I helped break down carcasses and sides of lamb, and learned to separate various bits for pâtes, others for stock, and so on. I developed a special love for the loin, particularly filled out like this with Mediterranean accents.

POSSIBLE DO-AHEAD STEPS

- Make the Light Chicken Stock and Veal Demi-Glace up to 1 week ahead.
- Make the Mint-and-Lemon Thyme Sauce and Sheep's Milk Yogurt up to 1 day ahead.

FOR THE LAMB LOIN

4 (4- or 5-ounce) lamb loins

2 garlic cloves

1 tablespoon olive oil

Large sprig of fresh thyme

Large sprig of fresh mint

FOR THE SOFRITO

4 plum (roma) tomatoes, halved, seeds and juices squeezed out, then minced

1 large red bell pepper, minced

2 shallots, minced

½ teaspoon roasted garlic puree, or 1 small garlic clove, minced

Large sprig of fresh thyme

1 dried bay leaf

Pinch of dried red chile flakes

1 tablespoon tomato paste

Pinch of saffron threads or powder

1 cup (8 ounces) Light Chicken Stock (see page xxviii)

¼ cup (2 ounces) orange juice

¼ cup (2 ounces) extra virgin olive oil

Grated zest of 1 lemon

2½ tablespoons minced green Taggiasche or Castelvetrano olives, or other briny green olives

Kosher salt and ground white pepper

FOR THE YOGURT

1 cup plain sheeps' milk yogurt

Pinch of cumin seeds, toasted and ground

4 dried apricot halves, chopped

2 tablespoons (1 ounce) walnut oil

Kosher salt and ground white pepper

FOR THE MINT-AND-LEMON THYME SAUCE

1 tablespoon olive oil

1 small onion, chopped

2 garlic cloves

½ head fennel or 3 ounces of chopped fennel tops

4 ounces mushroom stems or sliced button mushrooms

Large sprig of fresh mint

Large sprig of lemon thyme

1 cup (8 ounces) dry red wine

2 cups (1 pint) Veal Demi-Glace (see page xxviii)

Kosher salt and ground white pepper

FOR THE LAMB

4 tablespoons (2 ounces) olive oil

6 tablespoons (3 ounces) unsalted butter

3 garlic cloves

Large sprig of fresh thyme

Large sprig of fresh mint

3 ounces chopped fennel tops, optional

FOR THE FINISHED DISH

Fresh chervil leaves, red amaranth leaves, Bull's Blood beet tops or greens, or mustard blossoms

TO MARINATE THE LAMB

Combine the loins in a large zipper-lock bag with the garlic cloves, olive oil, thyme, and mint. Refrigerate for 1 hour.

TO PREPARE THE SOFRITO

1. Combine the tomatoes, bell pepper, shallots, garlic, thyme, bay leaf, red chile flakes, tomato paste, saffron, chicken stock, and orange juice in a saucepan. Simmer over medium-high heat until the liquid has nearly evaporated, 10–12 minutes.

2. Remove from the heat and fold in the rest of the ingredients. Reserve at room temperature.

TO PREPARE THE YOGURT

1. While the sofrito cooks, combine the ingredients for the yogurt in a blender and puree. Transfer to a bowl, cover, and refrigerate.

TO PREPARE THE SAUCE

1. Warm the oil in a medium saucepan over medium-high heat.

2. Stir in the onion, garlic, fennel, mushrooms, mint, and thyme, and cook until the onions are golden brown, about 7 minutes.

3. Pour in the wine and cook briefly until nearly evaporated.

4. Pour in the demi-glace and reduce the liquid by about half.

5. Strain the sauce through a fine-mesh sieve into a bowl, return the liquid to the pan, and keep warm over low heat.

TO COOK THE LAMB

1. Preheat the oven to 350°F. Season the lamb loins with salt and pepper.

2. Warm a 10- or 12-inch ovenproof skillet over high heat. Pour in the oil, swirl to coat evenly, and add the lamb loins. Sear until browned on all sides, about 6 minutes. Transfer the skillet with the lamb to the oven and roast for 6–7 minutes, or until medium-rare, 140°F–145°F on an instant-read thermometer.

3. Remove the skillet from the oven and add the butter, garlic, thyme, mint, and optional fennel tops. Baste the lamb for 30 seconds with the buttery pan juices. Transfer the lamb to paper towels to drain.

PUTTING IT ALL TOGETHER

Spoon 2 pools of sofrito on each of 4 plates. Slice each lamb loin into 4 pieces and arrange them in a line, partially over the sofrito. Spoon the yogurt around the lamb. Then spoon the sauce around the yogurt, with a bit drizzled over the lamb. Garnish with leaves and serve.

Kitchen Notes

In my kitchen, I use larger cuts of lamb and trim them down so that I have plenty of bones and trimmings for stock and jus. You can ask for lamb racks and trim them down to loins, or have the butcher do it for you, giving you the bones and trimmings along with the medallions.

restaurant embellishments

France was where I had a lot of opportunity to eat lamb accompanied by chickpea fries or fritters. In that spirit, I developed these deep-fried Goat Cheese and Chickpea Croquettes that we serve along with this lamb in the restaurant.

GOAT CHEESE AND CHICKPEA CROQUETTES

1 cup heavy cream

4 ounces fresh goat cheese, softened

1 ounce cream cheese, softened

4 ounces mashed cooked chickpeas
(canned ones are okay, drained and rinsed)

2 teaspoons minced fresh chives

1 teaspoon fresh thyme leaves

½ teaspoon roasted garlic puree

¼ teaspoon kosher salt

1 large egg

1 teaspoon water

1 cup unbleached all-purpose flour

1 cup panko bread crumbs

Canola or vegetable oil

1. Whip heavy cream in a stand electric mixer over high speed. When it holds soft peaks, reduce the speed to medium, and add goat cheese and cream cheese. When well-blended, stop the mixer and scrape down the sides.

2. Add chickpeas, chives, thyme, garlic puree, and salt, and mix over medium speed until combined.

3. Pipe or spoon the mixture into walnut-size balls on a wax paper-lined baking pan. Freeze for 20–30 minutes or until set. (The balls can be covered and frozen for up to 4 days.)

4. Mix together egg and water in a shallow dish. Place flour in another shallow dish, and bread crumbs in a third.

5. Heat at least 3 inches of oil in a medium saucepan to 350°F–355°F.

6. Roll each ball in egg wash, followed by flour, followed by bread crumbs, then repeat. You'll end up with golf-ball size croquettes.

7. Fry the croquettes, a few at a time, until brown and crisp, about 1 minute. Use a spider or slotted spoon to transfer the croquettes to a baking rack placed over paper towels, then serve warm.

In the restaurant kitchen, we use *sous vide* cooking to make the lamb extra silky before it is finished in a skillet. If you have *sous vide* equipment, combine the lamb with the marinade ingredients in a large vacuum bag and seal it at medium pressure. Cook in a 125°F circulating water bath for 80 minutes. Dry off the lamb before searing it.

SEARED LAMB RACK WITH CANNELLINI BEAN PUREE, RED PEPPER MARMALADE, AND KALAMATA OLIVE-LAMB JUS

SERVES 4

I reimagined a Middle Eastern stew here, so that each element will taste fresh, rather than melded together through slow cooking.

POSSIBLE DO-AHEAD STEPS
- Make the Light Chicken Stock and Veal Demi-Glace up to 1 week ahead.
- Make the Cannellini Bean Puree and the Red Pepper Marmalade up to 1 day ahead.

FOR THE PUREE

1 cup cooked cannellini beans (canned ones are okay, drained and rinsed)
1 cup (8 ounces) Light Chicken Stock (see page xxviii)
1 garlic clove, chopped
1 small shallot, chopped
¼ cup (2 ounces) heavy cream
4 tablespoons (2 ounces) unsalted butter
Kosher salt and ground white pepper

FOR THE MARMALADE

4 medium red bell peppers
2 tablespoons (1 ounce) olive oil
1 small shallot, minced
1 tablespoon granulated sugar
1 tablespoon tomato paste
1½ teaspoons Spanish smoked sweet paprika

3 tablespoons (1½ ounces) sherry vinegar
Kosher salt and ground white pepper
¼ cup (2 ounces) water

FOR THE JUS

2 cups (1 pint) Veal Demi-Glace (see page xxviii)
1 tablespoon minced black Kalamata olives
2 tablespoons (1 ounce) unsalted butter

FOR THE LAMB

2 (8- or 10-ounce) frenched lamb racks
Kosher salt and ground white pepper
Approximately 2 tablespoons olive oil

FOR THE FINISHED DISH

Small mint leaves, Thai basil leaves, or fennel or bronze fennel fronds

TO PREPARE THE BEAN PUREE

1. Combine the beans, stock, garlic, and shallot in a small saucepan. Warm over medium-low heat until the mixture comes to a boil and the beans are very soft.

2. Scrape the mixture into a blender, add the cream and butter and a pinch each of salt and pepper. Puree. Add more salt and pepper if you wish. Transfer to a bowl, cover, and refrigerate.

TO PREPARE THE RED PEPPER MARMALADE

1. Roast the peppers briefly over a stove burner or under the broiler until the skins are blackened. Turn with tongs as needed to blacken evenly.

2. Place the peppers in a plastic bag or covered bowl and let them steam until cool enough to handle. Steaming will loosen the skins.

3. Pull off the blackened skins, using a paper towel or 2 to help strip the skin away from the peppers.

4. Stem and seed the peppers and slice out the white veins that run lengthwise on the inside of the peppers. Discard all the trimmings. Finely dice the peppers.

5. Warm the oil in a small saucepan over medium heat, then sauté the shallot until beginning to soften, about 2 minutes. Stir in the remaining ingredients, reduce the heat to low, and cook until the peppers are very soft and the mixture is almost dry, about 10 minutes. Keep warm on low heat.

TO PREPARE THE JUS

1. Pour the veal demi-glace into a small saucepan and reduce by half over high heat. Whisk in the olives and butter and keep warm on low heat.

TO COOK THE LAMB

1. Preheat the oven to 350°F. Sprinkle the lamb racks with salt and pepper.

2. Warm a 10- or 12-ounce ovenproof skillet over high heat and add the oil. Sear the lamb racks deeply on all sides.

3. Transfer the skillet to the oven and roast the lamb for 7–8 minutes, or until medium-rare, 140°F–145°F on an instant-read thermometer.

4. Transfer the racks to paper towels and let them sit for several minutes.

PUTTING IT ALL TOGETHER

In the middle of each of 4 plates, spread about 3 tablespoons of the bean puree. Slice each rack into 4 thick chops and arrange a pair on each plate over the bean puree. Spoon a portion of marmalade between each pair of lamb chops. Drizzle jus over each. Garnish with leaves or fronds and serve right away.

restaurant embellishments

By now, you know I like eggplant. At the restaurant I may add wafer-like baked Eggplant Crisps as a garnish, with 2 or 3 per serving. To make them, I first line a baking sheet with a non-stick mat or parchment paper and then brush the mat or paper well with olive oil. I slice 2 Japanese eggplants or other long slim Asian eggplants (about 8 ounces each) paper-thin, lengthwise, with a mandoline. I lay the eggplant slices side-by-side on the baking sheet, then brush their tops lightly with more olive oil and sprinkle with kosher salt and ground white pepper. The eggplant bakes in a 225°F oven until crisp, 70–85 minutes.

Kitchen Notes

My lamb comes from a co-op of western lamb ranchers, Colorado-Based Mountain States Rosen (800-USA-LAMB, mountainstatesrosen.com). It's raised naturally and pasture-grazed in sustainable fashion. They oversee the production from field to delivery.

VENISON TENDERLOIN MEDALLIONS WITH CELERY ROOT PUREE AND HUCKLEBERRY SAUCE

SERVES 4

I love to serve venison for wine dinners. The lean but rich and deeply flavored meat stands up well to a variety of fine red wines. Many years ago, a fellow chef at the Eldorado Hotel introduced me to celery root paired with venison. I frequently return to that match.

POSSIBLE DO-AHEAD STEPS

- Make the Veal Demi-Glace and the Light Chicken Stock up to 1 week ahead.
- Make the Huckleberry Sauce to the point before adding the berries to it up to 1 day ahead. Add the berries when reheating so they don't disintegrate.

FOR THE HUCKLEBERRY SAUCE

2 tablespoons (1 ounce) olive oil

1 small red onion, cut in a 6 chunks

2 large sprigs of fresh thyme

1 small sprig of fresh rosemary

1 tablespoon juniper berries

1 tablespoon black peppercorns

1 tablespoon granulated sugar

2 tablespoons (1 ounce) red wine vinegar

1 cup (8 ounces) dry red wine

1 cup (8 ounces) Veal Demi-Glace (see page xxviii)

¼ cup fresh huckleberries, blueberries, or blackberries

Kosher salt and ground white pepper

FOR THE PUREE

2 tablespoons (1 ounce) olive oil

1 (12- or 14-ounce) celery root, peeled, then sliced thin

1 (6-ounce) parsnip, peeled, then sliced thin

1 large shallot

2 cups (1 pint) Light Chicken Stock (see page xxviii)

½ cup (4 ounces) heavy cream

4 tablespoons (2 ounces) unsalted butter

Kosher salt and ground white pepper

FOR THE VENISON

4 (4-ounce) venison tenderloin medallions

Kosher salt and ground white pepper

¼ cup (2 ounces) olive oil

Small sprig of fresh thyme

Small sprig of fresh rosemary

2 tablespoons (1 ounce) unsalted butter

1 tablespoon lavender honey

FOR THE FINISHED DISH

Fresh oregano blossoms, mustard flowers, dill fronds, small nasturtium leaves or small salad greens

TO PREPARE THE HUCKLEBERRY SAUCE

1. Warm the oil in a small saucepan over medium heat. Add the onion and sauté until soft, about 5 minutes.

2. Add the herbs, juniper berries, and peppercorns, and cook for another 3 minutes until the onion is medium brown.

3. Add the sugar and vinegar and simmer until almost dry.

4. Raise the heat to medium high, pour in the wine and reduce quickly to about half. Add the demi-glace and simmer for another 5–8 minutes, until reduced again by about half.

5. Strain the sauce through a fine-mesh sieve into a bowl and then return it to the saucepan. Stir in the huckleberries, season with salt and pepper, and keep warm on low heat.

TO PREPARE THE CELERY ROOT PUREE

1. Warm a small saucepan over high heat and add the oil. Add the celery root, parsnip, and shallot and sauté until soft and lightly colored in spots.

2. Pour in the stock and cream and bring to a boil. Reduce the heat to a simmer and cook the mixture for 10–15 minutes, until the vegetables are tender and the liquid has reduced to about ½ cup.

3. Transfer the mixture to a blender and add the butter. Puree, season with salt and pepper, and reserve.

TO COOK THE VENISON

1. Season the venison medallions with salt and pepper.

2. Warm a large heavy skillet, such as cast-iron, over high heat. Add the oil, swirl it around, and immediately add the venison medallions. Sear for about 2 minutes per side.

3. Reduce the heat to medium and continue cooking for about 2 minutes more per side until an instant-read thermometer inserted sideways into a couple of the medallions reaches 120°F. (The temperature will rise another 5 degrees or so while resting to medium-rare.)

4. Turn off the heat and add the herbs, butter, and honey. As the butter melts, baste the venison with the pan juices for about 30 seconds. Transfer the medallions to a cutting board and let the meat rest for several minutes.

PUTTING IT ALL TOGETHER

Spoon 2 mounds of celery root puree at opposite ends of each of 4 plates. Cut each venison medallion into 2 round slices, and place each over a mound of the puree. Spoon the sauce over the venison slices, let it pool up on the plates, garnish with blossoms, and serve right away.

restaurant embellishments

An Asian pear or nashi pear looks something like a yellow delicious apple and is crunchier than our more common pears. I pickle the pears and then smoke them briefly in a stovetop smoker. If you'd like to make Smoky Asian Pears too, here is my recipe.

SMOKY ASIAN PEARS

1 cup water

2 tablespoons granulated sugar

2 teaspoons kosher salt

2 teaspoons chopped fresh ginger

½ teaspoon black peppercorns

1 cinnamon stick

Juice of 1 lemon

2 skin-on Asian pears, cut in ¾-inch dice

1. Combine the pickling liquid ingredients (everything but the pears). Bring the liquid to a boil, then simmer for 2 minutes.

2. Add the pears and remove from the heat, placing a plate on top of the pears to keep them from floating. Cool the pears to room temperature in the pickling liquid. This can be done a day ahead of when you plan to smoke and serve the pears.

3. Shortly before serving, fire up a stovetop smoker, place the pear pieces in the smoker, and cook briefly until warmed through and slightly fragrant with smoke, 10–15 minutes.

desserts

POPCORN ICE CREAM WITH SWEET-AND-SALTY CARAMEL SAUCE

SERVES 8

This dessert brings out the kid in the most buttoned-up adult, and it's dead simple to make. When I took it to a friend's sixtieth birthday party, twenty-five adults looked like they had regressed to happy preschoolers. I fold caramel popcorn into a vanilla ice cream base, where it retains its crunch. I don't often use salted butter, because it throws off the salt balance in some dishes, but here it's perfect for the French-style salty caramel. If you are feeling ambitious, you can serve both of these with the Caramelized Banana and Milk Chocolate Tart (see page 287), or add shards of Caramel Glass, explained in Restaurant Embellishments. Like most of the dessert recipes, this serves eight instead of the usual four in case you're having a party.

POSSIBLE DO-AHEAD STEPS

- Make the Sweet-and-Salty Caramel up to 3 days ahead.
- Make the Popcorn Ice Cream up to 1 day ahead.

FOR THE POPCORN ICE CREAM

1 cup (8 ounces) half-and-half

2 cups (1 pint) heavy cream

1 tablespoon Nielson-Massey vanilla bean paste, preferably, or 1 tablespoon pure vanilla extract

3 cinnamon sticks

½ cup (6–7 large) egg yolks

¾ cup granulated sugar

1 cup caramel popcorn, from a specialty store or market, crushed in a plastic bag by hand or with a rolling pin (I like G.H. Cretor's Caramel Popcorn)

FOR THE CARAMEL SAUCE

¼ cup granulated sugar

1 tablespoon water

¼ cup (2 ounces) heavy cream

2 tablespoons (1 ounce) salted butter, diced into 8 pieces total

TO PREPARE THE POPCORN ICE CREAM

1. Combine the half-and-half, cream, vanilla, and cinnamon sticks in a medium saucepan. Over medium heat, bring the mixture just to scalding, when a few bubbles break at the rim.

2. In a medium bowl, whisk together the egg yolks and sugar. With a whisk in one hand and the warm cream-milk mixture in the other, drizzle the cream-milk mixture steadily into the egg yolk mixture, whisking rapidly.

3. Pour the combined mixture back into the saucepan and continue cooking over medium heat, stirring with a rubber spatula, until the mixture coats the back of the spatula heavily, about 10 minutes.

4. Strain the mixture through a fine-mesh sieve and chill over an ice bath or in the refrigerator for at least 1 hour.

5. Pour the mixture into an ice cream maker and follow the manufacturer's instructions. Freeze until the ice cream is softly holding its shape, then fold in caramel popcorn, and freeze until firm.

TO PREPARE THE CARAMEL

1. Combine the sugar and water in a heavy medium saucepan. Bring the mixture to a boil and watch the color until the sugar turns dark amber. Immediately remove the pan from the heat and add the cream, which will solidify the caramel. Continue stirring slowly until the mixture has liquefied again.

2. Return the pan to medium heat and simmer until the caramel has been reduced by half, approximately 5 minutes.

3. Whisk in the butter, a bit or 2 at a time, until the caramel has thickened and emulsified. Strain it through a fine-mesh sieve and let sit at room temperature.

PUTTING IT ALL TOGETHER

Paint a smear of caramel with a pastry brush across the center of 8 shallow bowls, then top with balls of ice cream. Alternatively, arrange ice cream balls in tall glasses and spoon caramel over. Serve right away.

restaurant embellishments

Caramel Glass is pretty much what it sounds like, thin amber see-through shards of sugar with a good crunch for contrast. If you want to make them, here's how.

CARAMEL GLASS

1 generous cup (8 ounces) granulated sugar	**¼ cup (2 ounces) light corn syrup**
	¼ cup (2 ounces) water

1. Line a rimmed baking sheet with a non-stick mat or lightly buttered parchment paper.

2. Combine all the ingredients in a small saucepan. Bring the mixture to a boil and continue boiling (it will darken in color) until it reaches 325°F–330°F degrees on a candy thermometer.

3. Carefully pour the hot caramel onto the middle of the baking sheet and allow it to cool completely.

4. While it is cooling, clean off the non-stick mat and return it to the baking sheet or, if using parchment paper, line the baking sheet with another piece and lightly butter it.

5. Preheat the oven to 325°F.

6. Once the caramel is cool and hard, break it up and transfer it to a blender or coffee grinder.

7. Grind to a powder, then dump the powder out on the baking sheet, smoothing it with a spatula in a thin fine layer.

8. Bake for about 3 minutes, or until melted again. When the mixture is cool, break it into shards.

STRAWBERRY SHORTCAKE WITH WHITE CHOCOLATE PARFAIT, VANILLA SPONGE CAKE, STRAWBERRY BROTH, AND CANDIED ALMONDS

SERVES 8

I find that a big hunk of cake or pie, no matter how good, gets a bit ho-hum to me within a few bites. That realization has pushed me to combine several elements on the same plate, generally something fruity, something creamy, something crunchy, and then maybe something cold or hot. If you want crunch but don't want to take the time to candy the almonds, buy some candied nuts. Most of the multiple steps for this and other dessert recipes can be made up to a day ahead, to help you with timing for an important meal. If you're not a person who whips up the perfect-looking pie or exquisitely decorated cake, you'll like these a lot. I tear cake into pieces for a bit of rusticity anyway.

POSSIBLE DO-AHEAD STEPS

- Make the White Chocolate Parfait, Candied Almonds, and Strawberry Broth up to 1 day ahead.

FOR THE PARFAIT

1½ cups (12 ounces) heavy cream (divided use)

5 ounces white chocolate, such as Valrhona Ivoire, finely chopped

1 large egg

3 large egg yolks

Scant ½ cup (3 ounces) granulated sugar

1 teaspoon Nielson-Massey vanilla bean paste, preferably, or 1 teaspoon pure vanilla extract

½ teaspoon grated orange zest

FOR THE STRAWBERRY BROTH

12 ounces fresh strawberries

Grated zest of 1 lemon

Grated zest of 1 lime

1 teaspoon Nielson-Massey vanilla bean paste, preferably, or 1 teaspoon pure vanilla extract

3 sprigs fresh mint

¼ cup granulated sugar

¾ cup (6 ounces) water

1 split (quarter bottle—187 milliliters) sparkling wine

FOR THE CANDIED ALMONDS

½ cup mild-flavored honey, such as orange blossom

½ cup sliced almonds

¼ teaspoon ground allspice

Pinch of kosher salt

FOR THE VANILLA SPONGE CAKE

3½ cups unbleached all-purpose flour

1⅜ teaspoons baking powder

1 teaspoon baking soda

1½ cups (12 ounces) buttermilk

1 teaspoon grated lemon zest plus ¼ cup (2 ounces) lemon juice

1 teaspoon Nielson-Massey vanilla bean paste, preferably, or 1 teaspoon pure vanilla extract

6 tablespoons (3 ounces) unsalted butter, softened

2 cups granulated sugar

2 large eggs

FOR THE FINISHED DISH

½ pint strawberries, sliced

Baby mint leaves or small mint sprigs or nasturtium leaves

Viola, nasturtium or borage blossoms, optional

TO PREPARE THE WHITE CHOCOLATE PARFAIT

1. Warm ¼ cup of the cream with the white chocolate in the top pan of a double boiler over its simmering water bath. Stir to help melt the white chocolate.

2. Remove the pan from the water bath just before the last of the white chocolate is melted, and keep stirring it off the heat to finish melting.

3. In the bowl of a stand mixer fitted with the whisk attachment, beat the egg and egg yolks with the sugar and vanilla at high speed until pale yellow and thick, almost like softly whipped cream, about 5 minutes.

4. Spoon the mixture into another bowl, rinse out the mixer bowl, and return it to the mixer. Pour the remaining 1¼ cup of heavy cream into the mixer bowl and whip it over high speed to soft peaks.

5. By hand, fold the egg mixture into the whipped cream, followed by the melted white chocolate mixture, and orange zest, mixing gently to avoid deflating the mixture.

6. Line a 9 x 12-inch rimmed baking sheet or similar size pan with plastic wrap. Spoon the mixture into the pan and freeze at least 2 hours.

TO BEGIN THE STRAWBERRY BROTH

Combine all the ingredients in a medium bowl, crushing the strawberries somewhat with your fingers or a pastry blender. Chill for at least 2 hours and up to overnight.

TO PREPARE THE CANDIED ALMONDS

1. Line a rimmed baking sheet with a non-stick mat or lightly buttered parchment paper.

2. Warm the honey in a small saucepan over high heat until the honey caramelizes and reaches 255°F–260°F measured on a candy thermometer.

3. Stir in the almonds and cook 1 minute, stirring constantly.

4. Stir in the allspice and salt, and scrape the mixture out onto the prepared baking sheet. Let it cool to room temperature.

TO PREPARE THE VANILLA SPONGE CAKE

1. Preheat the oven to 375°F.

2. Line a 9 x 12-inch rimmed baking sheet or similar size baking pan with lightly buttered parchment paper.

3. Combine the flour, baking powder, and baking soda in a small bowl and reserve.

4. Combine in another small bowl the buttermilk, lemon zest and juice, and vanilla paste and reserve it too.

5. In the stand mixer, this time fitted with the paddle attachment, cream the butter and sugar together at medium-high speed until smooth and fluffy, about 3 minutes.

6. Add the eggs, one at a time, stopping the mixer and scraping down the sides of the bowl between each addition.

7. Stop and add half of the flour mixture, then mix at medium speed until just combined. Then add half of the buttermilk mixture. Repeat with the rest of the dry and wet mixtures, and beat briefly, just until combined. The batter will be fairly thick and springy.

8. Spread the batter in the prepared baking pan. Bake for 18–22 minutes, or until the cake springs back at the center when you touch it. Cool in the pan on a baking rack.

PUTTING IT ALL TOGETHER

1. Arrange several layers of cheesecloth or a clean dishcloth over a medium bowl. Pour the strawberry mixture over the cloth and squeeze very hard to release all the juice from the berries. Discard the berry solids.

2. This is attractive in 8 large shallow bowls. Use a 3-inch biscuit cutter or round cookie cutter to cut out 8 rounds of parfait. Place one of them in the center of each plate. Tear the cake into some 16 sections, each on average a couple of inches square. Place 2 of them to the sides of each parfait round. Break up the candied almonds into uneven clusters and scatter several over each plate. Spoon broth on the plate and over the parfait rounds. Divide strawberries among the plates, garnish with some mint leaves, and serve right away.

restaurant embellishments

- If you have access to *sous vide* equipment, vacuum-seal the marinating strawberries for the broth in a medium *sous vide* bag sealed at medium pressure. It really infuses the berries with the flavorings so that the broth will be super tasty.

- I love herbal accents with fruit desserts. If you do too, make up this Basil Syrup. One of the secrets to its intense green is spinach blended in. Blanch a 2-ounce bunch of basil along with 4 ounces of fresh spinach. Squeeze out excess water, then place both in a blender with 1 cup of simple syrup (made with a half and half mixture of sugar in boiling water), 1 teaspoon of xanthan gum, and a pinch of kosher salt. Puree, then strain through a fine-mesh sieve and chill briefly or up to 1 day.

SERVES 8

This looks almost like one of our big fluffy cumulus clouds that float above Santa Fe on a summer's day, but it's much more substantial, and magnificent in taste.

POSSIBLE DO-AHEAD STEPS

- Make the Peach Parfait, Peach Crémeux, and White-Chocolate Orange Ice Cream up to 1 day ahead.
- Marinate the Gingered Peaches up to 4 hours ahead.

FOR THE PEACH PUREE (DIVIDED USE)

1 pound ripe yellow peaches, (about 3 medium), halved and pitted, but skin on

1 cup (8 ounces) water

½ teaspoon fresh lemon juice

FOR THE GOLDEN PEACH PARFAIT

1 heaping cup (8 ounces) granulated sugar (divided use)

¼ cup (2 ounces) light corn syrup

¼ cup plus 2 tablespoons (3 ounces) water

3 ounces egg yolks (4 to 5 large)

½ cup plus 2 tablespoons (5 ounces) heavy cream

3 ounces egg whites (about 3 large)

1 cup (8 ounces) Peach Puree (see above)

2 tablespoons (1 ounce) peach schnapps or orange liqueur such as Patrón Citrónge or triple sec

FOR THE ICE CREAM

2 cups (16 ounces) whole milk

1 cup (8 ounces) half-and-half

¾ cup granulated sugar

½ cup egg yolks (5–6 large)

½ teaspoon Nielsen-Massey vanilla bean paste, preferably, or pure vanilla extract

5 ounces white chocolate, such as Valrhona Ivoire, finely chopped

1 teaspoon grated orange zest

FOR THE CRÉMEUX

¼ cup plus 2 tablespoons (3 ounces) fresh lemon juice (divided use)

1 tablespoons unflavored powdered gelatin

10 ounces Peach Puree (see above)

¾ cup plus 2 tablespoons granulated sugar

5 ounces egg yolks (7 to 8 large)

Pinch kosher salt

3 ounces (6 tablespoons) unsalted butter

FOR THE MARINATED PEACHES

12 ounces (about 2 medium) ripe yellow peaches, sliced ½ inch thick

½ cup (4 ounces) simple syrup

1 tablespoon peeled and thinly sliced fresh ginger

½ teaspoon pink peppercorns

Small sprig of fresh mint

Small sprig of fresh tarragon

Chervil, mâche, tarragon, or mint leaves or sprigs

TO PREPARE THE PEACH PUREE

Combine the ingredients in a blender and puree. Measure out 1 cup (8 ounces) of the puree for the Golden Peach Parfait and 1 cup plus 2 tablespoons of it for the Golden Peach Crémeux. Any remaining puree can be for the cook to enjoy, or dotted on the dessert plates, or perhaps spooned over your morning yogurt.

TO PREPARE THE PEACH PARFAIT

1. Line a 9 x 12-inch rimmed baking sheet, or similar size pan with plastic wrap.

2. In a small saucepan over medium heat, warm ⅓ cup of the sugar with the corn syrup and water, and boil to a syrupy consistency, reducing by about a quarter.

3. In the bowl of a stand mixer fitted with the whisk attachment, beat the egg yolks at medium speed until light lemon color, a couple of minutes.

4. Slowly pour in the still hot sugar syrup. Immediately raise the mixer's speed to medium-high and keep beating until the mixture cools to warm room temperature, about 15 minutes. The mixture will get lighter in color and larger in volume and go through a stage where large bubbles break on the surface. The bubbles will subside as the egg mixture cooks slowly from the hot syrup. Spoon it into another large bowl carefully, to avoid deflating the mixture.

5. Rinse out the mixer bowl and the whisk attachment, returning both to the mixer. Pour in the heavy cream and beat over high speed until the cream forms soft peaks.

6. Fold the cream into the bowl of the egg mixture. Wash the mixer bowl and whisk attachment well, to get rid of any fat from the cream.

7. Whisk the egg whites over medium speed and, when foamy, pour in the remaining sugar, then beat on high speed until soft peaks of meringue form. (You want to beat the whites last because they deflate the easiest.)

8. Fold the egg white meringue into the bowl with the egg yolk and whipped cream mixture.

9. Lastly fold in the peach puree and schnapps.

10. Spoon into the prepared pan and freeze until set, at least at least 1 hour.

TO PREPARE THE ICE CREAM

1. Warm the milk and half-and-half in a small saucepan over medium heat. Bring the mixture just to scalding, when a few bubbles break at the rim.

2. Meanwhile, in a large bowl, whisk the sugar, egg yolks, and vanilla paste together until the eggs are in thick ribbons.

3. Pour the milk mixture slowly into the yolk mixture, whisking rapidly to temper, not scramble, the eggs. Transfer the custard mixture back to the pan and heat slowly, stirring with a rubber spatula until the custard heavily coats the back of the spatula.

4. Meanwhile, place the white chocolate in a bowl.

5. Strain the hot custard through a fine-mesh sieve into the bowl of chocolate and whisk well to melt the chocolate and emulsify the mixture. Stir in the orange zest.

6. Chill over an ice bath or refrigerate for at least 1 hour.

7. Pour the mixture into an ice cream maker and follow the manufacturer's instructions. Freeze until the ice cream is firm.

TO PREPARE THE CRÉMEUX

1. Pour 2 tablespoons of the lemon juice into a ramekin and sprinkle the gelatin powder over the juice. Set aside to soften for several minutes.

2. Warm the peach puree in a medium saucepan over medium heat just until scalding, when a few bubbles break at the rim.

3. Meanwhile, whisk together the sugar, egg yolks, the rest of the lemon juice, and salt.

4. When the puree is ready, whisk it slowly into the egg mixture, then return the tempered egg mixture back into the saucepan, and continue stirring with a rubber spatula until it starts to thicken. (It will feel a bit thick initially because of the peach puree.) Expect this to take about 10 minutes. The large bubbles that form around the edges will lessen, and the custard will coat the back of the spatula.

5. Whisk in the gelatin mixture, cook another minute, then whisk in the butter.

6. Strain the crémeux through a fine-meshed sieve into a bowl. Cool the crémeux in an ice bath, then cover and refrigerate it.

TO PREPARE THE PEACHES

Combine the ingredients in a bowl and marinate for at least 1 hour and up to 4 hours.

PUTTING IT ALL TOGETHER

Make 2 large smears of crémeux around the inside edge of each of 8 plates. Using a 1-inch round cookie cutter, doughnut hole cutter, or some similar cutter, cut out rounds of parfait and arrange 5 or so of the small disks on the plate, some laying down and some standing up on their edges. Arrange a couple scoops of ice cream on each plate. Drain the peach slices and arrange them equally among the plates, then tuck a few herb leaves in here and there. Serve immediately.

restaurant embellishments

If you have access to *sous vide* equipment, vacuum-seal the marinating peaches in a medium *sous vide* bag sealed at high pressure. The pressed peaches will really absorb the ginger and other spices.

The French cake called a financier for its rich buttery essence makes a perfect addition to this dessert plate. Traditionally, the cake is made in small molds that look like gold bars, but here I cook it up as one larger sheet cake that I can tear apart for these plates.

LEMON FINANCIER

8 ounces (2 sticks) butter

1½ cups confectioners' sugar

Scant ¾ cup unbleached all-purpose flour

1 scant cup almond flour

7 ounces egg whites (7–8 large)

1 teaspoon grated lemon zest

1. Preheat the oven to 375°F and line an 8-inch-square baking dish with parchment paper.

2. Brown the butter over medium heat in a small pan (preferably with a light-colored bottom so that you can easily see the butter change color). When the butter foams, swirl it around in the pan a few times, and watch it carefully as it turns from golden to nutty brown. The butter's aroma will become nutty too. Pour the butter into a heatproof bowl to stop its cooking.

3. In the bowl of a stand mixer fitted with the paddle attachment, mix together on low speed the confectioners' sugar, all-purpose flour, and almond flour.

4. Add the egg whites and increase the mixer speed to medium-high.

5. When the mixture is well blended, begin to mix in the brown butter. Add it about 1 ounce at a time, turning the mixer speed down to low while adding each portion of butter, then turning the speed back up to medium-high until the butter disappears into the batter. By hand, mix in the lemon zest.

6. Scrape the batter into the prepared pan. Bake the cake for 10 minutes. Reduce the heat to 350°F, then turn the cake around in the oven to ensure it cooks evenly, and bake for 5–8 more minutes until golden brown and fairly firm.

7. Cool the cake in the pan on a baking rack. Tear a couple of pieces of cake for each serving.

Kitchen Notes

- White chocolate can be a bit boring on its own, but I find it to be a terrific medium for adding silkiness to a dessert such as the ice cream here or the parfait in the recipe preceding this one. It takes both citrus and herbal flavors very well.

- The recipe includes quite a few egg yolks and whites. Large supermarkets often sell quart containers of yolks or whites, sometimes in the freezer section. They will work in this or my other recipes.

- The French word crémeux means something creamy, and in the case of pastry, usually refers to a mixture thicker than a sauce and runnier than a mousse, most like an American pudding. Sometimes it's thickened with gelatin, as I use here, but some of the body, and much of the creaminess, comes from multiple egg yolks.

BLACK FOREST "CAKE"

SERVES 8

I hate to use the word deconstructed to describe my spins on classic dishes. I rather think of them as reimagined and put back together in a new way. A traditional Black Forest cake combines layers of chocolate cake and cherries with cream. My "cake" is actually a lot simpler to make, and all the pieces can be assembled ahead. If you don't want to whip up anything quite this involved, make the sorbet and the cherries and you'll have plenty of Black Forest ambiance.

POSSIBLE DO-AHEAD STEPS

- Make the Chocolate-Cherry Crémeux, Chocolate Sponge Cake, and Chocolate Sorbet up to 1 day ahead.
- Marinate the Black Cherries up to 4 hours ahead.

FOR THE CRÉMEUX

8 ounces sweet dark cherries, pitted, fresh or thawed frozen

2 tablespoons (1 ounce) water

½ cup (4 ounces) whole milk

2 teaspoons unflavored powdered gelatin

2 ounces egg yolks (2–3 large)

2 tablespoons granulated sugar

½ cup (4 ounces) heavy cream

½ teaspoon Nielsen-Massey vanilla bean paste, preferably, or pure vanilla extract

½ teaspoon grated orange zest

Pinch kosher salt

6 ounces bittersweet chocolate (61–71 percent cacao), finely chopped

FOR THE SPONGE CAKE

4 ounces bittersweet chocolate (61–71 percent cacao), finely chopped

4 tablespoons (2 ounces) unsalted butter

1 cup granulated sugar

1 scant cup unbleached all-purpose flour

2 tablespoons plus 2 teaspoons cocoa powder

1 ¼ teaspoon baking powder

1 teaspoon baking soda

1 cup (8 ounces) buttermilk

2 large eggs

½ teaspoon Nielsen-Massey vanilla bean paste, preferably, or pure vanilla extract

FOR THE SORBET

9 ounces bittersweet chocolate (61–70 percent cacao), finely chopped

Generous ¾ cup granulated sugar

¼ cup plus 2 tablespoons glucose powder

½ teaspoon apple pectin powder

3 cups (24 ounces) water

FOR THE CHERRIES

8 ounces sweet dark cherries, pitted, fresh or thawed frozen

½ cup simple syrup

1 tablespoon sliced fresh ginger

Medium sprig of fresh lemon verbena

Medium sprig of fresh mint

FOR THE FINISHED DISH

Fresh mint sprigs or small mint leaves or lemon verbena leaves

TO PREPARE THE CHOCOLATE-CHERRY CRÉMEUX

1. Puree the cherries in a blender with the water. Strain through a fine-mesh sieve, pushing on the solids to get as much of them as possible through the sieve. Reserve.

2. Pour out about 2 tablespoons of the milk into a ramekin and sprinkle the gelatin over it. Set aside briefly to soften.

3. Combine the egg yolks and sugar in a medium bowl, and whisk to a light lemon color.

4. Heat the rest of the milk with the cream, vanilla, orange zest, and salt, and bring just to a simmer.

5. Whisk it slowly into the egg yolk mixture, then return the tempered mixture back into the saucepan, and continue stirring until it starts to thicken. Expect this to take about 10 minutes. The large bubbles that form around the edges will lessen, and you will be able to see a trail through the bottom of the pan when you are whisking.

6. Whisk in the chocolate, cherry puree, and gelatin. Strain through a fine-mesh sieve, chill in an ice bath, then refrigerate covered until needed.

TO PREPARE THE CHOCOLATE SPONGE CAKE

1. Preheat the oven to 375°F.

2. Line a 9 x 12-inch rimmed baking sheet or similar size baking pan with lightly buttered parchment paper.

3. Melt the chocolate and butter together in a small saucepan over low heat, whisking occasionally. Take the pan off the heat before all the chocolate has fully melted, and continue to whisk it off the heat until smooth.

4. In the bowl of a stand mixer fitted with the whisk attachment, combine the sugar, flour, cocoa powder, baking powder, and baking soda over low speed.

5. In another bowl, combine the buttermilk, eggs, and vanilla.

6. Pour the wet ingredients into the mixer, a bit at a time. When incorporated, beat over medium speed for about 30 seconds. Stop the mixer and scrape down the sides of the bowl.

7. Add the chocolate-butter mixture to the mixer and mix until just combined.

8. Transfer the batter to the prepared pan. Bake for 25–30 minutes, or until the cake springs back when pressed gently in the center. It will look like a pan of somewhat cakey brownies. Cool in the pan on a baking rack.

TO PREPARE THE SORBET

1. Place the chocolate in a large heatproof bowl.

2. Combine the sugar, glucose powder, and pectin in a medium saucepan. Pour in the water, whisking to avoid lumps. Bring the mixture to boil over medium heat, whisking occasionally.

3. Pour the hot liquid into the chocolate. Using a hand-held mixer or an immersion blender, mix the sorbet well.

4. Strain the mixture through a fine-mesh sieve. Chill over an ice bath, or refrigerate for at least 1 hour. Transfer to an ice cream machine and follow the manufacturer's instructions.

TO PREPARE THE CHERRIES

Combine all the ingredients together in a bowl and refrigerate for at least 1 hour.

PUTTING IT ALL TOGETHER

I like to serve this on 8 large white plates. Use a 3-inch biscuit cutter or round cookie cutter to cut out 8 rounds of crémeux. Place 1 of them in the center of each plate. Tear the cake into some 16 sections, each on average a couple of inches square. Place 2 of them to the sides of each crémeux round. Spoon the cherries onto each plate, drizzling some of the syrup around the cake and crémeux. Spoon a pair of scoops of sorbet onto each plate. Tuck in some mint leaves and serve right away.

restaurant embellishments

At the restaurant, I finish this plate off with Lavender Cream under it all. Lavender is just terrific in anything creamy. To make your own, follow this recipe.

LAVENDER CREAM

5 ounces (1 stick plus 2 tablespoons) unsalted butter

½ cup sour cream

½ cup granulated sugar

3 large eggs

2 large egg yolks

Pinch of kosher salt

½ teaspoon dried lavender buds

½ teaspoon grated lemon zest

½ teaspoon vanilla bean paste

1 bloomed silver gelatin sheet (or 1 teaspoon unflavored powdered gelatin softened in 1 tablespoon of water)

1. Combine in the top pan of a double boiler the butter, sour cream, sugar, eggs, egg yolks, and salt.

2. Place it over a simmering water bath. Whisk until everything has melded together.

3. Mix in lavender buds, lemon zest, vanilla bean paste, and gelatin.

4. Continue whisking until thick enough that the whisk leaves a trail across the bottom of the pan.

5. Strain through a fine-mesh sieve.

6. Chill in an ice bath, then refrigerate covered until serving time. Whisk well before swooshing it across the plates.

If you want a note of crunch, add shards of the Caramel Glass on page 263.

Kitchen Notes

"Sorbet stabilizer," chefs call it. It's a little miracle for making smoother sorbets that won't melt before you can get them to the table. The chefs who oversaw me and other stagiaires at Georges Blanc back in the 1990s added a mystery powder to our sorbets that they would never divulge. I knew that the frozen treats were ethereal, and that the identity of that powder had something to do with it, but I returned to the United States none the wiser about it. A few years later I attended a workshop in Colorado, where a couple of French pastry chefs demonstrated making sorbets. I was ecstatic when they showed us a combination of apple pectin powder and glucose powder, no doubt the mystery substance added by the secretive supervising chefs back in Vonnas. These days, it's a not-so-secret trick in restaurant kitchens, but it's still pretty much unknown to home cooks. You can buy "sorbet stabilizer" from many sources online, or purchase the apple pectin powder and glucose powder (available in most well-stocked supermarkets), and mix it yourself. Pectin is the naturally occurring substance in many fruits that helps their juices to gel when making jam or jelly. Apples contain a very high percentage of pectin, so their pectin is frequently used to help a mixture gel. Glucose or dextrose is a simple sugar found in many foods too. When mixed into sorbet, it helps retard the formation of ice crystals so that the final dessert stays lusciously creamy and extra smooth. I just call for the two ingredients separately, which lets me adjust the amounts based on what they are mixed with.

CARROT CAKE WITH YOGURT AND CREAM CHEESE FONDANT, CARAMELIZED WALNUTS, AND MOCHA ICE CREAM

SERVES 8

A dessert for all seasons, carrot cake has been on our menu in some form since we opened our doors. This cake is almost more carrots than batter, and instead of expected cream cheese frosting, pieces of cake sit beside a yogurt and cream cheese fondant, which is a bit richer than a crémeux, common to many of my other desserts. Crunchy walnuts and coffee-scented ice cream make this a happy dessert, or maybe even a happy-birthday dessert. You can swap in store-bought ice cream but this one is pretty fabulous.

POSSIBLE DO-AHEAD STEPS

- Make the Carrot Cake, Yogurt and Cream Cheese Fondant, Caramelized Walnuts, and Mocha Ice Cream up to 1 day ahead.

FOR THE CARROT CAKE

2 generous cups unbleached all-purpose flour

¾ teaspoon baking soda

½ teaspoon baking powder

½ teaspoon ground cinnamon

Pinch of kosher salt

4 large eggs

½ cup plus 2 tablespoons canola or vegetable oil

1 generous cup granulated sugar

2 cups packed grated carrots

1 teaspoon grated orange zest

FOR THE FONDANT

¾ cup plus 2 tablespoons (7 ounces) heavy cream (divided use)

2 teaspoons unflavored powdered gelatin

½ cup (4 ounces) mascarpone cheese

3 ounces plain full-fat Greek yogurt

3 ounces cream cheese

4 large egg yolks

Scant ½ cup granulated sugar

1 teaspoon grated orange zest

FOR THE ICE CREAM

2 cups (16 ounces) whole milk

1 cup (8 ounces) half-and-half

1 teaspoon Nielsen-Massey vanilla bean paste, preferably, or pure vanilla extract

Scant ¾ cup granulated sugar

½ cup egg yolks (5–6 large)

2 tablespoons instant espresso powder

FOR THE WALNUTS

½ cup mild-flavored honey, such as orange blossom

2 tablespoons packed brown sugar

½ cup walnut pieces

¼ teaspoon ground allspice

Pinch of kosher salt

Fresh mint sprigs or small mint leaves, or viola or borage blossoms

TO PREPARE THE CAKE

1. Preheat the oven to 350°F.

2. Line a 9 x 12-inch rimmed baking sheet or similar size baking pan with lightly buttered parchment paper.

3. Combine the flour, baking soda, baking powder, cinnamon, and salt in a medium bowl.

4. In the bowl of a stand mixer fitted with the whisk attachment, whisk the eggs on medium speed briefly until frothy, then slowly add the oil in a thin stream, like you are making mayonnaise.

5. Add the sugar in two steps, mixing to combine after each addition.

6. Remove the bowl from the mixer and fold in the bowl of dry ingredients. When just barely mixed, with a few streaks left, fold in the carrots and orange zest.

7. Scrape the batter into the prepared pan and bake for 15 minutes. Turn the oven temperature up to 375°F, and cook for another 12–15 minutes, or until the cake is springy in the center and nicely browned.

8. Cool in the baking pan on a baking rack.

TO PREPARE THE FONDANT

1. Pour 2 tablespoons of the cream into a ramekin, sprinkle the gelatin over it, and set aside to soften for several minutes.

2. Warm the mascarpone, yogurt, cream cheese, and ¼ cup of the heavy cream in a saucepan over medium heat until the ingredients have melted together and the mixture is steamy.

3. In a medium bowl, whisk together the egg yolks and sugar.

4. Pour the hot cream cheese mixture into the yolks, whisking the entire time, then transfer back to the saucepan. Cook over medium-low heat, stirring with a rubber spatula about 10 minutes, or until the mixture coats the back of the spatula.

5. Whisk in the gelatin mixture and cook for 1 minute more.

6. Chill the mixture in an ice bath.

7. Meanwhile, whip the remaining cream in the mixer fitted with the whisk attachment. Fold the whipped cream and grated orange zest into the chilled fondant mixture and refrigerate covered until needed.

TO PREPARE THE ICE CREAM

1. Warm the milk, half-and-half, and vanilla in a large saucepan over medium heat and bring just to scalding, when a few bubbles break at the rim.

2. Meanwhile, whisk together in a large bowl the sugar and egg yolks until the mixture is thick and pale yellow.

3. Pour the milk mixture into the yolk mixture, whisking continually to temper the eggs.

4. Transfer the mixture back to the saucepan. Cook over medium-low heat continuing to whisk until thickened, about 10 minutes, when you can see a trail across the bottom of the pan from the whisk.

5. Chill the mixture in an ice bath or refrigerate for at least 1 hour.

6. Once chilled, pour the mixture into an ice cream maker and follow the manufacturer's instructions. Store covered in the freezer if not using right away.

TO PREPARE THE WALNUTS

1. Line a baking sheet with a non-stick mat or parchment paper, lightly buttered.

2. Warm the honey and brown sugar in a small heavy saucepan over medium heat and caramelize to medium amber.

3. Stir in the walnuts, allspice, and salt, and cook for 1 minute more.

4. Scrape the mixture onto the baking sheet and let cool. Break up into small clusters.

PUTTING IT ALL TOGETHER

Tear the cake so that you have 24 similar pieces. Place 3 pieces of carrot cake in the center of 8 plates, place 1 scoop of fondant at the top of the plate and 1 scoop of ice cream towards the bottom. Sprinkle with the walnuts, garnish with mint, and serve right away.

restaurant embellishments

A pretty addition to the plates is Concord Grape Gel.

CONCORD GRAPE GEL

1 cup pureed Concord grapes (with skins and seeds)

½ cup simple syrup

1 teaspoon fresh lemon juice

2 bloomed silver gelatin sheets

¼ teaspoon agar agar

Pinch of kosher salt

Combine grapes, simple syrup, and lemon juice in a small saucepan, and bring to a boil. Whisk in gelatin, agar agar, and salt, and continue boiling for 2 minutes. Strain through a fine-mesh sieve and chill. Whisk again vigorously before using.

MASCARPONE CHEESECAKE WITH FIG-OLIVE OIL CAKE, DRIED BLACK PLUM JAM, AND RED CURRANT ICE CREAM

SERVES 8

This stars a cool creamy mousse. It's not quite a cheesecake in the New York sense, but you also don't have to bake it or worry about it cracking. I serve it with three fruits that always take me back to France.

POSSIBLE DO-AHEAD STEPS

- Make the Dried Black Plum Jam up to 2 days ahead.
- Make the Mascarpone Cheesecake, Fig-Olive Oil Cake, and Red Currant Ice Cream up to 1 day ahead.

FOR THE JAM

Scant ¾ cup granulated sugar

1 teaspoon apple pectin powder

8 ounces plump dried black plums (prunes), pitted

½ cup (4 ounces) water

½ cup (4 ounces) dry red wine

1 teaspoon fresh lemon juice

FOR THE CHEESECAKE

¼ cup (2 ounces) water

1 tablespoon unflavored powdered gelatin

1 cup (8 ounces) heavy cream

1 cup granulated sugar

Pinch kosher salt

3 ounces cream cheese, softened

5 ounces mascarpone cheese

1 tablespoon fresh lemon juice

½ teaspoon Nielsen-Massey vanilla bean paste, or pure vanilla extract

FOR THE CAKE

6 plump dried figs

¼ cup plus 2 tablespoons (3 ounces) olive oil

¼ cup (2 ounces) whole milk

1 large egg

¾ cup granulated sugar

Generous ¾ cup unbleached all-purpose flour

½ teaspoon baking powder

¼ teaspoon baking soda

Pinch kosher salt

FOR THE ICE CREAM

1 cup (8 ounces) half-and-half

2 cups (16 ounces) whole milk

1 teaspoon Nielsen-Massey vanilla bean paste, or 1 teaspoon pure vanilla extract

Scant ¾ cup granulated sugar

½ cup egg yolks (5 to 6 large)

½ cup fresh red currants, crushed lightly, or thawed frozen (no crushing needed)

PREPARE THE DRIED PLUM JAM

1. Line a 9 x 12-inch baking pan with plastic wrap.
2. In a small bowl, stir together the sugar and pectin. Make sure the pectin is well dispersed in the sugar. Reserve.
3. Puree the dried plums with the water in a food processor.
4. Scrape the puree into a medium saucepan and pour in the wine.
5. Whisk in the sugar-pectin mixture.

6. Place the pan on high heat and stir the mixture constantly until the jam reaches 215°F–220°F, measured on a candy thermometer.

7. Remove from the heat and stir in the lemon juice.

8. Pour the jam into the prepared pan. Place another piece of plastic wrap directly on its surface. Let cool to room temperature. Refrigerate until needed.

TO PREPARE THE CHEESECAKE

1. Line a 9 x 12-inch baking pan with plastic wrap.

2. Pour the water into a small saucepan or sauté pan. Sprinkle the gelatin over it and let stand for several minutes for the gelatin to soften.

3. Pour the cream into the bowl of an electric mixer with the whisk attachment. With high speed, whisk the cream until it is softly peaked. Refrigerate until needed. Scoop out into another bowl if you only have one bowl for your mixer, then rinse out the bowl.

4. Warm the pan of gelatin over medium heat and stir to dissolve it. Remove from the heat.

5. Combine in the bowl of a stand mixer fitted with the paddle attachment the sugar, salt, and cream cheese. Mix at low speed, occasionally scraping down the sides of the bowl.

6. Stop the mixer and add the mascarpone cheese, lemon juice, vanilla, and gelatin mixture. Mix again at low speed until combined. Raise the speed to medium high and beat for 2–3 minutes, until very silky, creamy, and thick.

7. Fold in the whipped cream by hand.

8. Spoon mixture into the prepared pan, cover and refrigerate.

TO PREPARE THE CAKE

1. Preheat the oven to 375°F. Line an 8-inch square baking pan with parchment paper, lightly buttered.

2. Puree the figs in a food processor. Reserve.

3. Whisk together in a small bowl the olive oil, milk, and egg. Reserve.

4. Combine in the bowl of a stand mixer fitted with the paddle attachment the sugar, flour, baking powder, baking soda, and salt. Using low speed, combine the dry ingredients.

5. Add the oil mixture in a slow steady stream, then raise the speed to medium and mix just until fully combined.

6. Stir in the pureed figs by hand.

7. Spoon the batter into the prepared pan. Bake 15–18 minutes, or until lightly golden and set. Cool the cake in the pan over a baking rack.

TO PREPARE THE ICE CREAM

1. Combine in a medium saucepan the half-and-half, milk, and vanilla. Warm the mixture over medium heat until it just comes to a boil.

2. Meanwhile, whisk together in a large bowl the sugar and egg yolks until thick and pale lemon in color.

3. Pour the milk mixture into the yolk mixture, whisking continually to temper the yolks, then transfer the mixture back to the pan. Continue cooking over medium-low heat, stirring with a rubber spatula, about 10 minutes, or until thick enough to coat the back of the spatula.

4. Strain through a fine-mesh sieve and chill over an ice bath or refrigerate for at least 1 hour.

5. Once chilled, pour into an ice cream machine and follow the manufacturer's instructions. When the ice cream is ready, but still a bit soft, fold in the currants. Mix only enough to get a marbled look to the ice cream. Use immediately or place in the freezer until needed.

PUTTING IT ALL TOGETHER

Cut the cheesecake into 8 slices about 1 x 6 inches and place them on 8 plates. (You will have some remaining that you can use for another dessert or a midnight snack.) Tear the cake into 24 more or less equal small pieces. Arrange 3 pieces of cake on each plate, somewhat covering the cheesecake. Spoon on a dollop of jam and scoop of currant ice cream to the side of each. Serve immediately.

restaurant embellishments

I love the playful enhancement of toasted marshmallow cream on the plate, burnished with the flame of a small kitchen torch. I make Toasted Orange Marshmallow this way.

TOASTED ORANGE MARSHMALLOW

6 bloomed silver gelatin sheets
½ cup (4 ounces) orange juice
1 teaspoon kosher salt
1 cup granulated sugar
¼ cup light corn syrup
1 cup water
½ teaspoon of grated orange zest

1. Warm orange juice salt in a small saucepan over medium heat. Whisk in the gelatin until dissolved. Pour into the bowl of a stand mixer fitted with the whisk attachment.

2. In another small saucepan, combine sugar, corn syrup, and water and bring to a boil over high heat. When the mixture reaches 220°F–225°F on a candy thermometer, remove it from the heat and add orange zest.

3. Start the mixer on low speed and pour the hot syrup slowly and carefully into the orange mixture. When combined, raise the speed to medium high and beat until the clear mixture turns foamy and then creamy and airy, like marshmallow cream, about 15 minutes.

4. The mixing bowl should be close to room temperature when it is ready.

5. Spoon the mixture into a plastic pastry bag and pipe onto the dessert plates in decorative mounds before adding the other ingredients. Toast the marshmallow cream with a few small blasts from a kitchen blowtorch, then add the rest of the ingredients, and serve.

Kitchen Notes

- In the cheesecake portion of this dessert the gelatin is cooked on its own rather than mixed in with other heated ingredients. That's because it is the only thickener—there are no eggs—so that the pure dairy taste of cream and cheese come through fully.

- If you have extra jam or ice cream, the two are great together for a simpler dessert later in the week.

KEY LIME VACHERIN WITH SZECHUAN PEPPERCORN MERINGUE AND ALMOND-COCONUT CRUMBS

SERVES 8

Key lime pie inspired this dish, but I think of it as a vacherin, the French dessert that combines crisp meringue with custard and fruit. Building from the bottom up, I make a cakey shortbread-style crust, add ground almond flour to bolster the sandy texture, and sprinkle in shredded coconut because I enjoy it with almonds. Then I break the baked shell into chunks evocative of the graham cracker crumbs many people enjoy in a piecrust. If you've ever worried about getting a piecrust to look just right, this crumbled style takes away all concerns, letting you play with your food. In the custard filling, I want an initial burst of lime quickly mellowed by the creamy essence. Key limes, also known as Mexican limes, or limones, are the tiny extra tangy limes that show up particularly in early winter and early summer. The meringue too is a key player for me. I love how that first bite of baked crispness dissolves in your mouth. To emphasize the effect, I bake the meringue into thin, stiff sheets so that there will be more of that crunchy surface in every bite. Szechuan peppercorns typically add zing and instant complexity to savory dishes. If you use them in something mild, like meringue, you taste their floral notes too, at least if you don't overdo it and numb your tongue. I break the meringue into shards and place two or three pieces in the cool custard leaning against each other.

FOR THE MERINGUE

6 ounces egg whites (about 7 large whites)

1 cup confectioners' sugar

¾ cup granulated sugar

1 tablespoon plus 2 teaspoons cornstarch

½ teaspoon ground Szechuan peppercorns

FOR THE CUSTARD

Zest of 2 key limes, plus 5 ounces (½ cup plus 2 tablespoons) fresh key lime juice

2 teaspoons unflavored gelatin powder

⅔ cup granulated sugar

Pinch of kosher salt

3 ounces egg yolks (3–4 large yolks)

1½ tablespoons unsalted butter

FOR THE ALMOND-COCONUT CRUMBS

1 cup unbleached all-purpose flour

¼ cup almond flour or almond meal

¼ cup shredded coconut

1 ½ teaspoons baking powder

1 teaspoon baking soda

1 teaspoon ground dried ginger

Pinch of kosher salt

½ cup granulated sugar

4 ounces (1 stick) butter, softened

1 large egg

FOR THE FINISHED DISH

Fresh mint sprigs or tarragon sprigs or nasturtium leaves

1 large lime, peeled and sliced into segments

TO PREPARE THE MERINGUE

1. Preheat the oven to 200°F. Line a rimmed baking sheet with a non-stick mat or parchment paper.

2. In the bowl of a stand mixer fitted with the whisk attachment, beat the egg whites at high speed until the mixture goes from clear and foamy to white.

3. Turn the mixer speed down to low and slowly add the confectioners' sugar, granulated sugar, cornstarch, and peppercorns. When incorporated, scrape down the sides of the mixer, then turn the speed back up to high and beat to stiff peaks.

4. Spread the meringue to approximately ½ inch in thickness on the baking sheet, smoothing it with an offset spatula or the back of a big spoon. Bake the meringue until dry and crisp, 70–80 minutes.

TO PREPARE THE LIME CUSTARD

1. Reserve the lime zest.

2. Measure out 2 tablespoons of the lime juice in a ramekin and sprinkle the gelatin over it. Let it sit for several minutes to soften.

3. Meanwhile, whisk together in the top pan of a double boiler the rest of the lime juice, sugar, salt, and egg yolks. Place the pan over the bottom pan of simmering water. Stir the mixture slowly until it begins to thicken and the whisk leaves a trail across the bottom of the pan.

4. Stir in the gelatin mixture, combining it well.

5. Add the butter in pieces, and continue whisking until all the butter is incorporated.

6. Strain through a fine-mesh sieve and fold in the grated lime zest.

7. Spoon into 6-ounce ramekins and let cool to room temperature. Cover and refrigerate at least 1 hour and up to overnight.

TO PREPARE THE ALMOND-COCONUT CRUMBS

1. Preheat the oven to 375°F.

2. Line a baking sheet with a non-stick mat or parchment paper.

3. Stir together in a medium bowl the flour, almond flour, coconut, baking powder, baking soda, ginger, and salt.

4. Using the stand mixer, this time fitted with the paddle attachment, cream the sugar and butter at high speed until the mixture is fluffy, about 2 minutes.

5. Add the egg and mix well.

6. Stop the mixer and scrape down the sides. Then add the dry ingredients in 2 additions, just mixing in each one. Scrape the dough from the bowl, wrap in plastic, and chill for at least 1 hour and up to overnight.

7. Roll the dough into a large oval or rectangle, ⅛ inch in thickness. Transfer the dough to the baking sheet in 1 piece, like 1 giant cookie. Bake for 7–9 minutes, or until golden brown and somewhat dry. Cool on the baking sheet on a baking rack. Break into large crumbles.

PUTTING IT ALL TOGETHER

Arrange 8 dessert plates on a work surface. Spoon about ⅓ cup of almond-coconut crumbs in the center of each plate. Run a small knife around the inside of a custard ramekin to loosen, then invert it and position it over the crumbs. Repeat with the rest of the remaining custards. Tear/break the meringue into free-form strips, making them at least 4 or so inches in height and an inch or so in width. Arrange several of the meringue shards so that they more or less cover the custard. Garnish with herbs and orange sections, and serve right away.

Kitchen Notes

Do give leaves of fresh tarragon a try as a dessert garnish. Don't overdo it, but the forward flavor of anise and the back hint of vanilla can complement a dish with creamy or tangy notes. Opt for sprigs of smaller whole leaves or slice larger leaves just before serving and sprinkle them over the dish.

CARAMELIZED BANANA AND MILK CHOCOLATE TART

SERVES 8

The question to myself was, "How can I elevate the everyday banana into a superb dessert?" Heating transforms the fruit's starchy texture to an almost silken state, which feels much more appealing on the tongue. A glassy caramelized sugar over the bananas makes a satisfying contrast, shattering like the top of crème brûlée. In today's world of designer chocolates, milk chocolate strikes people as rather ordinary too. But its gentle flavor plays well with others, and it echoes the banana's creamy essence. I add a hint of bittersweet chocolate too. It helps firm up the velvety milk chocolate just a touch and increases the depth of flavor without changing the luscious character. You can use any fine chocolate for this chilled pudding mixture, called on our menu a crémeux. To make the tart look grand, I layer a couple of pieces of a simple but delectable French sugar cookie, a sable, under everything else as a free-form crust.

POSSIBLE DO-AHEAD STEPS

- Make the dough for the sable cookies/tart crust up to 2 days ahead.
- Make the Almond Sable Cookies/Tart Crust and the Milk Chocolate Crémeux up to 1 day ahead.

FOR THE ALMOND COOKIES/TART CRUST

5 tablespoons unsalted butter, softened

2 tablespoons confectioners' sugar

1 large egg

½ cup unbleached all-purpose flour

3 tablespoons almond flour or almond meal

1¾ teaspoons baking powder

1 teaspoon ground cinnamon

Pinch kosher salt

FOR THE CRÉMEUX

1¾ cups (14 ounces) heavy cream (divided use)

2¾ cups milk chocolate, finely chopped

⅔ cup bittersweet chocolate (61–70 percent cacao), finely chopped

2 large egg yolks

¼ cup plus 1½ tablespoons granulated sugar

1 cup (8 ounces) whole milk

FOR THE CARAMELIZED BANANAS

2 large bananas, each peeled and cut into 4 lengthwise quarters

Raw turbinado sugar, about 2 tablespoons

FOR THE FINISHED DISH

Raspberry coulis or puree, such as Perfect Puree, optional

Tiny mint or basil leaves, optional

TO PREPARE THE COOKIES/CRUST

1. Cream the butter and sugar together in the bowl of a stand mixer fitted with the paddle attachment on high speed, until fluffy and smooth, about 1 minute. Stop and scrape down the mixture from the sides of the mixer, then beat in the egg.

2. Stir the flour, almond flour, baking powder, cinnamon, and salt together in a small bowl. Add to the mixer bowl in 2 additions, mixing each time at medium speed until just incorporated. Scrape the dough from the bowl onto a small plate. Cover with plastic and chill in the refrigerator for at least 30 minutes and up to overnight.

3. Preheat the oven to 350°F.

4. Line a baking sheet with a non-stick mat or parchment paper, lightly buttered.

5. Roll out the dough on a flour-dusted work surface with a flour-dusted rolling pin to ⅛ inch in thickness.

6. Cut the dough into 16 equal-size rectangles, about 1½ x 3 inches.

7. Place cookies on the baking sheet and bake for approximately 5–8 minutes, until lightly firm and golden.

8. Cool on the baking sheet for about 5 minutes, then transfer to a baking rack.

TO PREPARE THE CRÉMEUX

1. In the bowl of a stand mixer fitted with the whisk attachment, beat ¾ cup of the heavy cream to soft peaks. Refrigerate the whipped cream until needed.

2. Place the milk chocolate and bittersweet chocolate in a large heatproof bowl.

3. Whisk together in a medium bowl the egg yolks and sugar until the mixture forms thick ribbons and becomes a light lemon color.

4. Warm the remaining 1 cup of cream and milk in a medium saucepan over medium heat until scalding, when a few bubbles break at the rim.

5. With a whisk in one hand and the warm cream-milk mixture in the other, drizzle the cream-milk mixture steadily into the egg yolk mixture, whisking rapidly to temper and emulsify. Pour the combined mixture back into the saucepan and continue cooking over medium heat, stirring with a rubber spatula, until the mixture coats the back of the spatula.

6. Immediately strain the hot mixture through a fine-mesh sieve into the bowl of chocolate. Mix with the rubber spatula until the chocolate melts. Cool to room temperature.

7. Fold the whipped cream into the chocolate. Chill for at least 1 hour and up to a day. Transfer the filling to a pastry bag with a plain tip. Alternatively, spoon it into a plastic zipper-lock bag and snip off 1 lower corner of the bag.

TO PREPARE THE CARAMELIZED BANANAS

1. If you have a small kitchen torch, lay the banana pieces in a single layer in a greased small baking pan. If not, turn on the broiler and line a baking sheet with a non-stick mat or parchment paper, lightly buttered, and place the bananas on the sheet.

2. Sprinkle enough raw sugar over the bananas to cover them lightly but fully.

3. Caramelize the sugar using short bursts from the torch, until the sugar is deeply golden brown. Alternatively, place the pan under the broiler and broil briefly, a minute or 2.

PUTTING IT ALL TOGETHER

Arrange 8 dessert plates on a work surface. Arrange a sable cookie on each for the bottom crust. Pipe two thick lines of crémeux lengthwise over the cookie, practically covering it. Place another cookie directly over the filling and top with a caramelized banana section, about the same size as the sable cookies. Add dots of raspberry coulis, if you wish, and tuck in a few pretty herb leaves. Serve right away.

restaurant embellishments

Creamy, crunchy, salty, sweet. The restaurant staff says I'm always upping the ante and they are probably right. For more notes of caramel, I like to add Popcorn Ice Cream with Sweet-and-Salty Caramel (see page 262) to the plate as well. The classic stovetop caramel sauce echos the flavors here but brings a different texture and temperature. Arrange a scoop of ice cream to the side of each tart, then spoon some caramel over and around it.

Kitchen Notes

- I use Aalst Belgian chocolate for both the milk chocolate and the bittersweet. I love Valrhona chocolate too, which may be easier for a home cook to find, but it's a good bit more expensive.

- Sables are simple French cookies, with a sandy, tender texture. Replacing some of the usual wheat flour in a recipe with almond flour adds subtle nuttiness but also cuts down on the amount of gluten in the recipe, making an even more tender cookie. Almond flour and meal are the same thing, finely ground raw almonds.

PEAR SEMIFREDDO WITH CHAMPAGNE PEARS, TOASTED WALNUT SPONGE CAKE, AND PEAR-YOGURT PUDDING

SERVES 8

I always look forward to fall in New Mexico. The mountain aspens turn to shimmering gold and our yard's ash tree looks as if it's caught fire. The state's famous local green chiles turn as red as the tree too. Then there are pears and apples, many from trees that are relatives of ones planted by our area's original Spanish settlers. This dish fully celebrates those luscious pears. If you aren't feeling especially ambitious, try just the semifreddo with the Champagne pears.

POSSIBLE DO-AHEAD STEPS

- Make the Caramelized Pear Puree up to 2 days ahead.
- Make the Pear Semifreddo, Toasted Walnut Sponge Cake, and Pear-Yogurt Pudding up to 1 day ahead.
- Make the Champagne Pears up to 4 hours ahead.

FOR THE PUREE

4 Bosc or Anjou pears, unpeeled, but cored and chopped

¾ cup (6 ounces) water

⅔ cup granulated sugar

Juice of 1 lemon

FOR THE SEMIFREDDO

½ cup (4 ounces) heavy cream

1 cup (8 ounces) whole milk (divided use)

2 teaspoons unflavored powdered gelatin

7 ounces white chocolate, such as Valrhona Ivoire, finely chopped

½ cup (4 ounces) Caramelized Pear Puree (see above)

½ teaspoon Nielsen-Massey vanilla bean paste, preferably, or pure vanilla extract

4 ounces egg yolks (5–6 large)

Generous ¾ cup granulated sugar (divided use)

3 ounces egg whites (about 3 large)

FOR THE SPONGE CAKE

2 cups (1 pint) whole milk

1 cup (8 ounces) buttermilk

8 ounces (2 sticks) unsalted butter

3 cups unbleached all-purpose flour

1 cup granulated sugar

½ cup packed brown sugar

2 teaspoons baking powder

2 teaspoons baking soda

1 teaspoon ground cinnamon

3 large eggs

1 cup toasted chopped walnuts

FOR THE PEARS

2 Anjou, Comice, or other red-skinned pears, preferably, cut in different shapes (trimmings saved for pudding below)

1 cup (8 ounces) champagne, other sparkling wine, or dry white wine

½ cup granulated sugar

Pinch of kosher salt

1 tablespoon thinly sliced peeled fresh ginger

2-inch piece of lemon peel, about ½ inch wide

1 dried bay leaf

½ teaspoon Nielsen-Massey vanilla bean paste, preferably, or pure vanilla extract

Small sprig of fresh thyme

FOR THE PUDDING

1 cup (8 ounces) full-fat plain Greek yogurt

4 ounces minced skin-on pears (from pear trimmings above)

3 ounces (scant ½ cup) granulated sugar

1 teaspoon low-acyl gellan

¼ teaspoon agar agar

1 teaspoon Nielsen-Massey pure vanilla paste, preferably, or pure vanilla extract

Mint sprigs or small mint leaves

TO PREPARE THE PEAR PUREE

Combine all the ingredients in a small saucepan and bring to a boil. Reduce the heat to a simmer and cook until the liquid evaporates, about 10 minutes. Continue cooking a few minutes more, stirring frequently, until the pears have caramelized.

TO PREPARE THE SEMIFREDDO

1. Line a 9 x 12-inch rimmed baking sheet, or similar baking pan, with plastic wrap.

2. Whip the cream in the bowl of a stand mixer fitted with the whisk attachment at high speed. When the cream has soft peaks, spoon it into another bowl, cover, and refrigerate until needed. Wash the mixer's bowl and whisk attachment to use again shortly.

3. Pour about 2 tablespoons of the milk into a ramekin. Sprinkle the gelatin over the milk and let it sit several minutes to soften.

4. Meanwhile, warm the white chocolate and pear puree together in a medium saucepan over medium-low heat. Stir the mixture together as the chocolate melts. Remove from the heat just before the all the chocolate has melted and continue to stir until the mixture is smooth.

5. In another saucepan stir together the rest of the milk, vanilla, egg yolks, and ½ cup of the sugar. Cook over medium-low heat, whisking continually, until the mixture has thickened sufficiently for the whisk to leave a trail where you can see the bottom of the pan.

6. Whisk in the gelatin for an additional minute, then remove the pan from the heat.

7. Fold this mixture into the white chocolate mixture.

8. Using the mixer again fitted with the whisk attachment, beat the egg whites over high speed until they are foamy, slowly add the remaining ¼ cup of sugar, and continue beating until you have soft-peaked meringue.

9. Fold the meringue into the white chocolate mixture, followed by the whipped cream. Spoon it all into the prepared baking pan and freeze uncovered at least 1 hour. You can freeze the mixture up to 1 day but, in that case, cover it after it has set.

TO PREPARE THE CAKE

1. Preheat the oven to 335°F. Line a 9 x 12-inch rimmed baking sheet or similar baking pan with parchment paper, buttered lightly.

2. Warm the milk, buttermilk, and butter together in a medium saucepan over medium heat. Remove from the heat when the butter is melted. Reserve.

3. In the bowl of a stand mixer fitted with the paddle attachment, combine the flour, granulated and brown sugars, baking powder, baking soda, and cinnamon over low speed.

4. Pour the warm butter mixture into the mixing bowl, continuing to mix on low speed until combined.

5. Stop the mixer and scrape down the sides. Raise the speed to medium, then add the eggs one at a time.

6. Stop and scrape down the bowl again, then fold in the walnuts by hand.

7. Scrape the batter into the prepared baking pan and bake for 15–18 minutes, until lightly browned and set. Let the cake cool in the pan on a baking rack.

TO PREPARE THE PEARS

1. Place the pear pieces in a heatproof bowl.

2. Combine the champagne, sugar, salt, ginger, lemon peel, bay leaf, vanilla, and thyme in a small saucepan, and bring to a boil. Reduce the mixture by half, about 5 minutes, then pour the mixture over the pears. Let the mixture steep to room temperature. Cover and refrigerate until needed.

TO PREPARE THE PUDDING

1. Combine all the ingredients in a blender and puree.

2. Transfer to a medium saucepan and bring to a boil. Boil for 5 minutes, then strain through a fine-mesh sieve into a small bowl. Cool over an ice bath, then refrigerate covered if not using right away.

PUTTING IT ALL TOGETHER

Place 8 dessert plates on a work surface. Whisk the pudding to fluff it up a bit. Swoosh a big dollop of pudding across each plate. Using a 2- or 3-inch round biscuit cutter or cookie cutter, cut out rounds of semifreddo. Arrange a round or 2 of semifreddo in the center of each plate. Tear the cake into 16 somewhat equal pieces, and place 1 piece on each side of the semifreddo. Scatter a few pieces of the pears around the plate. Garnish with mint and serve.

restaurant embellishments

As I have done with much of the marinated fruit in this chapter, I would actually seal the champagne marinade and pears with *sous vide* equipment. If you are equipped to do that, seal in a *sous vide* bag at moderate pressure and refrigerate for at least 1 hour.

Why does pumpkin get all the autumn love? I really prefer butternut squash in many dishes, including this Spiced Butternut Sorbet that I add to the semifreddo and other fall dessert plates.

SPICED BUTTERNUT SORBET

2 cinnamon sticks	10 ounces pureed cooked butternut squash
2 star anise	Scant ½ cup granulated sugar
3 cloves	1 tablespoon grated orange zest
½ teaspoon black peppercorns	1 tablespoon glucose powder
1 cup (8 ounces) water	1 teaspoon apple pectin

1. Toast cinnamon sticks, star anise, cloves, and peppercorns in a medium saucepan over medium heat.

2. When fragrant add water, squash, sugar, orange zest, glucose powder, and apple pectin.

3. Bring to a boil, whisking occasionally to get rid of any lumps.

4. Remove from the heat and let steep until the mixture reaches room temperature. Strain through a fine-mesh sieve into a bowl. Chill in an ice bath or refrigerate for at least 1 hour, then transfer to an ice cream machine and follow the manufacturer's instructions.

MOLTEN BITTERSWEET CHOCOLATE CAKE WITH CARAMEL POPCORN TUILE, EARL GRAY TEA ICE CREAM, AND BANANA CARAMEL

SERVES 8

The class I enjoyed the most at the CIA was one simply called at the time "Experimental." We would conduct experiments like making a baguette with traditional wheat flours, then substitute buckwheat, rice, corn, or other flours, then do something like bake it in a microwave, just to see how each different ingredient or technique would change the outcome. We might make nut butters with raw or toasted peanuts, almonds, pecans, macadamias, walnuts, Brazil nuts, you name it. We'd caramelize different sugars and to different degrees. I loved it. Some of that old experimentation comes into play in this last dessert. The cake is always on the menu, but the way it's presented varies with the seasons and with my whims. You can save a little time by using a high-quality store-bought caramel sauce.

POSSIBLE DO-AHEAD STEPS

- Make the Molten Bittersweet Chocolate Cake, Earl Gray Tea Ice Cream, and Banana-Caramel Sauce up to 1 day ahead.
- Make the Caramel Popcorn Tuile up to 4 hours ahead.

FOR THE CAKE

8 ounces bittersweet chocolate (61–70 percent cacao), finely chopped

8 ounces (2 sticks) unsalted butter, softened

5 large eggs

¼ cup egg yolks (3–4 large)

Scant ½ cup granulated sugar

Generous ¾ cup unbleached all-purpose flour

FOR THE ICE CREAM

1 cup (8 ounces) half-and-half

2 cups (1 pint) whole milk

2 bags Earl Grey Tea

1 teaspoon Nielsen-Massey vanilla bean paste, preferably, or pure vanilla extract

Generous ¾ cup granulated sugar

4 ounces egg yolks (4–5 large)

FOR THE TUILE

1 cup plus 1 tablespoon (8 ounces) granulated sugar

¼ cup (2 ounces) light corn syrup

¼ cup (2 ounces) water

4 ounces popped popcorn, coarsely ground in a food processor

Pinch of kosher salt

FOR THE BANANA-CARAMEL SAUCE

½ cup granulated sugar

½ cup (4 ounces) water, plus approximately 2 tablespoons (divided use)

2 tablespoons (1 ounce) light corn syrup

2 medium bananas, chopped

1 teaspoon ground cinnamon

1 tablespoon fresh lemon juice

Pinch of kosher salt

TO PREPARE THE CAKE

1. Preheat the oven to 400°F.

2. Butter 8 ramekins, about 8 ounces in size.

3. Melt the chocolate and butter in the top pan of a double boiler placed over its simmering water bath. Stir the mixture to melt the evenly. Remove it from the heat shortly before all the chocolate has melted, and continue stirring until it is smooth.

4. In the bowl of a stand mixer fitted with the paddle attachment, beat the eggs and yolks over medium speed briefly until frothy.

5. Pour in the sugar in 2 additions, beating about 15 seconds after each.

6. Lower the speed to medium-low and mix in the melted chocolate mixture. Stop the mixer and scrape down the bowl's sides.

7. Add the flour, then mix again at medium-low until just combined.

8. Pour the cake batter into the prepared ramekins. Bake 6–9 minutes, until just set on the surface. You may serve the cakes in the ramekins or, just before serving, run a knife around each and invert it onto a plate.

TO PREPARE THE ICE CREAM

1. Combine the half-and-half, milk, tea bags, and vanilla in a medium saucepan. Warm the mixture over medium heat until just scalding, when a few bubbles break around the rim.

2. Meanwhile, whisk the sugar and egg yolks together in a large bowl until thick and pale lemon in color.

3. Pour the milk mixture into the yolk mixture, whisking continually to temper the yolks, then transfer the mixture back to the pan. Continue cooking over medium-low heat, stirring with a rubber spatula until the custard coats the back of the spatula.

4. Strain through a fine-mesh sieve and chill over an ice bath or refrigerate for at least 1 hour.

5. Process in an ice cream machine following the manufacturer's instructions. Use immediately or place in the freezer until needed.

TO PREPARE THE TUILES

1. Line a rimmed baking sheet with a non-stick mat or parchment paper, lightly buttered.

2. Combine the sugar, corn syrup, and water in a small saucepan. Bring the mixture to a boil and continue boiling (it will darken in color) until it reaches 325°F–330°F degrees.

3. Carefully pour the hot caramel onto the middle of the baking sheet and allow it to cool completely.

4. While it is cooling, clean off the non-stick mat and return it to the baking sheet or, if using parchment paper, line the baking sheet with another piece and lightly butter it.

5. Preheat the oven to 325°F.

6. Once the caramel is cool and hard, break up the caramel and transfer it to a blender or coffee grinder. Grind to a powder. Dump the powder out on a clean baking sheet, smoothing it with a spatula in a thin fine layer. Scatter the popcorn and salt over it. Bake for about 2 minutes, or until melted again.

7. When the mixture is just cool enough to handle, cut with a table knife into at least 8 pieces longer than they are wide. Bend them in curlicues as you wish and let them cool to room temperature.

TO PREPARE THE BANANA CARAMEL SAUCE

1. Combine the sugar, ½ cup water, and corn syrup in a small saucepan. Bring to a boil and boil to a medium caramel color, then immediately stir in the rest of the ingredients, which will cause some sputtering.

2. Reduce the mixture by about half. The bananas will get very soft and begin to melt into the caramel syrup.

3. Transfer to a blender and puree until smooth. If the caramel is not pureeing easily, add an additional tablespoon or 2 of water and blend again. Spoon into a bowl and reserve at room temperature.

PUTTING IT ALL TOGETHER

If the cakes have cooled, you can reheat them for a couple of minutes in a low oven if you wish. Arrange 8 plates on a work surface. Spoon caramel across each plate. Place a cake to one side of the plate and top it with a tuile. Add a scoop of ice cream across from the cake and serve right away.

restaurant embellishments

We freeze blackberries and raspberries in season so that we can use them for dessert syrups and gels when the desire arises. To add a Blackberry Gel to the dessert, follow this recipe.

BLACKBERRY GEL

6 ounces fresh or thawed frozen
   blackberries

¼ cup plus 2 tablespoons (3 ounces) water

1 or 2 tablespoons granulated sugar

1 teaspoon vanilla bean paste

½ teaspoon low-acyl gellan

¼ teaspoon xanthan gum

1. Puree blackberries, water, 1 or 2 tablespoons of granulated sugar (depending on the berries' sweetness), vanilla bean paste, gellan, and xanthan gum in a blender.

2. Transfer to a saucepan, bring to boil, and boil for 3 minutes.

3. Strain through a fine-mesh sieve into a small bowl and cool it over an ice bath. When cool, cover and refrigerate until needed.

Kitchen Notes

Tuiles are thin wafer-like cookies with curved up edges, said to resemble French country roof tiles. Almost anything else thin, delicate, and curved can be called a *tuile* too, such as the confection topping the cake here.

resources

I hope you will patronize stores in your own locale when feasible, but here are some sources that ship nationally and carry some of my more distinctive items. You can find nearly everything listed here by going to amazon.com, but we all need to support small businesses too.

Asian Food Grocer
Asianfoodgrocer.com
(888) 482-2742
Dried bonito flakes, furikake, togarashi shichimi, nori, hijiki (and other dried seaweed), yuzu, yuzu kosho, sudachi juice, maitake and enoki mushrooms, white soy sauce

Black Star Gourmet
Blackstargourmet.com
(888) 336-4441
Wasabi tobiko, cheeses of the world

John Boos & Company
Johnboos.com
(888) 431-2667
Cutting boards, butcher blocks, tables, and more.

Bulk Foods
Bulkfoods.com
(888) 285-5266
Apple pectin powder, dried fruit, nuts, and coconut products

Chef's Garden
Chefs-garden.com
(800) 289-4644
Edible flowers and pea shoots, shiso, sorrel, other herbs, amaranth, mustard greens, micro-greens, and much more

Cowgirl Creamery
Cowgirlcreamery.com
(866) 433-7834
Humboldt Fog, Point Reyes Blue, Mt Tam, and other fresh and aged cheeses

D'Artagnan
Dartagnan.com
(800) 327-8246
Duck fat, quail, squab, truffle juice, truffle butter, Tarbais beans, fresh and dried mushrooms in many varieties

Gourmet-Delights.com
Gourmet-delights.com
Aji panca paste, aji panca chiles, olive oils, champagne vinegar, sherry vinegar, rice vinegar, saffron, smoked sweet paprika, carnaroli rice

Heath Ceramics
Heathceramics.com
(415) 361-5552
Dinnerware, serving ware, glassware

Johnny's Select Seeds
Johnnyseeds.com
(877) 564-6697
Seeds for unusual varieties of organic and heirloom vegetables, fruits, legumes, and herbs

Kalustyan's
Kalustyans.com
(800) 352-3451
Dried spices and herbs, mustard oil, beans, grains, French green lentils, Earl Grey tea, iota carrageenan

King Arthur Flour Company
Kingarthurflour.com
(800) 827-6836
Almond flour, durum flour, semolina flour, top-quality all-purpose flour, espresso powder, meringue powder

La Tienda
Tienda.com
(800) 710-4304
Aji panca sauce, dried chiles, canned chipotle chiles en adobo, serrano ham, manchego cheese, squid ink, other Mexican, Latin, and Spanish ingredients

Maple Leaf Farms
Mapleleaffarms.com
(800) 348-2812
Duck breasts, duck fat

Melissa's Produce
Melissas.com
(800) 588-0151
Organic produce in exotic heirloom varieties, organic farro

Modernist Pantry
Modernistpantry.com
(469) 443-6634
Agar agar, xanthan gum, iota carrageenan, low-acyl gellan gum, soy lecithin, sucrose, dextrose, silver gelatin sheets

Nambé
Nambe.com
(800) 443-0339
Flatware, serving ware, other tableware

Santa Fe School of Cooking
Santafeschoolofcooking.com
(505) 983-4511
Dried chiles, Nielsen-Massey vanilla bean paste, asadors, stovetop smokers, dinnerware, serving ware, and flatware

Savory Spice Shop
(505) 819-5659 (Santa Fe location)
Savoryspiceshop.com
Mayan chocolate; white pepper; pink, green, and black peppercorns; smoked salt; shichimi togarashi; dried spices and herbs

Spectrum Organics
Spectrumorganics.com
(866) 595-8917
Organic canola oil, cooking sprays, and specialty oils and vinegars

The Spanish Table
Spanishtable.com
Piment d'Espelette, smoked sweet paprika, Spanish chorizo, serrano ham, manchego cheese, saffron, squid ink, anchovies, sherry vinegar, Marcona almonds, grains, dinnerware, serving ware

The Spice House
Thespicehouse.com
(847) 328-3711
White pepper; pink, black, and green peppercorns; salts; dried spices and herbs

WillPowder
Willpowder.com
(866) 249-0400
Xanthan gum, agar agar, iota carrageenan, low-acyl gellan gum, soy lecithin, sorbet stabilizer, egg white powder

Zingerman's
Zingermans.com
(888) 636-8162
Piment d'Espelette, grains, agrumato lemon oil, great olive oils, vinegars, and mustards, cheeses of the world

index

about the authors

CHEF MARTÍN RIOS has been repeatedly honored for his innovative and pleasing combinations of flavors, colors, and presentations. His unique style emphasizes fresh, local produce and organic meats and poultry, and reflects not only Southwestern and Asian influences but also his classic training in French technique. His list of accolades includes the following:

Chef Martín with his family. From left: daughter Emma, wife Jennifer, and daughter Anneliese.

Finalist for the 2015 "Best Chef of the Southwest" Awards

Semi-finalist for the 2010 James Beard "Best New Restaurant in the US" Award

Semi-finalist for the 2011, 2012, 2013, and 2014 "Best Chef of the Southwest" Awards

Appeared on the Cooking Channel's 2012 season of "United Tastes of America"

Appeared on the BBC America's 2012 season of "Chef Race: UK vs. US"

Named one of *Saveur* magazine's 2012 top 25 Nationwide "Tastemakers"

Featured in the 2008 season of Iron Chef America

The only chef from New Mexico to have won the Robert Mondavi Culinary Award of Excellence

Chef of the Year by the City of Santa Fe

Chef of the Year twice by the State of New Mexico

Chef of the Year twice by the New Mexico Lodger's Association

Named "Celebrated Chef" by the National Pork Council

Featured in the *Bon Appétit* magazine cover story "The American Restaurant: Our Favorite Places"

Under his leadership the Old House Restaurant was listed by Zagat's Restaurant Survey as the best dining experience in New Mexico, and one of the best restaurants in the United States.

CHERYL AND BILL JAMISON are the authors of eighteen cookbook and travel guides and write with passion and wit about the food and culture of the Southwest. They are among the nation's most-lauded culinary professionals, with honors that include four James Beard Awards, an IACP award, and multiple New Mexico Book Awards. Cheryl and Bill make frequent guest instructor appearances at top cooking schools. Cheryl is the culinary editor at *New Mexico* magazine. The Jamisons live in Tesuque, New Mexico. Visit them at CookingWithTheJamisons.com

about the photographer

Kate Russell is a nationally recognized photographer based in Santa Fe. Known for her ability to create evocative images and elevate simplicity, Russell's sensitivity to light and the moment can be seen in her photos. Her work has appeared in numerous regional and national publications, including *The New York Times, Western Interiors, Trend Magazine, The Santa Fean, Western Art and Architecture,* and the books *Old World Interiors,* by David Naylor, and *Designers Here and There,* by Michele Keith. Kate can be found at katerussellphotography.com